LINCOLN CHRISTIAN C

W9-CCW-245

The CHRISTIAN and AMERICAN LAW

The CHRISTIAN and AMERICAN LAW

Christianity's Impact
on America's
Founding Documents
and Future Direction

H. Wayne House

General Editor

kregel
PUBLICATIONS

Grand Rapids, MI 49501

The Christian and American Law: Christianity's Impact on America's Founding Documents and Future Direction

Copyright © 1998 by H. Wayne House

Published by Kregel Publications, a division of Kregel, Inc., P.O. Box 2607, Grand Rapids, MI 49501. Kregel Publications provides trusted, biblical publications for Christian growth and service. Your comments and suggestions are valued.

All rights reserved. No part of this book may be reproduced, stored in a retrieval system, or transmitted in any form or by any means—electronic, mechanical, photocopy, recording, or otherwise—without written permission of the publisher, except for brief quotations in printed reviews.

For more information about Kregel Publications, visit our web site at http://www.kregel.com.

Cover design: Alan G. Hartman
Book design: Nicholas G. Richardson

Library of Congress Cataloging-in-Publication Data
House, H. Wayne
    The Christian and American law / H. Wayne House.
        p.   cm.
    Includes bibliographical references.
        1. Religion and law—United States. 2. Christianity and law. 3. Constitutional law—Religious aspects—Christianity. 4. United States—History—Religious aspects—Christianity. 5. Constitutional history—United States. I. House, H. Wayne.
KF379.C47   1997   340'.11—dc21   97-7912
                                                                            CIP

ISBN 0-8254-2875-0

Printed in the United States of America

1 2 3 / 04 03 02 01 00 99 98

Contents

97648

Contributors

Gary Amos, J.D., attorney at law, Visiting Professor of Law and Government, College of Law and Government, Regent University, Virginia Beach, Virginia

Harold O. J. Brown, Ph.D., Professor of Theology and Ethics, Trinity Evangelical Divinity School, Deerfield, Illinois

Edmund P. Clowney, S.T.M., D.D., former President of Westminster Theological Seminary, Escondido, California

John Eidsmoe, J.D., D.Min., attorney at law, Professor of Law, Jones School of Law, Faulkner University, Montgomery, Alabama

Arthur F. Glasser, M.Div, D.D., Senior Professor and Dean Emeritus, School of World Mission, Fuller Theological Seminary, Pasadena, California

Carl F. H. Henry, Ph.D., evangelical theologian and author, has been Visiting Professor at Trinity Evangelical Divinity School and is Research Scholar at Southern Baptist Theological Seminary, Louisville, Kentucky

H. Wayne House, Th.D., J.D., Professor of Law, Trinity Law School, and Professor of Theology and Culture, Trinity Graduate School, Trinity International University

Douglas Kelly, Ph.D., Professor of Systematic Theology, Reformed Theological Seminary, Charlotte, North Carolina

R. C. Sproul, Th.D., Adjunct Professor, Reformed Theological Seminary, Orlando, Florida, President of Ligonier Ministries

7

William J. Stuntz, Professor of Law, University of Virginia School of
Law, Charlottesville, Virginia

Herbert W. Titus, J.D., attorney at law, editor and publisher of *The
Foreaster*, formerly Dean and Professor of Law, College of Law
and Government, Regent University, Virginia Beach, Virginia

Larry Walker, Ph.D., author, lecturer, former seminary professor

Introduction

AMERICA HAS A RICH tradition of commitment to the rule of law. This respect was fostered in the early days of the Republic by a common belief in absolute values, which were considered part and parcel of God's divine order of the universe. He was the great lawgiver, and men were to emulate His laws in their midst so as to have an orderly society. Laws enacted according to human whims more often than not resulted in tyranny rather than equality, and enslavement rather than liberty.

The American experiment was built on the acceptance of law from two sources, both reflecting adherence to divine law. The first was the law of nature, generally known as natural law. The second was the law of Scripture. Early framers of American government such as Jefferson and Madison, echoed the thinking of John Locke, William Blackstone, Edward Coke, and Charles de Montesquieu, who advocated many ideas that were based on a belief in the laws of nature and of nature's God.

At the heart of America's constitutional government lies a third source: the common law tradition, which authorities such as Coke and Blackstone saw as based on Holy Scripture. Themes of equality and liberty were further drawn from natural law perspectives of men such as Locke. The blending of the common law tradition and natural law, affirmed at the beginning of the Declaration of Independence, has provided many of the blessings enjoyed by Americans for over two hundred years.

A sad state of affairs has developed, however, as we approach the beginning of a new century and millennium. The underpinnings of our legal system, which once recognized the law of God, absolute ethics, and similar values are eroding rapidly. The law has become little more than the subjective dictates of legislators and judges captured by the philosophy of relativism. Since laws no longer have an objective point of reference, man now has the arbitrary rule rather than the standard law of God.

In the midst of this upheaval do Christians have anything to offer? Critics often point to historical issues such as slavery, upon which many Christians did act inconsistently, in an effort to invalidate Christian participation in contemporary social issues. The Christian principles on which the country was primarily founded are rarely consulted other than for formalities of state, derision, or for the purpose of contrasts in the making of new laws. For a good part of this century, Christians committed to biblical truth abandoned the public sphere as a result of social intimidation and fear or as a result of theological views that elevated the Lord's imminent return and subsequent judgment.

We who believe in Jesus Christ as Savior and Lord, however, surely have truth to offer that will provide a better foundation than the shifting sand of contemporary relativism and postmodernism. As Christians we need to examine our historical impact upon America if we are to provide future direction for the enactment and enforcement of law. In view of this need, the National Association of Evangelicals convened in Washington, D.C. in 1993. The participating scholars discussed how Christians should evaluate the current state of American law and government. They examined the past influence of Christianity on the law, determined ways in which Christians should relate to current laws, and proposed ways Christians might influence the future laws. They especially wanted to determine in what ways we as Christians could work within the secular legal community, promote better laws, and ensure greater opportunity for the preaching of the Gospel within the public forum.

The participants also set forth a series of affirmations and denials that we believe reflect a biblical view of law and government. Our desire is that these efforts will promote a growing awareness of the need for Christians to recapture the best aspects of the past and to foster moral and just government in our nation's future.

PART ONE

How Christianity Has
Influenced American Law

ONE

God's Revelation: Foundation for the Common Law

Herbert W. Titus

"[W]HILE THE ROMAN LAW was a deathbed convert to Christianity, the common law was a cradle Christian."[1] So wrote John C. H. Wu in his 1955 encomium to the Anglo-American legal system known as the common law. Wu, a convert to Christianity in the 1930s and a noted international statesman, jurist, and law professor, documented this claim by tracing the history of the English common law from Bracton through Coke to Blackstone.

Bracton, named by Wu as the "Father of the Common Law,"[2] was a churchman, learned in both the canon and Roman law. Remembered for his great thirteenth-century treatise, *De Legibus et Consuetudinibus Angliae,* the first systematic treatment of the English common law, Bracton laid down an unmistakably Christian philosophy of law:

> The king himself . . . ought not to be under man but under God, and under the law, because the law makes the king. . . . [F]or there is no king where will, and not law, wields dominion. That as a vicar of God he [the king] ought to be under the law is clearly shown by the example of Jesus Christ . . . [f]or although there lay open to God, for the salvation of the human race, many ways and means . . . He used, not the force of his power, but the counsel of His justice. Thus He was willing to be under the Law, "that he might redeem those who were under the Law." For He was unwilling to use power, but judgment.[3]

Coke, whom Wu praised as "the incarnate common law"[4] or the savior of the common law, showed incomparable courage when he cited Bracton in his momentous encounter with King James I, who claimed that he personified the law as king.[5] Well prepared to defend the common law against tyranny even from the highest place in the kingdom, Coke, like Bracton, understood that God, not man, was the ultimate source of law, even of that law that governed the civil realm. Before his confrontation with the king, Coke had confidently proclaimed that "the law of nature is part of the law of England,"[6] that this "law of nature was before any judicial or municipal law,"[7] and that this "law of nature is immutable."[8] What was this law of nature? Coke described it eloquently:

> The law of nature is that which God at the time of creation of the nature of man infused into his heart, for his preservation and direction; . . . this is *lex aeterna*, the moral law, called also the law of nature. And by this law written with the finger of God in the heart of man, were the people of God a long time governed, before the law was written by Moses, who was the first reporter or writer of law in the world.[9]

Coke's law of nature, the eternal law of God, written on the heart of every man, paralleled John Calvin's moral law, which the theologian characterized as "nothing else than a testimony of natural law and of that of conscience which God has engraved upon the minds of men."[10] Coke's law of nature and Calvin's moral law, in turn, drew support from the apostle Paul's letter to the church at Rome: "For when the Gentiles, which have not the [written] law, do by nature the things contained in the law, these, having not the law, are a law unto themselves which shew the work of the law written in their hearts, their conscience also bearing witness" (Rom. 2:14–15).[11]

This Christian philosophy of law came to full bloom in England with the work of Sir William Blackstone in his monumental *Commentaries on the Law of England*. In his seminal chapter on "the Nature of Laws in General," Blackstone stated his Christian thesis with unmistakable clarity:

> Man, considered as a creature, must necessarily be subject to the law of his creator, for he is entirely a dependent being . . . [A] state of dependence will inevitably oblige the inferior to take the will of him, on whom he depends, as the rule of his conduct . . . And consequently, as man depends absolutely upon his maker for every thing, it is necessary that he should in all points conform to his maker's will.
> This will of his maker is called the law of nature. . . .
> This law of nature, being coeval with mankind and dictated by God himself, is of course superior in obligation to all other.

It is binding over all the globe, in all countries, and at all times; no human laws are of any validity, if contrary to this; and such of them as are valid derive all their force, and all their authority, mediately or immediately, from this original.[12]

Published in 1765, Blackstone's *Commentaries* quickly became the definitive treatise on the common law both in England and in America. Blackstone's statement of the meaning and significance of the law of nature served not only the cause of the common law, but providentially the cause of the American War of Independence. As for the common law, Blackstone provided to Associate United States Justice Joseph Story ample evidence to support the justice's firm opinion that "[t]here never has been a period, in which the Common Law did not recognise Christianity as lying at its foundations."[13] As for America's claim to independence, Thomas Jefferson unhesitantly and confidently rested his case on "the laws of nature and of nature's God."[14]

For over one hundred years, however, this godly heritage of American law has been neglected. It is no longer generally acknowledged by her lawyers or her judges. The purpose of this chapter is twofold: (1) to document and to explain how God's revelation provided the basic foundation for the Anglo-American common law system; and (2) to urge its renewal and restoration.

The first section of the chapter contains a succinct summary of the biblical philosophy that laid the foundation for the common law at the time of America's founding. It concludes with a brief account of its demise, occasioned by a late nineteenth-century Darwinian revolution, and with a forecast of a coming Christian counterrevolution.

To illustrate how this biblical philosophy was applied in the past, and how, if restored, it would make a difference in the future, the second and third sections address two subjects, private property and civil jurisdiction. Both of these sections document the biblical roots of the common law of property and of jurisdiction, and urge a return to them to preserve economic stability and to reestablish true liberty in America.

1. GOD'S REVELATION AND THE COMMON LAW

The Law of Nature and of Nature's God

The Declaration of Independence's reliance on the laws of "nature's God"[15] as well as on "the laws of nature"[16] reflected the faith of America's founders in a "God Who is there and Who is not silent."[17]

They believed without reservation that God had created all humanity, that God had endowed them with certain rights, and that God actively judged and superintended the affairs of humans, including that of nations.[18] Their faith in God and in His revelation in support of their revolutionary cause mirrored Blackstone's faith in God's will as revealed in nature and in the holy Scriptures. Not surprisingly, America's founders endeavored to preserve and to purify Blackstone's philosophy of the common law even as they were leading the United States of America in a war against the mother country. Jesse Root, in his "remarkable preface to the first volume of systematic *Reports* on Connecticut cases,"[19] explained the revelational epistemology on which all Americans understood the common law to rest:

> What is common law? . . . Common law is the perfection of reason, arising from the nature of God, of man, and of things, and from their relations, dependencies, and connections: It is universal. . . . It is in itself perfect . . . it is immutable, . . . it is superior to all other laws and regulations. . . . It is immemorial . . . it is co-existent with the nature of man, . . . It is most energetic and coercive. . . .
>
> [W]ho will ascend into heaven to bring it down, or descend into the depths to bring it up, or traverse the Atlantic to import it? It is near us, it is within us, written on the tablet of our hearts, in lively and indelible characters; . . . It is visible in the volume of nature, in all the works and ways of God. Its sound is gone forth into all the earth, and there is no people or nation so barbarous, where its language is not understood.
>
> The dignity of its original, the sublimity of its principles, the purity, excellency and perpetuity of its precepts are most clearly made known and delineated in the book of divine revelations; heaven and earth may pass away and all the systems and works of man sink into oblivion, but not a jot or tittle of this law shall ever fall.[20]

Root's explicit revelational epistemology was presupposed by Blackstone in his *Commentaries*. Thus, Blackstone unapologetically began his chapter on the nature of laws in general with propositional statements derived from the Genesis account of creation:

> Law . . . signifies a . . . rule of action, which is prescribed by some superior, and which the inferior is bound to obey.
>
> Thus when the supreme being formed the universe, and created matter out of nothing, he impressed certain principles

on that matter, from which it can never depart, and without which it would cease to be. When he put that matter into motion, he established certain laws of motion, to which all moveable bodies must conform.[21]

Continuing this Genesis theme of creation, Blackstone moved quickly from the laws of the Creator governing the inanimate world to the rules of the same Creator governing the animate world:

If we farther advance, from mere inactive matter to vegetable and animal life, we shall find them still governed by laws . . . equally fixed and invariable. The whole progress of plants . . . the method of animal nutrition, . . . and all other branches of vital economy . . . are not left to chance, or the will of the creature itself, but are performed in a wondrous involuntary manner, and guided by unerring rules laid down by the great creator.[22]

Again without hesitation, Blackstone moved from the rules governing the animate world to those applying to human action or conduct. While he acknowledged that humanity, unlike the animals, is "a creature endowed with both reason and freewill,"[23] Blackstone drew a straight line from the laws governing the inanimate and animate worlds to the laws governing the "image-bearing nature world"[24] peculiar to humans:

For as God, when he created matter, and endued it with a principle of mobility, established certain rules for the perpetual direction of that motion; so, when he created man, and endued him with freewill to conduct himself in all parts of life, he laid down certain immutable laws of human nature, whereby that freewill is in degree regulated and restrained.[25]

By relating God's laws governing humanity to those governing the inanimate physical world, Blackstone—whether advertently or inadvertently I do not know—followed God's revelatory strategy in His dealing with Job. For in response to Job's complaint, God answered by declaring His sovereign power as Creator over inanimate nature and, consequently, His rule of that inanimate world: "Where wast thou when I laid the foundations of the earth? . . . Who hath laid the measures thereof? . . . or who hath stretched the line on it? . . . Knowest thou the ordinances of heaven? Canst thou set the dominion thereof in the earth?" (Job 38:4–5, 33).

God repeats this revelatory strategy throughout Scripture both in His relationships with Israel (e.g., Jer. 10:2–15) and with individual human beings. In a most telling passage in the book of James, God likens His physical laws governing water quality to His moral laws governing what humanity speaks with its mouth:

> [T]he tongue can no man tame; it is an unruly evil, full of deadly poison. Therewith bless we God . . . and therewith curse we men, which are made after the similitude of God. Out of the same mouth proceedeth blessing and cursing. My brethren these things ought not so to be. Doth a fountain send forth at the same place sweet water and bitter? (James 3:8–11).

Given these revelations of identity between the laws governing the physical world and those governing humanity's free will, Blackstone envisioned the job of the lawyer or jurist to be like that of the physical scientist; namely, to use God's gift of "reason to discover the purport of those laws" governing humanity's freewill.[26] Blackstone had faith that God "has enabled human reason to discover" these laws "so far as they are necessary for the conduct of human actions."[27]

First, Blackstone contended that God created each individual human being in such a way that he but by his own self-love will discover the rules that lead to happiness.[28] According to Blackstone, one need not be a metaphysician in order to know what is good and what is evil.[29] Likewise, Jesse Root claimed that the law of nature created by God could be known through reason because God had created all human beings with the capacity to know those laws:

> [T]he law exists . . . [not as] a matter of speculative reasoning merely; but of knowledge and feeling. We know that we have a property in our persons . . . we know that we have a right to think and believe as we choose . . . we know the value of a good name . . . we know that every man's peace and happiness is his own. Nay, more when our persons are assaulted, our lives attached, our liberties infringed . . . our property . . . spoiled, we feel the injury that is done to us. . . . We know also that other men have the same rights. . . . When their rights are violated, this law is therefore evidenced both by the knowledge and the feelings of men.[30]

Notwithstanding the fact that God had revealed His laws clearly in nature and had created each human being with the capacity to discover those laws, both Blackstone and Root agreed that God's revelation of His laws in the natural world was not the only source of humanity's knowledge of the rules governing his free will. Both claimed that there was a better source than nature to consult, namely, the Holy Scriptures. Indeed, Root called the "book of divine revelations . . . the Magna Charta of all our natural and religious rights and liberties."[31]

Calling the Bible the Magna Charta of justice and liberty did not mean that God had failed to make known His laws through the natural world; nor did it mean that God had failed to give humanity sufficient reasoning and emotional capacity to discover those laws in nature. To the contrary, God's ways in nature were still discoverable by humanity through reason. Nevertheless, God, in His mercy, provided a more sure guide. Blackstone captured best the reason why God took these laws already sufficiently revealed in nature and revealed them also in writing:

> [I]f our reason were always, as in our first ancestor before his transgression, clear and perfect, unruffled by passions, unclouded by prejudice, unimpaired by disease or intemperance, the task would be pleasant and easy; we should need no other guide but this [i.e., the law of nature]. But every man now finds the contrary in his own experience; that his reason is corrupt, and his understanding full of ignorance and error.
>
> This has given manifold occasion for the benign interposition of divine providence; which, in compassion to the frailty, the imperfection, and the blindness of human reason, hath been pleased . . . to discover and enforce its laws by an immediate and direct revelation. The doctrines thus delivered we call the revealed or divine law, and they are to be found only in the holy scriptures.[32]

For Blackstone and Root, then, the biblical revelation did not displace the natural revelation, but confirmed it and made it possible for man, even though his reason had been corrupted by sin, to continue to discover the special rules that the Creator had imposed on humans as beings created in the image of God. Again, Blackstone is most explicit:

> These precepts [the ones written in the holy Scriptures] . . . , when revealed, are found on comparison to be really a part of the original law of nature, as they tend in all their consequences

to man's felicity. But we are not from thence to conclude that the knowledge of these truths was attainable by reason, in its present corrupted state; since we find that, until they were revealed [in writing], they were hid from the wisdom of ages. As then the moral precepts of this law are indeed of the same original with those of the law of nature, so their intrinsic obligation is of equal strength and perpetuity.[33]

In other words, God's putting in written form, "Thou shalt not murder" (Ex. 20:13) did not make murder wrong, but His putting the rule in writing revealed more effectively to fallen people the original law protecting the sanctity of human life that God had placed and revealed in the created order from the beginning. Murder was wrong, therefore, because it was contrary to the nature of people and to the very nature of God's creation.

The Municipal or Civil Law

By presupposing God's revelation in both nature and in the Holy Scriptures, Blackstone and Root established the common-law heritage as rooted in an objective legal order that preexisted civil society and the writings of men. That objective legal order Blackstone identified as "the law of nature and the law of revelation."[34] As for the laws of civil order, Blackstone claimed that such laws were wholly dependent on the law of nature and the law of revelation and that "no human laws should be suffered to contradict these."[35] As for the writings of men, these were only "what, by the assistance of human reason, we imagine to be" the law of nature.[36] Blackstone called these writings the "natural law"[37] and distinguished them from the law of nature, which he stated is "expressly declared . . . to be [Law] by God himself."[38]

Having begun with God's revelation in nature and in the Holy Scriptures to define law generally, Blackstone turned to the subject of "municipal or civil law; that is, the rule by which particular . . . nations are governed."[39] Before proposing a definition of municipal law, however, Blackstone laid one final building block from God's revelation. While no human law could be law if it contradicted the law of nature and the law of revelation, there were, Blackstone claimed, "a great number of indifferent points, in which both the divine and the natural leave a man at his own liberty; but which are found necessary for the benefit of society."[40] In other words, God's revelation does not command every single human law, jot and tittle; rather, God, having created people in His own image, has allowed them freedom to adopt some rules that they find efficacious about which God is indifferent.

To illustrate this point, Blackstone contrasted those human laws prohibiting murder and those laws governing the export of wool into foreign countries. As for murder Blackstone noted:

> [T]his is expressly forbidden by the divine, and demonstrably by the natural law; and from these prohibitions arises the true unlawfulness of this crime. Those human laws, that annex a punishment to it, do not at all increase its moral guilt, or superadd any fresh obligation in foro conscientiae to abstain from its perpetuation. Nay, if any human law should allow or enjoin us to commit it, we are bound to transgress that human law, or else we must offend both the natural and the divine.[41]

In two later chapters Blackstone returned to the subject of murder with explicit reliance on God's revelation in the Holy Scriptures. On the question of civil authority to impose the death penalty, Blackstone rested his case squarely on Genesis 9:6: "[C]apital punishments are in some instances inflicted by the immediate command of God himself to all mankind; as, in the case of murder, by the precept delivered to Noah, their common ancestor and representative, 'whoso sheddeth man's blood, by man shall his blood be shed.'"[42]

On the question of authority to pardon a convicted murderer, Blackstone claimed that it was prohibited, citing Numbers 35:31: "Moreover ye shall take no satisfaction for the life of a murderer, who is guilty of death, but he shall surely be put to death; for the land cannot be cleansed of the blood that is shed therein but by the blood of him that shed it."[43]

With these two revelations Blackstone supported his observation that murder was a "crime at which human nature starts, and which is . . . punished almost universally throughout the world with death,"[44] and his critique of the "Polish monarch . . . who thought it proper to remit penalties of murder to all the nobility, in an edict with this arrogant preamble, 'nos divini juris rigorum moderantes, etc.'"[45]

In contrast to the authority of civil rulers to impose the death penalty on convicted murderers, Blackstone claimed that no civil ruler had authority to impose such a penalty for "offenses against the municipal law only, and not against the law of nature; since no individual has, naturally, a power of inflicting death on himself or others for actions in themselves indifferent."[46] Whether or not an offense is "indifferent," i.e., within the discretion of humanity to prohibit, was, however, determined by God's revelation: "[W]ith regard to matters that are in themselves indifferent, and are not commanded or forbidden by those superior laws [the law of nature and the law of revelation] . . . here the inferior legislature has scope and opportunity to interpose, and to make that action unlawful which before was not so."[47]

Armed with this foundational distinction from God's revelation, Blackstone proceeded to define municipal or civil law as "a rule of civil conduct prescribed by the supreme power in a state, commanding what is right, and prohibiting what is wrong."[48] This definition tracked that of law generally: "Law . . . is that rule of action, which is prescribed by some superior, and which the inferior is bound to obey,"[49] but it specified the criteria by which one determined if he was bound to obey.

With God all of His rules of action are binding on all of His creatures because His authority is universal and because His rules are inherently good: "As therefore the Creator is a being, not only of infinite power, and wisdom, but also of infinite goodness, . . . he has . . . inseparably interwoven the laws of eternal justice with the happiness of each individual, that the latter cannot be attained but by observing the former."[50]

In contrast, the civil ruler, being both finite and limited in authority, could prescribe rules extending only to matters of civil conduct that, according to Blackstone, distinguished "municipal law from the law of nature, or revealed; the former of which is the rule of moral conduct, and the latter not only the rule of moral conduct, but also the rule of faith."[51] Such rules of morality and faith

> regard man as a creature, and point out his duty to God, to himself, and to his neighbor, considered in light of an individual. But municipal or civil law regards him also as a citizen, and bound to other duties towards his neighbor, than those of mere nature and religion: duties . . . which amount to no more, than . . . the subsistence and peace of the society.[52]

Whether a duty was moral only or faith only, as contrasted with civil, was in Blackstone's view determined by God's revelation, just as the distinction between duties commanded by God and those commanded solely by the civil ruler was determined by God's revelation.

Blackstone reiterated this latter point in his discussion of the criteria governing what is right and what is wrong for the purpose of determining whether one was bound to obey a rule prescribed by municipal or civil law. On this point, Blackstone was clearly not a positivist; that is, he did not claim that a human law was binding solely because a lawful civil ruler had properly prescribed it. To the contrary, Blackstone expressly noted that "no human legislature has power to abridge or destroy . . . [t]hose rights which God and nature has established."[53]

Notwithstanding, "with regard to things in themselves indifferent . . . [t]hese become either right or wrong, just or unjust . . . according as the municipal legislator sees proper, for promoting the welfare of the society, and more effectually carrying on the purposes of civil life."[54] Again Blackstone provided an example to illustrate this crucial distinction and once again the example rested on God's revelation: "[I]n civil duties; obedience to superiors is the doctrine of revealed as well as natural religion: but who those superiors shall be, and in what circumstances, or to what degrees they shall be obeyed, is in the province of human laws to determine."[55]

The Common Law of England and America

Having drawn on God's revelation to define both the jurisdiction and the substance of municipal or civil law generally, Blackstone turned in the next section, chapter 2 of volume 1 of his *Commentaries*, to the municipal law of England, which he claimed could be divided into "the unwritten, or common law" and "the written, or statute law."[56] In this section, Blackstone devoted over two-thirds of his discussion to the common law as "contained in the records of the several courts of justice, in books of reports and judicial decisions, and in the treatises of learned sages of the profession."[57]

Blackstone noted first that the common law was considered to be unwritten because that law had become law *not* because it had been put into writing by judges in their opinions or by legislators as statutes, but rather, the common law had become law "by long and immemorial usage" or by custom.[58] Thus, Blackstone claimed that common-law judges in England did not make law, but only discovered and stated it.[59] A court opinion, therefore, was only evidence of law, not law itself. As "living oracles," judges were "bound by oath to decide according to the law of the land."[60] Should a judge's opinion be found not in conformity with that law, then that opinion was considered not to be "bad law" but to be "not law" at all.[61]

The common law contained two kinds of rules. First, there were the rules commanded by God and required of all nations and at all times. Second, there were the rules adopted by the community because they were felicitous to the societal order. These were known as customs, indifferent to God. As for the former, such rules were clearly subject to the rule of reason. If a court opinion setting forth such a rule was found "contrary to reason" or "much more . . . contrary to the divine law," then it was incumbent on a "subsequent" judge to disregard that ruling as "not law, that is, that it is not the established custom of the realm, as has been erroneously determined."[62] As for customs "indifferent to God," a judge could never justify a departure from rules that were "fixed and established . . . without a breach of his oath and the law . . . [f]or herein there is nothing repugnant to natural justice."[63]

The common law of England, then, was but one form of the municipal or civil law of the nation and subject to the same limitations as to jurisdiction and as to substance. The customs of the realm could extend only to *civil* conduct, not to exclusively moral or exclusively religious conduct. And the customs could not proscribe what God has commanded or command or permit what God has prohibited.

Blackstone's view of the common law and the role of the judge was accepted without debate in America at the time of its founding. Jesse Root, in answering the questions, "What is the common law of America? Have we any common law in Connecticut?,"[64] began first to describe those rules found "in the book of divine revelations"[65] that are common to all people:

> By this we are taught the dignity, the character, the rights and duties of man. . . . This teaches us, so to use our own as not to injure the rights of others. This enables us, to . . . construe contracts and agreements. . . . This designates crimes. . . . This defines the obligations and duties between husbands and wives, parents and children . . . between the rulers and the people, and the people or citizens towards each other. This is the Magna Charta of all our natural and religious rights and liberties—and the only solid basis of our civil constitution and privileges . . . the usages and customs of men and the decisions of the courts of justice serve to declare and illustrate the principles of this law.[66]

Root, like Blackstone, found that the common law also included customs not reflected in Holy Writ, but binding nonetheless. Customs were rules "adopted in practice by the citizens at large, or by particular classes of men, as the farmers, the merchants . . . which are reasonable and beneficial."[67] Root explained that

> the courts of justice take notice of [these customs] as rules of right, and as having the force of laws formed and adopted under the authority of the people, [for] as statutes are positive laws enacted by authority of the legislature . . . [as]

representatives of the people, ... [s]o these unwritten customs
... have the force of law under the authority of the people.[68]

This view of the Anglo-American common law prevailed in both
England and America into the early period of the twentieth century.[69]
At the end of the nineteenth century, however, God's revelation as
the foundation and framework of the common law came under
relentless attack from the pens of Oliver Wendell Holmes Jr. and his
Harvard colleague, John Chipman Gray, as well as from the new "case
method" of teaching law installed by Dean Christopher Columbus
Langdell at Harvard.

Langdell led the way in 1870 by recasting the science of law in
evolutionary terms, thereby discarding the revelation of God as the
source of laws governing the universe. Langdell wrote in 1879 in the
Preface to his *Cases on Contracts*, the first law casebook ever published:
"Law, considered as a science, consists of certain principles or
doctrines. . . . Each of these doctrines has arrived at its present state
by slow degrees; in other words, it is a growth, extending in many
cases through centuries."[70]

Two years later Holmes published his book on the common law.
He tracked Langdell's evolutionary scientific view of law with neither
explanation nor justification:

> The life of the law has not been logic: it has been experience.
> The felt necessities of the time, the prevalent moral and
> political theories, intuitions of public policy . . . even the
> prejudices which judges share with their fellow-men, have
> had a good deal more to do than the syllogism in determining
> the rules by which men should be governed. The law embodies
> the story of a nation's development through many centuries,
> and it cannot be dealt with as if it contained only the axioms
> and corollaries of a book of mathematics. In order to know
> what it is, we must know what it has been, and what it tends
> to become.[71]

With God's revelation cast aside as "a brooding omnipresence in
the sky" not an "articulate voice of some sovereign . . . that can be
identified,"[72] Gray put on the finishing touches by disposing of
Blackstone's view that judges discover but do not create law. He
contended that there is no mysterious entity, "the Law," apart from
the rules of conduct that the courts apply, and that judges are the
creators rather than the discoverers of the law.[73]

This shift from a common-law system founded and framed by God's revelation to a common law system determined by judge's opinions was not accidental. Indeed, Christopher Columbus Langdell had been chosen by Harvard president Charles William Eliot for the specific purpose of establishing a new method of teaching law based on the Darwinian revolution that had taken hold of American higher education in the late nineteenth century. As Eliot put it in his address celebrating the inauguration of the first president of Johns Hopkins University:

> They [the new schools of which Johns Hopkins was one] can show how . . . biology with its principle of evolution through natural selection, [has] brought about within thirty years a wonderful change in men's conception of the universe. If the universe, as science teaches, be an organism which has by slow degrees grown to its form of today on its way to its form of tomorrow, with slowly formed habits which we call laws, . . . then, as science also teaches, the life principle or soul of that organism, for which science has no better name than God, pervades and informs it so absolutely that there is no separating God from nature.[74]

Nearly one hundred years later American historian, Henry Steele Commager, would write:

> Fundamental changes in culture . . . were affected . . . decisively by the intellectual and philosophical revolution we associate with Darwin's *Origin of Species* (1859). . . .
>
> This shift, both inspired and dramatized by the speedy acceptance of the hypothesis of Darwin, was fundamental. It was a shift from the old teleologically oriented moral and natural philosophy to the scientific. . . .
>
> "My generation," wrote the philosopher James Hayden Tufts, who had been born in the midst of the Civil War, "has seen the passing of systems of thought which reigned since Augustus. The conception of a world ruled by God and subject to his laws . . . has dissolved."
>
> What shattered that traditional world was science, which in almost every arena—including . . . the law . . . —substituted the operations of the law of evolution for the laws of God.[75]

As the twentieth century closes, man's faith in evolutionary science is itself being challenged. Not only is the Darwinian hypothesis under siege,[76] but the common-law system that evolutionary science transformed is breaking down. At the same time there is a resurgence of Christian scholarship in law that is taking a second look at the Blackstonian legacy of the common law based on a revelatory epistemology centered on the Genesis account of creation in the Holy Scriptures. To illustrate the significance of this coming counterrevolution, I turn now to two major subjects that have long captured the minds of legal scholars; the law of private property and the law of freedom of religion.

2. THE COMMON LAW AND PRIVATE PROPERTY

A Biblical Heritage

In his introduction to book 1 of the University of Chicago's facsimile of Blackstone's *Commentaries on the Laws of England*, the late Stanley N. Katz, professor of law at Chicago, dismissed Blackstone's chapter, "On the Nature of Laws in General" as "a brief and unconvincing essay on the natural law background of the English legal system . . . [and as] an obligatory eighteenth-century exercise, in which Blackstone accords to natural and revealed law about the same importance as Newton accorded God in the operation of the physical universe."[77]

Calling Blackstone's view of law a "modern positivist one,"[78] in which God's revelation played no real part, Katz simply ignored large chunks of the *Commentaries* that were laced with references to God's revelation. Nowhere was this oversight more significant than in Blackstone's section on the common law of property.

In the opening chapter of his second book, addressing "the Rights of Things," Blackstone devoted fifteen full pages to exploring the origin and foundation of the right of property, namely "that sole and despotic dominion which one man claims and exercises over the external things of the world, in total exclusion of the right of any other individual in the universe."[79] Without hesitation or apology, Blackstone began his search by quoting Genesis 1:28: "In the beginning of the world, we are informed by holy writ, the all-bountiful creator gave to man 'dominion over all the earth; and over the fish of the sea, and over the fowl of the air, and over every living thing that moveth on the earth.'"[80]

Blackstone chose to begin with the biblical mandate to exercise dominion, not because he had no other possible source, but rather, he began with Genesis because he believed that book to be "the only true and solid foundation of man's dominion over external Óings, whatever airy metaphysical notion may have been started by fanciful writers on this subject."[81] While Blackstone did not identify these "fanciful writers" by name, America's Blackstone, Chancellor James Kent of New York, did in the introduction to the common law of property in his *Commentaries on American Law:*

> To suppose a state of man prior to the existence of any notions of separate property . . . when men throughout the world lived without law or government, in innocence and simplicity, is a mere dream of the imagination. It is the golden age of the poets which forms such a delightful picture in the fictions, adorned by the muse of Hesiod, Lucretius, Ovid, and Virgil.[82]

And what were these "dreams" of a "golden age" in which man lived in "innocence and simplicity?" Hesiod, the Greek poet mentioned first by Kent, lived in the eighth century before Christ. In his epic poem, *Works and Days,* he imagined a golden age of history in which all human beings lived happily on a fruitful earth that spontaneously satisfied all men's needs. Hesiod bemoaned the loss of this age of innocence. He blamed this loss on the gods who had failed to create humanity in such a way as to prevent it from falling into evil. Because evil had entered into the world, Hesiod claimed, humans were condemned to hard work to exercise dominion.[83]

As for Lucretius, this Roman poet who lived in the first century before Christ claimed that the earth, not gods, had given birth to humankind through a process of natural selection of species. He hypothesized a time when human's lived communally

> after the roving fashion of wild beasts. No one then was a sturdy guider of the bent plough or knew how to labor the fields with iron or plant in the ground young saplings or lop with pruning hooks old boughs from the high trees. What the sun and rains had given, what the earth had produced spontaneously, was guerdon sufficient to content their hearts.[84]

Only later did humanity invent laws and government as it evolved from a state of nature to a civilized creature with a spoken language. According to Lucretius, "mankind, tired out with a life of brute force, lay exhausted from its feuds; and therefore the more readily it submitted of its own freewill to laws and stringent codes."[85]

Ovid, like Lucretius, staked man's origin in Mother Nature, personified by the goddess "Venus . . . the spirit of desire, mating, fertility."[86] In his *Metamorphoses,* Ovid "recounted in engaging hexameters the renounced transformations of inanimate objects, animals, mortals, and gods . . . and range[d] through the whole realm of classical mythology from the creation of the world to the deification of Caesar."[87]

Virgil, in the *Aeniad,* also wrote a "sacred scripture for Rome." Although "he oscillates between Jove and an impersonal Fate as the ruler of all things," he repeated the same "mythological background" as the Greek poets before him. In earlier works he predicted the coming of a utopia that, in reality, was simply a wishful forecast of a return to a mythological golden age.[88]

Kent dismissed all of these poetic musings with a brief, but telling, reference to the Genesis account of Cain's murder of Abel following the fall of humanity in the Garden of Eden: "It has been truly observed, that the first man who was born into the world killed the second; and when did the times of simplicity begin?"[89] The significance of this citation cannot be overestimated. With it Kent not only dismissed the possibility of some utopian past, but he rejected the poet's anthropological speculations and evolutionary hypotheses as well. No wonder Kent, after citing Genesis 4, proceeded to endorse that entire book as the only authentic account of the origin of the world and of humankind. This endorsement came as he turned from his critique of the Roman and Greek poets to a similar critique of their historians and philosophers.

Claiming that the works of Homer, Herodotus, and Livy rivaled that of their poetic compatriots in "their descriptions of some imaginary state of nature," Kent found these men attempting to know the impossible and, therefore, to have spent their energies in conjecture.[90] Kent's appraisal of these three men's work has proved remarkably prescient. In his monumental work on *The Story of Civilization,* Will Durant came to similar conclusions. On Homer, Durant wrote that no one can be sure that he even existed and that Homer's work contained but "legends of an Heroic Age" in which gods and men interacted with each other, even in acts of sexual intercourse to sire those who were destined to rule on the earth.[91] As for the Greek historian, Herodotus, Durant found "much nonsense" in his work, including the claim that "Nebuchadnezzar was a woman."[92] Durant also observed that the Roman historian Livy "accepts almost any superstition" and "litters his pages with omens, portents, and oracles . . . [so that] as in Virgil the real actors are the gods."[93] So zealous to establish the absolute righteousness of Rome, Durant finally noted that Livy "ceases to distinguish legend from history."[94]

Having dismissed this Roman and Greek heritage, Kent proceeded to endorse God's revelation in the book of Genesis as the only true account of the origin of the universe, and, consequently, of the origin of private property. "No such state [of man prior to the existence of any notions of separate property] was intended for man in the benevolent dispensation of Providence; and in following the migrations of nations, apart from the book of Genesis, human curiosity is unable to penetrate beyond the pages of genuine history."[95]

Having identified Genesis as his starting point, Kent, for reasons unknown, shifted his focus from God's revelation in the Holy Scriptures to God's revelation in every person's heart: "The sense of property is inherent in the human breast. . . . Man was fitted and intended by the [A]uthor of his being . . . for the acquisitions and enjoyment of property. It is, to speak correctly, the law of his nature."[96] Perhaps Kent believed that this sense of property was so self-evident it needed no support from Scripture. Perhaps he believed that Scripture's endorsement of private property was so clear that it needed no exegesis. After all, had not Cain owned the land that he tilled and the crops that he grew (Gen. 4:2–3)? And had not Abel owned the land on which he grazed his sheep and the sheep as well (Gen. 4:2–4)? And were not Cain and Abel the first generation after Adam and Eve, so there was no room for any wandering nomads or communal property in between (Gen. 4:1)?

Blackstone, however, was not so sure. First, he was uncertain that Cain and Abel owned the land because there was so much of it and so few to claim it. It was not until the population of the world increased that conflicts over land arose. Even so, Blackstone stuck with Genesis as he cited the controversies between Abraham and Abimilech and Abraham and Lot as the earliest examples of how such conflicts were resolved, for he, like Kent, considered the book of Genesis "the most venerable monument of antiquity, considered merely with a view of history."[97]

Even before Blackstone, other apologists for the institution of private property, most notably John Locke, also found Genesis to be the beginning of any effort to justify any man's right to exercise exclusive dominion over things. Locke began his discussion of the subject by referring not only to God's revelation in nature but also to His revelation in the Scriptures: "Whether we consider natural reason, which tells us, that men, being once born, have a right to their preservation, and consequently to meat and drink, and such other things as nature affords for their subsistence: or revelation, which gives us an account of those grants God made of the world to Adam, and to Noah and his sons."[98]

Locke, unlike Kent, did not believe, however, that the right of private property was self-evident. So he, like Blackstone, sought to explain how, and to justify why, an individual human being could claim exclusive right to a piece of land or to a thing. And Locke, like Blackstone, relied on the Genesis creation story and utilized the Genesis accounts of Cain and Abel, Abraham and Lot, and Esau and Jacob to support his theory of private property.[99]

Other common-law scholars followed suit. But their common starting point in Genesis and their affirmation of Genesis as the authoritative account of the early history of humankind did not result in agreement in the foundational principles of the common law of property.

Private Property: Unalienable Right or Societal Convention

Blackstone and Locke inferred from the Holy Scriptures that in the beginning God had given the earth and all it contains to all humankind in common. While Blackstone rested his case on Genesis 1:28,[100] Locke based this first principle on Psalm 115:16: "[I]t is very clear, that God, as [K]ing David says, 'has given the earth to the children of men;' given it to mankind in common."[101] From this foundational principle Blackstone and Locke sought to demonstrate how the institution of private property came about. Both claimed that it had arisen out of necessity, in that as people multiplied on the earth there was not enough land to meet every person's needs. To illustrate this historical process, both cited passages from the book of Genesis dealing with conflicts over property.[102]

While Blackstone and Locke agreed that "necessity begat property,"[103] they did not agree on the justification for an individual human being to claim exclusive right to a plot of land or a thing to the exclusion of all others. Drawing on the Genesis history, Blackstone determined that exclusive ownership began with first possession and that the system of laws protecting private property were designed to keep the peace by preserving possessory interest from claims of those who came later. In effect, Blackstone simply accepted as fact that the "first taker" had a superior right to the property possessed and that anyone with a contrary claim had the burden of proving that his claim was better. Because Blackstone found nothing inherently right in the first taker's claim, he concluded that the common law of property was a matter of societal convention, not a matter of natural right. He favored a system of private property partly because it best met people's needs and partly because it was clearly practiced in the book of Genesis. But he did not believe that the system of private property as portrayed in Genesis had been specifically prescribed by God; it was one of those areas of "indifference" where humanity had freedom to choose a variety of rules depending on its assessment of their efficacy.[104]

Locke thought otherwise. While God gave "the world to men in common," He also gave each man "reason to make use of it to the best advantage of life and convenience."[105] This ability to reason and, thereby, to exercise dominion was each individual man's property in which "nobody has any right to but himself. The labor of his body and the work of his hands, we may say, are properly his."[106] From this God-given right, Locke reasoned that whatever a man, by his labor, "removes out of the state that nature has provided" he has, by mixing his labor with the thing removed, made the thing "his property."[107] To ensure that all humans would have opportunity to mix their labor with some external thing, Locke claimed that a human's claim of ownership could not exceed the bounds of reason, i.e., could not go beyond what he could use to the advantage of life. To be sure, no one could claim ownership to anything if one did not work for it, but no one could claim so much that it kept others from having opportunity to own things for their use and enjoyment.[108]

While Blackstone's view allowed that humans could adopt any system of property ownership so long as it proved efficacious, Locke's view required a system of private property governed by rules that protected claims based on one's work tempered by rules that limited those claims to reasonable use and enjoyment. Both came to their positions because of their first proposition that God had given to all humankind in common the earth and all that it contains.

Kent disagreed with this first postulate. He emphatically denied that there ever was time when humans owned all things in common. To the contrary, he claimed that God fitted and intended each individual person from the beginning to acquire and to enjoy separate property. Kent did not bother to support this proposition with a careful scriptural account; he was content to state it as self-evident: "There is no person, even in his rudest state, who does not feel and acknowledge . . . the justice of this title of the one who occupies something first."[109] It was occupancy, not labor, that gave rise to a claim of title, Kent claimed, because God "graciously bestowed [the sense of property] on mankind for the purpose of rousing them from sloth, and stimulating them to action."[110] He further asserted that private property rights "ought to be sacredly protected," not subordinated to claims of injustice whether they are based on inequalities of wealth or on unreasonable use and enjoyment:

> A state of equality as to property is impossible to be maintained, for it is against the laws of our nature; and if it could be reduced to practice, it would place the human race in a state of tasteless enjoyment and stupid inactivity, which

would degrade the mind, and destroy the happiness of social life.[111]

Who was right, Blackstone, Locke, or Kent? Or were any of them right? Had Kent bothered to examine the Holy Scriptures carefully, he would have found ample evidence to refute both Blackstone and Locke. As for their first postulate, that God had given the earth and all it contains to humankind in common, neither Genesis 1:28 nor Psalm 115:16 or any other verse in Scripture supports that proposition. Rightfully understood, Genesis 1:28 along with Genesis 1:26 is a grant of authority, not a conveyance of title. True, the language of each verse is in the form of a command—man must rule—but the operative word, *rule*, is not one that connotes an "immediate gift" as Blackstone contended. Rather, *rule*, literally "rule ye" (the command to man as male and female), is not a possession word or an ownership word, but an authority word, meaning to "have dominion, rule, dominate."[112]

As for Psalm 115:16, it must be read in context of the whole of Scripture. It cannot be read in isolation from Genesis 1:26–28, nor from the Genesis account of property ownership as evidenced in the lives of real people.

Family Free Enterprise

The grant of authority contained in Genesis 1:28 is not to humankind in general, but to humankind through the family unit. The command to exercise dominion is linked directly to the command for humans, male and female, to multiply and replenish the earth. By conferring authority on the family, God chose the one human institution uniquely suited to meet the terms of the dominion mandate. Given the vastness of the earth and its contents, the mandate could not possibly be fulfilled without the multiplication of human beings through the natural reproductive method prescribed by God. Thus, God placed Adam and Eve in the Garden of Eden, thereby conveying title and ownership to the "first family farm" with the expectation that from this humble beginning with one family the earth and all its contents would be "kept and tilled" (Gen. 1:26–28; 2:7–10, 15).

This grant of family authority sets the norm as chronicled by Moses in the book of Genesis. Family ownership begins with Adam and Eve, continues with their offspring and begins again with Noah and his sons, interrupted only by Pharaoh, who obtained all the land and property of his Egyptian subjects, thereby placing them in slavery (Gen. 4; 9:18–20; 13:1–6; 26:12–32; 31; 47:11, 27). Significantly,

Jacob and his progeny escaped this enslavement only to be enslaved later by a "Pharaoh who knew not Joseph" (Gen. 47:11, 27). By the opening of Exodus we are introduced to this Pharoah's "final solution" to the Jewish problem—a systematic extermination of all new-born sons (Ex. 1:8–16). The enslavement of the Israelites began with the taking of their labor and their property, but it could only be completed by abolition of the Jewish family units. Providentially, God led the people of Israel out of slavery and into the Promised Land where property ownership was restored family by family (Num. 26:1–56; 27:1–11; 33:53–54; see, e.g., Josh. 15:1, 20).

This Old Testament normative view of family free enterprise is affirmed propositionally by the writer of Proverbs: "Houses and riches are the inheritance of fathers . . ." (Prov. 19:14). It is also confirmed by one of the teaching parables wherein Jesus drew on the family free-enterprise system to illustrate a certain basic principle in the kingdom of God. In the parable of the vineyard owner who leased out his vineyard, the right of the son to inherit his father's property is utilized to demonstrate the right of Jesus as the Father's Son to inherit the whole of creation (Luke 20:9–16).

This right of a son or other child to inherit the property of the father or parent was considered by Locke, Kent, and other common-law authorities to be God given.[113] This follows from the foundational proposition that God authorized the family through the generations to exercise dominion. But with the right of inheritance comes also the duty to meet the needs of one's parents. Jesus confirmed this by condemning the pharisaical practice of "Corban," i.e., of dedicating property to God but neglecting to honor one's father and mother by meeting their needs in their old age (Mark 7:10–13). Paul followed this teaching with one of the most severe rebukes that one can find in his many letters to believers: "But if any provide not for his own, and especially for those of his own house, he hath denied the faith, and is worse than an infidel" (1 Tim. 5:8). Of course, this passage applies not only to the duty of sons and daughters to aged parents but also to the duty of fathers and mothers to their children. Paul illustrates this point with his reminder to the church at Corinth that as their spiritual father, he had a responsibility to meet their needs, not vice versa: "[F]or the children ought not to lay up for the parents, but the parents for the children" (2 Cor. 12:14).

In short, God selected the family as the primary economic unit of society—not the individual, not the state, not the corporation, and not the church. The common law was designed to foster and protect the family, not only through rules protecting private-property ownership and facilitating its voluntary transfer but also through criminal sanctions prohibiting adultery, fornication, sodomy, and bigamy.

Since the Darwinian revolution, however, this understanding of the common law has deteriorated. In the late nineteenth century the system of family free enterprise was first eroded by the selfish, individualist capitalist who, invoking Darwin's theory of the survival of the fittest, disclaimed any responsibility for the welfare of the poor and claimed immunity from all state regulation.[114] In reaction to this perverted view of free enterprise and private property came the cry for socialism, or short of that, for redistribution of wealth by the state for the benefit of the less fortunate.[115]

The most extreme reaction to individualistic capitalism came from Karl Marx in his *Communist Manifesto:* "Aboli[sh] . . . Private Property. . . . Aboli[sh] . . . the family!"[116] While these communist ideals have never triumphed, these ideas still claim the imaginations of scholars, fuel the visionary schemes of utopian reformers, and undergird various government entitlement programs that have dominated American national politics since the New Deal. With the advent of social security in the 1930s, the God-ordained responsibility for children to care for their aged and infirm parents has slowly eroded to the point where parents claim with pride that they are not a burden to their children in their old age. This erosion of family responsibility has also created a generational conflict of significant proportion as younger workers pay the bill for an ever escalating Social Security benefit system that is being exhausted by a retired generation whose life span continues to lengthen.

No longer the cornerstone of economic prosperity, the family has become increasingly viewed as a place for retreat and pleasure away from the work place. With the sexual revolution of the 1960s and 1970s, the family has become even more irrelevant because young people are lured into sexual activity outside of the marriage commitment, which is seen by many experts as the antithesis of pleasure.[117] This change of sexual mores has been accompanied by the systematic failure of the state to enforce its criminal sanctions against adultery, fornication, sodomy, and bigamy. Such laws are considered to be relics of an outmoded "Victorian morality"[118] rather than essential to protect the primary economic unit of society, the family.

Having divorced the family from the economy, America's leaders, both Republican and Democrat, have placed the social issues on the back burner to concentrate on the economic issues. But the issues of abortion and homosexual behavior, to name just two, are keys to the economic future of the nation. Activities designed to destroy America's posterity by ridding it of its so-called unwanted children, and by protecting the unproductive lifestyle of homosexual couples, are already devastating America's work force, so essential to America's continuing economic prosperity. By elevating a woman's selfishness to choose death for her baby to the level of a constitutional right, America has endorsed the unnatural use of the woman over that ordained by nature (Rom. 1:26; 1 Tim. 2:15). If America elevates the homosexual's right to similar heights, and many of America's leaders are doing everything they can to do just that, then we will see policies enacted into law that encourage men to elevate the unnatural use of their bodies over the natural. The apostle Paul warned the readers in his letter to the church at Rome that this exchange—the unnatural for the natural—would introduce an avalanche of ungodly behavior, including covetousness and covenant breaking (Rom. 1:27–32).

Respect for the property of others and the keeping of one's promises are foundational moral principles essential to the economic health and prosperity of a nation. The common-law protection of the monogamous family reflected a biblical understanding that family free enterprise protected by the law of private property was the only economic system sanctioned by God. Given this biblical endorsement of private-property ownership through the family, America's founders included "the pursuit of happiness" or "property" along with life and liberty as one of the three major God-given rights to be "secured" by civil government.[119] To secure a right granted by God does not mean that the civil ruler may define what that right is. A God-given right is defined by revelation in nature and in the Holy Scriptures; the duty of the civil ruler is to discover that right and to enact rules that facilitate its exercise and protect it from wrongful acts of others.[120]

Thus, James Kent denied to the civil ruler any authority to enact "sumptuary laws," that is, rules dictating to property owners how they should use and dispose of that property. He also objected to any legislative enactment limiting "the extent of the acquisition of property."[121] Such laws, along with policies designed to redistribute the wealth, did not belong to the civil realm, but to "Providence."[122] In drawing this jurisdictional line, Kent endorsed another common-law principle, the law that limited civil authority to duties that are by nature and by Scripture enforceable by civil sanction. It was that law of jurisdiction, well developed in the common law, that ultimately led to the constitutional protection of freedom of religion in America.

3. THE COMMON LAW OF CIVIL JURISDICTION

Civil Conduct, Not Moral or Faith Conduct

As noted earlier, Blackstone, in his *Commentaries*, defined municipal or civil law as those rules governing civil conduct, as contrasted with moral and faith conduct.[123] In drawing this distinction among different kinds of conduct, Blackstone was simply following a well-established, common-law rule that not all of humanity's duties were enforceable by the civil ruler. That principle was well established in those areas of life exclusively governed by the biblical admonition to love one's neighbor as oneself (Matt. 22:39). Love, rightly understood, must be both unconditional and voluntary. This is clearly what Jesus taught in the parable of the Good Samaritan. The man who came to the aid of the man in need did so without condition, and the man in need had no power or authority to require the other to help him (Luke 10:25–37). Likewise, the common law did not sanction any human being for failing to rescue another nor authorize a person in need to sue another for having failed to rescue him.[124]

But this jurisdictional principle was not well established in the common law when it came to matters of faith, i.e., in those duties owed to God. Thus, Blackstone devoted an entire chapter of his *Commentaries* to "offenses against God and religion." In this chapter, Blackstone affirmed the common-law crimes of apostasy, heresy, reviling the ordinances of the church, blasphemy, witchcraft, Sabbath breaking, and so forth.[125] Blackstone's endorsement of these duties as subject to civil sanction caused him some uneasiness as he acknowledged that certain acts of nonconformity with the rules of the established church of England could very well be matters of "private conscience." Nevertheless, Blackstone allowed only that such nonconforming acts could be "tolerated" so long as they did not disturb the good order of the established church and of society.[126] In short, Blackstone endorsed the principle of freedom of "faith conduct," but he could not bring himself to the point of endorsing its practice.

The Advent of Freedom of Religion

It was not until the eve of the American Revolution that this common-law principle of limited civil jurisdiction was applied to matters of religion by any political state. Adopted in 1776, the Virginia Declaration of Rights captured the essence of the principle with the following language:

> That religion, or the duty which we owe to our CREATOR,
> and the manner of discharging it, can be directed only by

reason and conviction, not by force or violence; and therefore
all men are entitled to free exercise of religion, according to
the dictates of conscience; and that it is the mutual duty of
all to practice Christian forbearance, love and charity towards
each other.[127]

An earlier draft, written by George Mason, had contained the
typical language of religious toleration: "that all men should enjoy
the fullest Toleration in the Exercise of Religion . . . unpunished and
unrestrained . . . unless . . . any Man disturb the Peace, the Happiness
or Safety of Society or of Individuals."[128] But this language was rejected
and the absolute jurisdictional guarantee of free exercise of religion
was inserted. Freedom of religion was to be determined by the nature
of the duty, i.e., whether or not it was enforceable only by "reason
and conviction" as dictated by the law of the Creator.[129] It could not
be balanced away or modified by any societal considerations.

It was James Madison who led his fellow Virginia statesmen to
make this significant break with the past. Had he been more successful,
he would also have included language of disestablishment. That battle
would have to be won on another day, and it was on January 19,
1786, when the Virginia Assembly passed Thomas Jefferson's *Act for
Establishing Religions Freedom*.[130] The operative section of this act
specifically prohibited the civil ruler from levying a tax to support
Christian teachers. But Jefferson's preamble to that section, also
adopted by the Virginia Assembly, embraced a principle that went
beyond that specific prohibition.

Beginning with the observation that Almighty God had created
the mind free from all coercive sanctions, even in humanity's
relationship with Him, Jefferson concluded that "to compel a man to
furnish contributions of money for the propagation of opinions which
he disbelieves, is sinful and tyrannical."[131] It is sinful because it violates
the law of God's limiting the authority of the civil ruler: "Render
therefore unto Caesar the things which be Caesar's and unto God
which be God's" (Luke 20:25). And it is tyrannical because true liberty
is found only when humanity's law conforms to the law of God. This
latter proposition was clearly derived from the teachings of Bracton,
the father of the common law, who claimed that there was no king
"where will, not law, wields dominion."[132] The former proposition,
likewise, stemmed from Bracton's use of Christ as the supreme example
of a man with all power and dominion but who nevertheless was
committed to obey the law so that He might redeem those who were
under the law.[133]

These common-law antecedents found in Jefferson's preamble are also evident in James Madison's famous *Memorial and Remonstrance*, written in support of the Act that, in effect, disestablished religion in Virginia. If a man failed to pay his tithe as he ought, Madison claimed that "it is an offence against God, not against man" for the payment of the tithe was a duty "precedent, both in order of time and in degree of obligation, to the claims of Civil Society."[134] Here, Madison's reliance on Blackstone's view of the law of nature, i.e., God's will revealed in nature, limits the authority of the human lawmaker who cannot enact any rule into law contrary to natural revelation. To do so would not create "bad law," but would create a rule that was not law at all.[135]

This philosophical premise enabled Madison to learn from his predecessors but not to be bound by their practices. For example, John Locke provided a fertile seedbed for true freedom of religion with his arguments in *A Letter Concerning Toleration*. In that letter Locke defined civil authority as extending to the protection of life, health, liberty, and the possession of outward things, property. These interests were protectible by the use of force and coercion because the civil magistrate had been created by the consent of the governed for the very purpose of securing such rights. But the civil jurisdiction was not without limits: "Now that the whole jurisdiction of the magistrate reaches only to these civil concernments; and that all civil power, right, and dominion, is bounded and confined to the only care of promoting these things; and that it neither can nor ought in any manner to be extended to the salvation of souls."[136]

Locke did not limit the civil religious immunity to only inward beliefs, but extended it to some acts as well. However, he never broke from the English practice of toleration.

Freedom of Religion and the Law of Revelation

While neither Jefferson nor Madison cited God's revelation in the Holy Scripture, both clearly embraced the Genesis account of creation as the foundation for their views on freedom of religion. While they knew that they were departing from the English practice of toleration and establishment of religion, they believed that by doing so they would be more true to the common-law jurisdictional principle than those who had gone before them. But their reliance on God's revelation in nature, unaccompanied by explicit justification based on the Scriptures, meant that the full implications of this new experiment in church and state would not be realized either in their lifetimes or in the next two hundred years.

As the great Lord Acton has so clearly stated it, the key to understanding true freedom of religion is found in the teachings and life of Jesus Christ.[137] It was Christ who taught the basic principle: "Render therefore unto Caesar the things which be Caesar's, and unto God the things which be God's" (Luke 20:25). It was also Christ who embraced this principle at his own trial before Pilate when Pilate asked him if He was the King of the Jews. Pilate's question was obviously directed to Jesus to determine if he was guilty of treason, for the Roman emperor was the king of everyone in the Roman Empire, including the Jews. Jesus replies that He is the King of the Jews, but that His Kingdom "is not of this world"; rather His Kingdom is "truth" (John 18:36–37). In light of this response, Pilate could not and did not find Jesus guilty of treason: "I find in him no fault at all" (John 18:33–38). In effect, Pilate acknowledged that neither he nor the Roman emperor as civil ruler had any authority over what is truth.

The significance of this jurisdictional limitation on the power of the civil ruler was soon revealed in the life of the early church. In Acts 4 and 5, it is recorded that the church was twice ordered by the ruling religious council of the Jews "not to speak at all nor teach in the name of Jesus" (Acts 4:17; 5:28). The religious council backed its order with the exercise of civil power first by threatening to imprison the church leaders, Peter and John, and then by beating them (Acts 4:3, 21, 40). But led by the Holy Spirit to Psalm 2, Peter and John claimed that their authority to teach came from God, not Caesar, so that they could not help but teach what they had heard, for they must obey God, not men, in this matter (Acts 4:19–31; 5:29).

This biblical heritage affirming the exclusive sovereignty of God over the work of the church is clearly the foundation of America's early formative embracement of a constitutional guarantee of the free exercise of religion. At the heart of that guarantee is the right to choose one's religious faith without fear of civil sanction. Madison put it this way in his *Remonstrance:* To use civil power as a "means of salvation . . . is a contradiction to the Christian [r]eligion itself, for every page of it disavows a dependence on the powers of this world."[138] Not only did Madison rest his case for freedom of religion on this explicitly biblical base, he further observed that the Christian religion, not having been invented by men, was not in need of enforcement by men. Indeed, Madison reminded the reader "that this religion [Christianity] both existed and flourished, not only without the support of human laws, but in spite of every opposition from them, and not only during the period of miraculous aid, but long after it had been left to its own evidence and the ordinary care of Providence."[139]

Finally, Madison returned to the creation theme struck by the text of Virginia's constitutional guarantee, that religion is a duty owed to the Creator, enforceable only by reason and conviction: "[I]t is a contradiction in terms; for a [r]eligion not invented by human policy, must have pre-existed and been supported, before it was established by human policy."[140]

But was Madison's view of freedom of religion limited to religious matters, such as the "means of salvation"? Almost all legal and political scholars have assumed that Madison and Jefferson claimed protection only for humanity's "religious opinions" under the constitutional guarantee of free exercise of religion. That assumption is clearly false and has given rise to one of the most pernicious infringements on the rights of conscience in the history of humankind: the system of tax-supported public schools in America.

For nearly one hundred years, American education has been dominated by a tax-supported and civilly supervised program. This system has been assumed to be consistent with constitutional guarantees of freedom of religion so long as religious activities are not conducted and religious opinions are not inculcated in the public schools. Because citizens are taxed to support the system, they are inevitably forced to support the teaching of some ideas with which they disagree. As for Bible-believing Christians, they are forced to support a system of education that "constitutionally requires," according to the United States Supreme Court, that their ideas be excluded from the classroom dialogue.[141] No one in America would require an atheist or agnostic to pay taxes to support the church or the church school. Yet millions of American Christians are required to pay for an educational program that assumes that there is no God, or that, if He exists, He is irrelevant to history, science, and language. American school~hildren study subjects as if the Author of these subjects does not even exist.

This was not what Jefferson and Madison had in mind when they endorsed freedom of religion. Jefferson put it most succinctly when he stated "[t]hat to compel a man to furnish contributions of money for the propagation of *opinions* with which he disbelieves, is sinful and tyrannical."[142] Religion, for Jefferson, embraced *all* opinions, not just religious ones. Madison agreed. He wrote that the civil magistrate could not be "a competent [j]udge of [r]eligious [t]ruth" and that, therefore, he could not use religion as an engine of civil policy.[143] What is tax supported education but an "engine" of "civil policy" whereby the public school teacher "inculcates" the "fundamental values necessary to the maintenance of a democratic political system."[144] In fact, this is the very description that has been consistently attached to the role of the public school system by even the most liberal justices of the United States Supreme Court.

Madison's and Jefferson's view of civil immunity for all of the opinions of humankind rests squarely on Christ's claim that He is the King of truth and that His kingdom encompasses all of truth, not just matters of salvation. The apostle Paul summarized this foundational principle in his letter to the Colossians: In Christ "are hid *all* the treasures of wisdom and knowledge" (Col. 2:3). And Paul practiced what he preached as is evidenced by his sermon on Mars Hill in Athens, the intellectual capitol of the Roman Empire. In that brief message Paul spoke of history, philosophy, and the natural sciences; of politics, anthropology, and psychology; and of gerontology, futurology, and theology (Acts 17:22–31). All disciplines, all truth, are subject to God's Holy Spirit, immune from the sanctions of human tyrants pretending to exercise civil power.

Jefferson's preamble to his *Statute for Religious Freedom* echoes Paul's comprehensive understanding of the nature of religion as embodying all of truth. He wrote that the opinions of men are not the "object" of civil government because "our civil rights have no dependence on our religious opinions, anymore than our opinions in physics or geometry."[145] Jefferson claimed that truth would prevail only in an arena free from civil regulation or subsidy. He, therefore, concluded that the civil magistrate could exercise power only after the breaking out of "overt acts against peace and good order."[146] All of this followed from Jefferson's having embraced the same principle of liberty as had Jesus Christ and the early church, and in words that are unmistakably biblical:

> Well aware that Almighty God hath created the mind free; that all attempts to influence it by temporal punishments or burdens, or by civil incapacitations, tend only to beget habits of hypocrisy and meanness, and are a departure from the plan of the Holy Author of our religion, who, being Lord both of body and mind, yet chose not to propagate it by coercions on either, as was in His Almighty power to do.[147]

CONCLUSION

As evidenced by this opening statement in Jefferson's preamble to his 1786 *Statute for Religious Freedom*, America's founding fathers embraced a philosophy of law and government explicitly based on God's revelation in nature and in the Holy Scriptures. This philosophy was deeply rooted in the English common-law heritage to which America's founders clung even as they sought independence from the mother country. It is a philosophy that served America well in the beginning by establishing both economic liberty on the common law of private property and political liberty on a constitutional guarantee of freedom of religion.

These liberties have been put in jeopardy in America in the last one hundred years because the nation's leaders and its people have drifted from a Godly heritage of a created order with fixed, uniform, and universal rules to a scientific future of a changing technological order with an evolving set of values. This shift in philosophy has ushered America into an age of uncertainty and of escalating costs as legal, political, and economic norms break down. God's revelation offers to the nation a set of "self-evident truths" that, if embraced, will insure to all humankind God-given rights of life, liberty, and the pursuit of happiness.

NOTES

1. This chapter, originally given at the Consultation on the Christian and Law, subsequently was published by Regent University Law Review 4 (Spring 1994) and is used by permission. It was decided to retain the legal form for the endnotes of this chapter unlike the remainder of the book. For consistency, the legal citation style follows *The Chicago Manual of Style*, 15.312–15.320. John C. H. Wu, *Fountain of Justice: A Study in the Natural Law* 65 (1955).

2. Ibid., 71.

3. Henry Bracton, *De Legibus er Consuetudinibus Angliae* 39 (Sir Travers Twiss ed. 1878).

4. Wu, *Fountain of Justice*, 93.

5. Ibid., 91–93.

6. Ibid., 91.

7. Ibid.

8. Ibid.

9. Wu, *Fountain of Justice*, 91 (quoting *Calvin v Smith*, Eng. Rep. 377 [K. B. 1610]).

10. John Calvin, *Institutes of the Christian Religion*, 1504 ed. J. T. McNeill, trans. F. L. Battles (Westminster 1960).

11. All Scripture in this chapter is from the King James Version of the Bible.

12. William Blackstone, 1 *Commentaries* *39, 41.

13. Joseph Story, "Discourse Pronounced upon the Inauguration of the Author as Dane Professor of Law in Harvard University, August 25, 1829," in *The Legal Mind in America*, ed. Perry Miller 176, 178 (1962).

14. The Declaration of Independence ¶ 1 (U.S. 1776).

15. Ibid.

16. Ibid.

17. The phrase has been inspired by Dr. Francis Schaeffer's books, *The God Who Is There* (1968), and *He Is There and He Is Not Silent* (1972).

18. See generally, Gary Amos, *Defending the Declaration* (Wolgemuth & Hyatt, 1989).

19. Jesse Root, "The Origin of Government and Laws in Connecticut, 1789," in Miller, *The Legal Mind in America*, 31.

20. Ibid., 34–35.

21. Blackstone, 1 *Commentaries*, *38–39.

22. Ibid.

23. Ibid., 39.

24. This term reflects the realm of nature that was made in the image of God (Gen. 1:27). The term emphasized the distinction between humans and animals. The emphasis is necessary in this modern age so enamored with the Darwinian belief that a human is only a "human animal."

25. Blackstone, 1 *Commentaries*, 39–40.

26. Ibid., *40.

27. Ibid.

28. Ibid.

29. Ibid., *40–41.

30. Root, "The Origin of Government," 36.

31. Ibid., 35–36.

32. Blackstone, 1 *Commentaries*, *41–42.

33. Ibid., *42.

34. Ibid.

35. Ibid.

36. Ibid.

37. Ibid.

38. Ibid.

39. Ibid., *44.

40. Ibid., *42.

41. Ibid., *42–43.

42. Blackstone, 4 *Commentaries*, *9 (quoting Gen. 9:6).

43. Ibid., *194 (quoting Num. 35:31).

44. Ibid.

45. Ibid. *Nos divini juris rigorum moderantes* is translated as "We are those who moderate the rigor of divine law."

46. Ibid., *9.

47. Blackstone, 1 *Commentaries*, *43.

48. Ibid., *44.

49. Ibid., *38.

50. Ibid., *40.

51. Ibid., *45.

52. Ibid.

53. Ibid., *54.

54. Ibid., *55.
55. Ibid.
56. Ibid., *63.
57. Ibid., *63–64.
58. Ibid., 64.
59. Ibid., *69–70.
60. Ibid., *69.
61. Ibid., *69–71.
62. Ibid., *70.
63. Ibid., *70–71.
64. Root, "The Origin of Government," 34.
65. Ibid., 35.
66. Ibid., 35–36.
67. Ibid., 37.
68. Ibid., 37–38.
69. See, e.g., James C. Carter, *Law Its Origin Growth and Function* (DaCapo Press, 1974).
70. Christopher C. Langdell, *A Selection of Cases on the Law of Contracts* vi (Little, Brown, & Company, The Legal Classics Library ed. 1983).
71. Oliver Wendell Holmes Jr., *The Common Law* 1 (1887).
72. *South Pacific Co. v Jensen*, 244 U.S. 205, 222 (1917) (Holmes, J., dissenting).
73. John C. Gray, *The Nature and Sources of Law* 99 (2d ed. 1921).
74. Hugh Hawkins, *Between Harvard and America* 129–30 (1972).
75. Henry S. Commager, 1978: "The World of the Mind," 64 *American Bar Association Journal* 1003, 1005–6 (1978).
76. See, e.g., Phillip E. Johnson, *Darwin on Trial* (1991).
77. Stanley N. Katz, "Introduction," in Blackstone, 1 *Commentaries* vi (University of Chicago Press, facsimile ed. 1979).
78. Ibid.
79. Blackstone, 2 *Commentaries*, *2.
80. Ibid., *2–3 (paraphrasing Gen. 1:28).
81. Ibid., *3.
82. James Kent, 2 *Commentaries on American Law* *317.
83. See Will Durant, *The Life of Greece* 102 (1939).
84. Lucretius, "On the Nature of Things," in *Man and the Universe The Philosophers of Science*, ed. S. Commins and R. N. Linscott 27 (Random House 1947).
85. Ibid., 33.
86. Will Durant, *Caesar and Christ* (1944), 61; see also Lucretius, "On the Nature of Things," 28–29.
87. Durant, *Caesar and Christ*, 256.
88. Ibid., 236–42.

89. Kent, *Commentaries on American Law*, *317–18.
90. Ibid., *318.
91. Durant, *Caesar and Christ*, 38–39.
92. Durant, *The Life of Greece*, 431–32.
93. Durant, *Caesar and Christ*, 251.
94. Ibid.
95. Kent, *Commentaries on American Law*, *318.
96. Ibid.
97. Blackstone, 2 *Commentaries*, *5–6.
98. John Locke, *Second Treatise of Government*, ed. C. B. McPherson 18 (1980).
99. Ibid., 24–25.
100. "The earth . . . and all things therein, are the general property of mankind, exclusive of other beings, from the immediate gift of the Creator." Blackstone, 2 *Commentaries*, *3.
101. Locke, *Second Treatise of Government*, 105 (quoting Ps. 115:16).
102. Blackstone, 2 *Commentaries*, *5–6; Locke, *Second Treatise of Government*, *23-24.
103. Blackstone, 2 *Commentaries*, *8; Locke, *Second Treatise of Government*, *27-30.
104. Blackstone, 2 *Commentaries*, *3–15.
105. Locke, *Second Treatise of Government*, *18.
106. Ibid., *19.
107. Ibid.
108. Ibid.
109. Kent, *Commentaries on American Law*, 319.
110. Ibid.
111. Ibid., 328.
112. William Gesenius, *A Hebrew and English Lexicon of the Old Testament*, ed. F. Brown, trans. E. Robinson (1907), 921–22.
113. Locke, *Second Treatise of Government*, 105; Kent, *Commentaries on American Law*, *326. George Tucker, Virginia lawyer and professor of law at The College of William and Mary, wrote in a footnote in his edition of Blackstone's *Commentaries* that he disagreed with Blackstone's view that family inheritance was a matter of societal convention. Blackstone, 3 *Commentaries* 10 n (William Birch Young & Abraham Small 1803).
114. See Richard Hofstadter, *Social Darwinism in American Thought* (rev. ed. 1959), 3–66.
115. See, e.g., Upton Sinclair, *The Goose Step* (rev. ed. 1922), 15–18, 436–40.
116. Karl Marx, *Communist Manifesto* (1848), reprinted in *The Portable Karl Marx*, trans. E. Kamenka (Viking Press 1983), 219, 223.

117. See Melvin Maddocks, *Brave New Marriage*, 230 Atlantic Monthly 66–69 (1972); see also Harry D. Krause, *Family Law Cases Comments and Questions* 123–72 (3d ed. 1990).

118. See American Law Institute, 1 pt. 2 *Model Penal Code and Commentaries* 430 (1980).

119. Amos, *Defending the Declaration*, 128–29.

120. Blackstone, 1 *Commentaries*, *39–43.

121. Kent, *Commentaries on American Law*, 328–29.

122. Ibid., 330.

123. See Blackstone, 4 *Commentaries*, *9, *38, *40, *43, *44,*45 as well as the accompanying text from notes 46–52 in this chapter.

124. See, e.g., *Buch v Amory Mfg. Co.*, 44 A. 809, 811 (N.H. 1898).

125. Blackstone, 4 *Commentaries*, *41–45.

126. Ibid., *51–53.

127. Virginia Const., Art I, § 16.

128. George Mason's "Proposal for the Virginia Declaration of Rights (June 12, 1776)," in *James Madison on Religious Liberty*, ed. R. S. Alley (1985), 51.

129. James Madison, "Memorial and Remonstrance against Religious Assessments (circa June 20, 1785)," in *James Madison on Religious Liberty*, 56.

130. Thomas Jefferson, "An Act for Establishing Religious Freedom," in 12 Hening 84 (1786).

131. Ibid.

132. Bracton, *De Legibus*, 39.

133. See the text accompanying note 3 in this chapter.

134. Madison, "Memorial and Remonstrance," 56–57.

135. Blackstone, 1 *Commentaries*, *70.

136. John Locke, "A Letter Concerning Toleration (1689)," in *The Locke Reader*, ed. John W. Yolton (1977), 246.

137. John E. E. D. Acton, *Essays on Freedom and Power* 81 (1956); see also Herbert W. Titus, "Education, Caesar's or God's: A Constitutional Question of Jurisdiction," 3 *Journal of Christian Jurisprudence 101* (1982).

138. Madison, "Memorial and Remonstrance," 57.

139. Ibid.

140. Ibid.

141. See *Edwards v Aguillard*, 482 U.S. 578, 584, 597 (1987).

142. Jefferson, "An Act for Establishing Religious Freedom," 84 (emphasis added).

143. Madison, "Memorial and Remonstrance," 57.

144. The words are from *Ambach v Norwick*, 441 U.S. 68, 77 (1979), an opinion written by moderately conservative Justice Lewis Powell J.,

and they were quoted with approval and without reservation by former Justice William J. Brennan J., in *Board of Education v Pico*, 457 U.S. 853, 864 (1982).

145. Jefferson, "An Act for Establishing Religious Freedom," 84.
146. Ibid.
147. Ibid.

TWO

The Philosophical and Biblical Perspectives That Shaped the Declaration of Independence

Gary Amos

INTRODUCTION: CONVENTIONAL APPROACH PRE-1980s

Prior to the decade of the 1980s, the claim posed by the above title would have been refuted quite simply. First, the philosophical perspectives that shaped the Declaration of Independence were those of Renaissance and Enlightenment humanism, with their roots in classical Roman and Greek philosophy. Second, there were no biblical perspectives that shaped the Declaration of Independence, and any apparent mention of theological ideas in the document was mere lip service—a culturally required exercise of civil religion.[1]

This view still dominates in political science textbooks and in selected reading assignments in high schools, colleges, and universities across America. The conventional wisdom, in a nutshell, is that Thomas Jefferson and the coauthors of the Declaration of Independence were philosophically and intellectually Deists and Enlightenment humanists in their view of law, government, rights, and politics. Behind this general persuasion is the widespread notion that all of America's constitutional and democratic institutions trace their intellectual and philosophical heritage to the philosophies of the seventeenth-century Enlightenment and from there to the influence of ancient Greco-Roman culture. This type of view has held sway in American academia at least since the early 1920s and only recently has been challenged in any significant way.

The MacPherson Analysis: A Typical Example of the Dominant View

When C. B. MacPherson wrote *The Political Theory of Possessive Individualism* in 1962, his highly acclaimed work dealing with rights theory contained a number of basic assumptions.[2] The first is that Western rights theory in the twentieth century—including American rights theory—is drawn squarely from such thinkers as Jeremy Bentham in the eighteenth century, by way of John Stuart Mill in the nineteenth century. The second major assumption is that Mill and Bentham built on a seventeenth-century rights-theory foundation provided by Locke, Hobbes, and Grotius, who were assumed to be Enlightenment rationalists with a humanist worldview. There was no need to look earlier than the seventeenth century for rights theory because there was nothing there. Rights theory traces to the seventeenth century and its humanism, and there the search stops.

During the 1960s and 1970s it was widely accepted that America is indebted to John Stuart Mill for the modern notions of individualism and individual rights. Mill was seen as a great expositor of the ideas of Jefferson and Madison. That view is mistaken, however. Twentieth-century America has departed radically from the rights theory of its founders and from the Declaration of Independence. Indeed the entire libertarian political movement, which attempts to trace its heritage to Jefferson and Madison, more accurately traces its heritage to Mill and Bentham, who were outside the Jeffersonian stream of thought. It is a mistake to read back onto Jefferson and the Declaration the current notions of rights, which have been reduced to mere "civil liberties" or positivistic "constitutional rights" that have no existence apart from political action and are valid only if the government chooses to protect them.

As Abraham Lincoln advocated, we must begin taking the Declaration of Independence seriously and stop acting as if it were a mere propaganda tract of no political significance. After all, it is part of our organic law, and a civil war was fought over its claims. Anyone who undertakes a reexamination of the philosophical heritage of the Declaration must discard the MacPherson thesis as entirely inadequate. A new approach must be used based on more accurate assumptions.

Secular Philosophical Roots Only

The MacPherson thesis is only typical of the dominant approach. His thesis was widely respected because it built on or agreed with imposing precedents. One of those was the seminal work on the Declaration of Independence done by Carl Becker in 1922.[3] Becker was the darling of a leading intellectual movement of his day. That movement, emanating from such places as Harvard, Columbia, and Yale, promoted the revision in pragmatic Darwinian evolutionary terms of every aspect of American history and culture. Becker was one of its premier foot soldiers.[4] Besides being a committed Darwinian revisionist, Becker was also enamored with the Hegelian dialectic, and early on, he embraced the Marxist application of that dialectic. In the first version of Becker's book on the Declaration of Independence, he explained that the American Revolution along with the French Revolution was just one more step in an evolutionary chain of the dialectic of history, leading to the final synthesis that was the Bolshevik Revolution of 1917. In 1922, Becker saw Communism as the final and purest form of what the French Revolution, and to a lesser extent the American Revolution, aimed for. Becker became publicly embarrassed by that conclusion and revised it in subsequent editions of his book; but he never departed from using the underlying dialectical philosophy as an analytical hook in dealing with the facts of history. That is why Becker's book is in some respects more of a propaganda tract about the Declaration than an objective attempt to explain its meaning and structure.

Stripped to its bare essentials, the Becker thesis is simply that Jefferson and the founders were secular and rationalist in their philosophy of law and rights. They were self-consciously Deists and Enlightenment humanists. They longed for the day when the masses would be enlightened and not be prone to thinking in religious and biblical terms all the time; but they were cynical as well. They used religious metaphors in the same way that Locke supposedly used them—insincerely and as an unavoidable requirement for winning the allegiance of the masses of religiously convinced colonists, whose help must be enlisted for the cause to succeed.

Declaration of Independence—Nonbiblical or Antibiblical

The Becker thesis has seemed all but unassailable for seventy years. It has had many subscribers. In this group are a number of evangelicals who feel duty bound to attack or repudiate the Declaration of Independence for having a nonbiblical or antibiblical foundation. As of 1989, few examples in this regard are Greg Singer and a number of the followers of Gary North as well as Gary North himself. Another group also exists that ought to be mentioned, although they are important to a lesser degree. It is composed of those evangelicals who are present-day partisans of southern secession. They attack the Declaration of Independence for all the reasons mentioned above, as well as because Abraham Lincoln was for it and radical secessionists were against it. They are influenced by such spokesmen as Otto Scott, as well as by a score of conspiracy writers who attack the founders on other grounds, such as being guilty of Masonic influence.

Classical Roman and Greek Epistemological Roots

At the core of the prevailing denial of any biblical influence on the Declaration is the conviction that classical Roman and Greek ideas underlie it. Those who want the Declaration to be non-Christian or nonbiblical emphasize the supposed Deist or Enlightenment humanist influence on its philosophy and structure. Such an influence, it is said, traces directly to the Greco-Roman view of the universe. Those who wish that the Declaration were Christian or biblical, but are convinced that it is not and are embarrassed that it is nonbiblical or antibiblical, also believe that classical ideas rather than biblical ideas underlie it. Both sides generally agree than a pagan epistemology rather than a Christian one is at the heart of the Declaration's meaning and structure.

RECENT CHALLENGE FROM MEDIEVAL SCHOLARS

Recent scholarship from experts of the medieval period directly refutes the MacPherson thesis along with the dominant conventional wisdom of the past several decades. Indirectly it challenges the Becker thesis and the prevailing view of the Declaration of Independence.

Michel Villey—Modern Rights Theories Traced to the Fourteenth Century

French scholar Michel Villey spent four decades doing exhaustive research and writing about the rights perspectives of classical Rome and Greece.[5] His groundbreaking work was the first in this generation to call into serious question the conventional wisdom that all rights theory had its beginnings with the humanist Enlightenment in the seventeenth century. This fact is particularly important, since Villey himself is an avowed humanist and devotee of Aristotelian jurisprudence. For those familiar with his work, there was no question that Villey had shown conclusively that Western rights theories[6] could not be traced to classical Rome and Greece. He demonstrated that although some of the language of rights existed in Rome and Greece, the fundamental philosophical concepts, indispensable to the English and America experience, were entirely lacking from the Greek and Roman worldview and experience.

Since Greece and Rome could not be accredited with the birth of Western rights theories, Villey was forced to look elsewhere. In his attempt to show where the crucial shift began, Villey settled on the fourteenth-century figure, William of Ockham, a nominalist theologian of the Roman Catholic Church.

Richard Tuck—Modern Rights Theory Preexisted Ockham

The next groundbreaking work in the area of rights history was done in England by Richard Tuck of Cambridge. Tuck agreed with

Villey that the transitional ideas that gave rise to modern rights theory could not be traced to the Greeks or the Romans. But Tuck's study of the medieval period revealed to him that Villey had overlooked sources of modern rights theory that were much earlier than Ockham and the fourteenth century. Tuck's research showed that the necessary elements of Western rights were current by at least the twelfth century.[7]

Brian Tierney—Locating Transitional Elements Even Earlier

Rights expert Brian Tierney uncovered sources and evidences that led him to be dissatisfied with the conclusions of both Villey and Tuck.[8] Whereas Tuck had located the transitional ideas in the twelfth century, Tierney demonstrated that the transitional ideas existed as early as the eleventh century.[9] As for the twelfth century, not only did the transitional ideas exist as Tuck had shown; but full-blown, highly developed concepts of individual, personal, active rights existed in the twelfth century.

REASONS FOR DOUBTING THE GREEK-ROMAN CONNECTION

When we examine the ancients' beliefs about rights, we find that their views of rights are quite different and distinct from the kind of thinking that gave rise to the idea of inalienable rights. The Greeks had no concept of inalienable rights. And the ideas of claim rights, subjective rights, and active rights were either weak or nonexistent, depending on what period of history one studies. Yet, all these concepts can be found in the Scriptures.

The Declaration's words, "all men are created equal and are endowed by their Creator with certain unalienable rights," cannot be traced to the Greeks for the following reasons. First, the Greeks had no clear concept of a creator. The Greeks were polytheists who believed in an eternally existing universe in which matter and divinity shared the same essence. The Greeks did not believe in a personal creator god. The Bible and biblical religion teach about God the Creator, who is separate and distinct from His creatures. The Declaration rests on such a concept of the Creator and, thus, cannot be Greek.

Second, the overall Greek view of the universe did not allow for the notion that the universe or men were created. For the most part, the Greeks believed that the universe emanated or sprang from an impersonal divine force that permeates the universe. At best, Zeus pervades all things, and nature is an extension of his being.[10] All men and things participate in this essence and possess divinity in differing degrees. All men are thus inherently unequal. Some men are more divine than others.

Third, there was no room in Greek philosophy or religion for the notion of endowment because creatures and divinity were never separated. Creatures were believed to be visible manifestations of divine energy. Matter was viewed as an infusion and generation of divine force, not as endowed by a transcendent and separate creator. The Greek worldview provided for a belief in magic and divination whereby men could manipulate cosmic forces and the powers of inferior deities. But it made no place for the belief in a divine endowment of authority or power from a creator. Greek religion rested on the notion of the "chain of being" in which all things share in the same divine essence. God was the universe, and the universe was divine.

Fourth, the nature of Greek philosophy and religion rendered rights unfixed or uncertain. Greek mystery religion made truth unknowable and inscrutable. Humanity's existence was subject to the whim and caprice of the gods and fate. The heart of Greek belief was not certainty but tragedy. Man's status in the universe was always tenuous, never fixed. His rights, where such were even mentioned, were never certain.

Fifth, the Greeks could not conceive of inalienable rights. The same Greek beliefs about mystery, fate, and tragedy made all human characteristics and attributes mutable and alienable. The Greek world operated on the principle of might rather than right. The gods of the Greeks were heroes or giants of force, power, and might. The Greeks gloried in might and power. Weak men deserved to be slaves of strong men because the strong were more like the gods.

Sixth, the Greeks could not conceive of rights that were god given. The Greeks believed that rights were a product of society and state. Only free men had rights, because free men were able to participate in the government of the *polis*, the "city." Slaves, women, and children did not share those rights because they had no political voice. What rights men had were created by the state and could be ended by the state. Rights were politically given and subject to the political process, rather than god given.

Seventh, only in biblical religion do we find all the component parts that make up the Declaration's phrase that "all men are created equal and are endowed by the Creator with certain unalienable rights." The message of the Bible is about a Creator who created all men equal because all men are made in the image and likeness of God. He is separate from His creatures and over them in all things. This view of God stands in complete distinction to the Greek belief in an eternally existing universe where god and matter share the same essence.[11] And the Bible's view of man stands in stark contrast to that of the Greeks in which men belong at different levels in a great mystical hierarchy where they participate in the divine essence of the universe.

Neither Aristotle nor Plato believed that all men were created or that they were created equal or that they were endowed by a creator with rights or that such rights were inalienable. Both still held to Greek polytheism that declared all men inherently unequal. Even the gods were unequal for the Greeks.

Aristotle thought that some men ought to be slaves. Plato believed that women and children had no rights because they had nothing to contribute to the political life of the state. Both agreed with the natural character of slavery and with the Greek practice of dividing the human race into distinct and unequal political and ethnic groups. Only males who could make the state a more perfect state had rights. In Greece, people were deemed to be inherently unequal.

The Greeks did not believe in rights by nature any more than they believed in law by nature. According to Antiphon, the Sophists held nature to be in opposition to law, custom, and conventions.[12] For the Greeks, law was antithetical to nature. Men create law by convention, and whatever rights men have (in the distributive sense) are at the grace of the state. They are state created. Socrates, for example, believed that rights were a product of convention.[13] The same can be said of Plato. It is impossible to link law and rights in the Greek view the way they are linked in the Declaration.

In the Greek view all rights are alienable because all rights are politically given rather than god given.[14] Humanity's right is to receive the justice due it as determined by the state. The state is higher and more important than the human even though the purpose of the state is to perfect humans. A man is only fully human when he is being directed by another superior man who is a statesman, legislator, or other civil ruler.[15] Of the Greek view, Leo Strauss writes, "Political activity is then properly directed if it is directed toward human perfection or virtue."[16]

It is well known that the Greeks had no doctrine of equality.[17] Strauss correctly observes: "Equal rights for all appeared to the classics as most unjust."[18] The Greeks, and later the Romans, believed that some men by nature were superior to others and had an inherent right to rule others. The Roman Stoic, Cicero, did not change this view. Thus, equal rights cannot be traced to Cicero either.

Tuck maintains that the Romans not only had a very weak theory of subjective rights, but they also lacked the modern elements of an active-right/claim-right theory.[19] At least the concept of subjective right was very weak in Rome. According to Tuck, all Roman rights were passive rights and as such made "liberty a relatively unimportant concept."[20]

The Romans did not see property as a right at all, much less as an inalienable right.[21] They followed the Greeks for whom "justice [was] incompatible with what is generally understood by private ownership."[22] Tuck says that the notion of *iura ad rem*, or rights in a thing, "would have been utterly incomprehensible to the Roman jurist, but it obviously followed from the idea of a right as a claim."[23] Tuck also says that the "classical Romans did not have a theory about legal relationships in which the modern notion of a subjective right played any part."[24]

The idea of active and subjective claim rights, not merely passive but prosecutable rights, had to come from something other than a Greek or Roman source. Some change in Western thinking had to mark the shift from passive rights to claim rights, where all rights are juridically identifiable and legally redressable. Rights had to become a demand that one man could make on another man who owed him a duty. Without this shift, there could be no concept of inalienable rights.

That shift was initiated in the entrenched Hellenism of Greece and Rome by the coming of the Gospel. Prior to the Gospel, the state was the religion. The regime was coextensive with creation, and its purpose was to become the "best regime" by making men virtuous.[25] Redemption was to be brought to men through political action and state activism. All of this was in the name and service of the local deity whose chief priest was also the chief magistrate of the city or *polis*. Greek religion knew nothing of the separation of church and state.

Christianity meant that the state was no longer the religion. The purpose of the state became completely transformed in biblical religion. No longer was the *polis* or government to bring about redemption, but redemption and virtue in humanity was to be produced by God's supernatural activity.[26] The state became an administrator of justice under God's divine law, and men were to render to Caesar only those things that were Caesar's and to God what was God's. Christ did not equate the kingdom of God with a particular government or political party. Christianity made possible the jurisdictional separation of church and state.

THE NATURE OF THE TWELFTH-CENTURY CHANGE AND WHY IT HAPPENED

It is important to describe the nature of the change that happened in the twelfth century and attempt to account for why it took place.

Scholars generally use the term *twelfth-century humanism* to describe the cultural and intellectual shift of the period. The term can be misleading, and it must be carefully distinguished from seventeenth- and eighteenth-century Enlightenment humanism. Twelfth-century humanism describes a new appreciation for the dignity of the human person and for the sanctity of life that began to permeate European culture due to the preaching of the Gospel. Enlightenment humanism was a completely different phenomenon in that it sought to elevate humanity's importance by denying the relevance or existence of God. It also eradicated all norms, rules, and morals that were rooted in a Christian worldview.

Twelfth-century humanism was brought about by a new appreciation for the fact that humans are created in the image of God and are of inestimable value. Twelfth-century humanism marked a point in history where the stranglehold on culture caused by the brutal and fatalistic Greco-Roman view of humanity and society was finally being broken. Prior to the twelfth century, the Mediterranean traditions of brutality and valuelessness of humans, held over from the classical age and pagan religion, prevented the development of such ideas as the inalienable rights of the person and the equality of all.

It is also important to note that there was a change in Western Christianity itself. At least from the time of Augustine in the early fifth century, Christians generally expected the return of Christ by the end of the first millennium. When that event did not take place, tremendous upheavals occurred within Christianity itself. Christianity in Western Europe began to depart from its otherworldly spirituality. In A.D. 1054, the church split east and west, the eastern church retaining its eastern or Mediterranean ideals, and the western church becoming more western or less otherworldly.

This change in the church's posture toward the world and society is by far the most fundamental reason for the transition from East to West in the character and definition of European culture. There came to be an ever-widening gap between the Western Roman Catholic Church and the Eastern Orthodox Church. Consequently, both the common law and Western rights theory developed in the west entirely, and in the east not at all. This, of course, explains the predicament of Eastern Europe and the countries of the former Soviet Union.

THE GREGORIAN REFORM AND ITS FRUIT

Harold Berman explains in *Law and Revolution* (1983) that these changes came about due to the papal revolution begun by Pope Gregory VII in 1075.[27] I suspect that Pope Gregory came to an important realization, namely, since Christ had not returned at the end of the first millennium as had been expected, this meant that God had a long-range plan for the church in the world and society. The mysticism of the ninth and tenth centuries was not enough. Consequently, he directed that theologians and Bible scholars set about the task of applying the principles of Scripture to every practical area of human life and experience. The reform lasted for approximately two hundred years.

Not until the Gregorian Reform and the Investiture Struggle (1075–1122) did the biblical model begin to dominate Western political theory and become the central focus of debate about rights. This was the time in which "the Bishop of Rome sought to emancipate the clergy from the control of emperor, kings, and feudal lords, and sharply to differentiate the church as a political and legal entity from secular politics."[28] The modern Christian theory of rights was born in this period, due to the work of Christian jurists and legal scholars, even though the principles had been present in the linguistics of Scripture for more than a thousand years.

After the Gregorian Reform we enter an entirely different atmosphere. Whereas the classicists could never easily equate property and right, or *dominium* and *ius*, the "medieval lawyer always regarded property (*dominium*) as a right (*ius*)."[29] Irnerius, who founded the law school at Bologna at the end of the eleventh century, specifically equated *dominium* with *ius* following the biblical model.[30] Later, Irnerius's successor Azo insisted that property is not only a right (*dominium* is a *ius*) but a *ius* or right is also a *meritum* (claim).

Gregorian Reform and Western Culture

The theological and intellectual posture of the Gregorian Reform represented a decidedly Western shift in Christian theology that led to a decidedly Western shift in European culture. One need only compare the tenor of the writings of the Greek fathers of the church with the writings of Gregorian clerics and specialists of the eleventh and twelfth centuries to see the difference. It is more than just a difference between Greek and Latin languages; there is an obvious difference between Eastern and Western outlook and perspective. The new aggressive and activistic policy of the Western Roman Catholic Church toward culture and society, and the new mandate to Christianize existing institutions or charter entirely new ones, are distinctly different from the earlier mysticism and aloofness toward the world, a posture that remained dominant in the various Eastern Christian sects after the eleventh century.

Gregorian Reform and the Scholastic Worldview

One of the distinctive characteristics of the Gregorian Reform was the Scholastic methodology and worldview that prevailed. Throughout the period of the reform, namely the twelfth and thirteenth centuries, the clerics and theologians who applied the Bible to all of life did so with the tenacity of a modern-day Internal Revenue Service auditor or a special prosecutor. The reformers were men of incredible creative energy with encyclopedic abilities to analyze, organize, scrutinize, dissect, compare, and compile.

Because of the centuries of experience in the church councils in dealing with the minute matters of orthodoxy versus heresy, and the belief that there was nothing of more value and importance than the Word of God, there was already in the church a passion for detail and for highly technical specificity with regard to the use and application of every "word." Also, in this Gregorian-Scholastic worldview there were no seams. There was one unified view of all of life, whatever the subcategories might be. There was a direct correlation in the minds and practice of these reformers among theology, law, rights theory, polity, morality, and so forth. Legal theory was not chopped off and separated from theology. They were part of the same body of truth, to be understood and systematized in light of the Word of God.

The Common Law and Jurisprudence

It is easy to overlook the fact that the father of the common law, Henri de Bracton, was a reformer in the Gregorian tradition. He was an archdeacon in the church who ordained priests and who also introduced the writ system to England—a simple, yet elaborate, precise, and highly technical process of law. In one sense, this is entirely predictable, coming from a tireless Scholastic.

Scholastic Methodology and Key Terms

As should be expected, the common-law system of England, which was birthed by Scholastics, was thoroughly Scholastic in its methodology and treatment of key terms. The earliest judges were priests or bishops. The administrative officers or "clerks" (i.e., clerics) were from the lower clergy. They used as legal terms words that were part and parcel of the regular language of theology, and they distinguished between shades of meanings with all the care of theologians arguing the finer points of formal doctrinal disputations.

As Herb Titus has explained in his chapter in this work (see pp. 9–19), the common law was a cradle Christian. It was born in a Scholastic cradle, and dandled on Gregorian knees. This meant that from the outset, the common law had the typical Scholastic traits—

a unified approach to theology, law, rights, and political theory. The common law was more than just common law, it was a completely integrated view of all of life and society from a jural aspect laid in a Scholastic Christian matrix. It applied in the legal context the rigor of the church-council tradition where the incessant pursuit of truth was concerned. Moreover, it resolved differences in legal principles with the same approach used by the clergy to settle contemporary doctrinal controversies. This culture of the court left its mark so deeply on the later common law, that it survived the Protestantizing of the British nation with practically no change. So the common law contained more than just a legal theory. It contained a whole view of law, life, society, culture.

Impact of the Scholastic Method on the Common Law

It is very easy to see the impact of the Scholastic method on the common law when one looks at the system of pleading, with its highly technical requirements, and at common-law legal methodology. The practice of law and the common law was one of the last areas in society in which a vibrant Scholastic tradition and methodology remained. Because of this fact, the practice of law remained highly technical and Scholastic in method all the way up to the time of the American Revolution.

Simultaneous Development of Rights Theory

Because the common law was Scholastic from the beginning and continued to be so through the centuries, one should not be surprised to learn that there occurred a simultaneous development of rights theory as well as political theory within the common-law tradition. In the Scholastic worldview, these were all aspects of a single reality. Often the key persons in the development of rights theories were the same persons who were important in the development of theology or of law. As with the practice of law, pleading, the issuing of writs, and so forth, the language of rights was highly Scholastic and technical in methodology and terminology.

Some of the key players in the development of rights theory were the Dominicans and Franciscans. The Dominican, Thomas Aquinas, wrote the *Summa*, which presented a unified view of law and theology. Dominicans also articulated political theory and were probably the first to articulate the concept of inalienable rights of the person. The Franciscans made sure that the weakest and least powerful were deemed fully equal in every way to the most powerful or privileged in society.

Scholastic Methodology and Key Terms

There was no such thing as Western rights theory prior to the Gregorian Reform and prior to the activism of Gregorian clerics and technical specialists of the eleventh through the thirteenth centuries. But as Tuck and Tierney have shown, throughout the twelfth and thirteenth centuries an impressive and technical language of rights was developed, particularly by the Dominicans and the Franciscans. The same thinkers who provided the seminal work in canon law and the common law provided the seminal work in rights theory. The Latin Bible played a large role in this development. The Bible contained concepts that were entirely foreign to Greek and Roman thought. Thus, when the Bible was translated into Latin, new meanings were poured into Latin words, changing the nature of the Latin words themselves. Where rights language is concerned, the key was in first changing the Latin word *ius* to mean "a right," and the second in linking the Latin word *dominium* or property with the word *ius*.

In classical Latin, *ius* was a law. In medieval Latin under the influence of theologians, *ius* became a right. In classical Latin, *dominium* was the degree of power or control that a man exercised over a piece of land or a chattel. In medieval Latin—the world of abstract theorizing from a Trinitarian perspective—*dominium* took on its modern definition of being a complex bundle of rights, either to one's person, or goods, or relationships, or land, and among individuals, families, communities, and the state. In its use of the Latin Bible, the Scholastic culture and methodology from the Gregorian Reform in the Western Roman Catholic Church was just as central to the development of rights theory as it was to the common law. Indeed, the development of law and rights were two aspects of the same phenomenon.

Christian Streams

Dominican

There were two crucially important Christian streams in the birth and development of Western rights theory. The first was the Dominican stream. The Dominicans were the ones who defended the notion of property (*dominium*) as being part of humanity's God-given authority or rights prior to the fall into sin. Therefore, having and exercising property rights was not sinful in and of itself. A running feud took place among various groups of theologians for several centuries, centering around the passage in Scripture where God gave dominion (i.e., property) to humankind:

And God said, Let us make man in our image, after our
likeness: and let them have *dominion* over the fish of the sea,
and over the birds of the heavens, and over the cattle, and
over all the earth, and over every creeping thing that creepeth
upon the earth. And God created man in his own image, in
the *image of God* created he him; male and female created he
them. And God blessed them: and God said unto them, Be
fruitful, and multiply, and replenish the earth, and subdue it;
and have *dominion* over the fish of the sea, and over the birds
of the heavens, and over every living thing that moveth upon
the earth. (Gen. 1:26–28 ASV, emphasis added)

Some thought that property (*dominium*) resulted from man's fall into
sin. Therefore anything more than mere possession of nonconsumable
goods or use of consumable goods was inherently sinful and contrary to
the law of nature. The Dominicans finally won the feud, and in A.D.
1329 the pope officially approved the Dominican approach to
interpreting the dominion mandate stated in Genesis chapter one. The
church's position was that God gave humans *dominium* and all that it
entailed prior to the time that they fell into sin. Therefore humans
could exercise dominion innocently and not be viewed as sinning for
exercising property rights. Without this historical development, the
growth of rights theories in the West would have been considerably
stunted and may not have succeeded all.

Franciscan

The Franciscans were in one sense the arch enemies of the
Dominicans and in another their best ally. The Franciscans believed
that *dominium* was a result of the Fall; and therefore for a Christian to
live innocently in the world, he or she must renounce all property
rights or property ownership of any kind. The Dominicans and
Franciscans battled with each other over this matter for more than
two centuries. The Franciscans, at least on this point, were forerunners
of present-day Christian Marxists.

But the Franciscans placed a great deal of emphasis on the
importance of each individual person before God because each person
is created in God's image. Therefore, all men are created equal, and
there should be no class divisions or race divisions among humans.
The Dominicans came to accept this part of the Franciscan outlook
and incorporated it into the overall Dominican theory of law and
rights.

This high regard for the individual because of the image of God
being stamped on each person led the Dominicans to formulate the

basic concept of inalienable rights. Those rights of the person that were annexed to men's personality by the fact that God created them in his own image cannot be annulled by the actions of humans. Therefore, whatever is part of the image of God in people and part of people's dominion authority (i.e., rights) from the Creator is inalienable—it cannot be unconditionally sold, divested, diluted, or transferred either by people or by governments without displeasing the Maker.[31]

Defining the Scope of Dominium

The other feud that had to be settled involved how the Latin word *dominium* would be defined. In classical Latin, *dominium* had simply meant total control. If God gave humanity *dominium* in the pagan Latin sense, then humanity had unrestricted control over every aspect of its being, including the rights of its person. The Dominicans insisted that only God was sovereign and that only God has total control, therefore any *dominium* given to humans is partial and limited. Accursius coined the term *dominium utile*, which meant beneficial ownership rather than direct ownership. Therefore humanity is a trustee, rather than an owner, of its rights and dominion.

The reason this dispute is important is as follows: If *dominium* means that humanity has total control over its rights, then all rights are alienable. But if *dominium* means less-than-total control, then some rights would be inalienable. A human would not have enough *dominium* to transfer, sell, or give away that which was reserved by God. To the extent that humanity is a mere steward or trustee over God's property, it cannot sell or divest what belongs to God. Since the image of God in humans belongs to God and not to them, and because the life in humans belongs to God and not to them, humanity has a duty to live its life for God and a duty to live fully in the image of God. Such duty is inalienable duty toward God and, therefore, an inalienable right toward other people.

Dominion by Grace—i.e., Only Christians Have Rights

One of the earliest forms of rights theory was that of John Wycliffe who advocated dominion by grace. Those who believed in dominion by grace agreed that God had given dominion (property and rights) to Adam in the first chapter of Genesis, but they insisted that when Adam fell into sin, he forfeited all dominion. Therefore, since every descendent of Adam is born in sin, every human being is born without dominion. According to this view, only the saved or redeemed have been restored to the dominion, which Adam lost by his fall, through the redeeming grace of Jesus Christ. Consequently, only Christians have rights and have a right to take dominion over the earth. The dominion-by-grace philosophy created a two-class society with Christians in a superior social position and unbelievers in an inferior social position. This theory is still advocated in a modern form by such writers as James Jordan of the Reconstructionist movement.

Dominion by Nature—i.e., All Persons Have Rights

The dominion-by-grace explanation of Genesis 1 eventually failed to carry the day because it was not adopted by the Catholic Church as the best way to understand the dominion mandate in Scripture. The Dominican approach was adopted instead. The Dominican approach survived the clashes between Catholics and Protestants. It came to be accepted by both and, later, by the drafters of the Declaration of Independence.

The essence of the Dominican position was that God gave humanity dominion prior to the Fall, therefore dominion is not inherently sinful; and through the covenant with Noah, God renewed that dominion for all of Noah's progeny in spite of their corruption by sin. This meant, of course, that dominion is part of God's creation order rather than the redemption order. Dominion is still by grace, in one manner of speaking, but through ordinary grace that God shows to all humankind through the Noahic covenant. Dominion is not by the special grace that brings salvation. Dominion is still a part of God's creation law—the law of nature, which is prior in time to God's plan of salvation and the redemptive scheme of things. When God restored the ordinary course of nature and the law of nature through His covenant with Noah as the federal head of the race, he also reissued the basic creation mandate to every descendent of Noah forever.

By viewing dominion as pertaining to all humans rather than just the redeemed, the logical conclusion is that all humans have rights. This view of dominion and rights does not create a class-conscious structure in which Christians view themselves as special or superior when compared to unbelievers. The Christian view of rights means that there are rights for all, not for Christians only.

For centuries after this debate, the matter was considered settled. *Dominium* or property "was not a phenomenon of social intercourse, still less of civil law; it was a basic fact about human beings, on which their social and political relationships had to be posited."[32] *Dominium* or property dealt with the very character of humans and God's plan for them in the world. The Dominican view was received by the Calvinists in the Protestant Reformation and by the English common law so that in America and England the right to property was called inalienable. To deny humans the right of property is to deny an aspect of their personhood.

THE HUMANIST RESPONSE

Quattrocento Humanists

The humanist response was entirely predictable. The humanists of the fourteenth century rejected the Bible as a legitimate foundation for law theory, rights theory, and political theory. Instead they sought to return to the Greco-Roman view (e.g., Cicero and Aristotle) that exalted the state and public order as the ultimate expression of the good in society. The private individual was of little significance, and, therefore, rights should not even be a concern. The most important concern is public order, public law, and insuring that the power of the government is not unnecessarily challenged, thus endangering political stability and the status quo. The Quattrocento humanists had a low view of personal rights and did not accept the principle of inalienability.

Continental Humanists

The same conclusion is true about the humanists of the eighteenth-century Enlightenment. Enlightenment humanist intellectuals in France and England rejected the Christian heritage and rationale for rights theory. Instead they yearned for a return to the empire of classical Rome's glory days. This fact is somewhat obscured by the way in which the French Revolution began. The rallying cry of the French Revolution was "liberty, equality, and fraternity," based on the declaration of the "Rights of Man." However, it is clear from the words and deeds of the revolutionary leaders that their appeal to personal rights had been more or less plagiarized from the American colonial experience thirteen years earlier. It is also clear that the language of rights had been stripped of its epistemological core by bloodthirsty opportunists who directed that awful disaster.

The Renaissance

The humanists of the Renaissance did not believe in the creation account, natural law, or rights from nature or creation.[33] They rejected the Catholic ideas, based on the biblical account of creation and society, of the naturalness of rights and the principle of inalienability. They also rejected the link between the law of nature and inalienable rights—the fundamental basis of the Declaration's preamble.

"The humanists instead simply accepted the classical Roman view," says Tuck, "[that] all real moral relationships belonged to the stage of civilisation."[34] They "found it virtually impossible to talk about natural rights."[35] Humanist intellectuals of the Renaissance stood in the Quattrocento stream and were positivists: "What was important to them was not natural law but humanly constructed law, not natural rights but civil remedies."[36] Indeed, they viewed the Christian way of thinking about law and rights with "contempt."[37] Tuck rightly concludes, "Given the general attitude of the humanist lawyers, there was obviously no place in their thinking for natural rights of any kind. Man's natural life was simply not an appropriate setting for such things as *dominium*."[38]

Tuck reinforces his explanation by showing how Aquinas's view of the naturalness of property rested on "post classical" (later than Greek or Roman) developments in legal thinking, which in turn was based on "unclassical" (not Greek or Roman) notions of property and rights.[39] The Catholic developments were of a wholly different kind of thought than those passed down from Greece and Rome. In effect, the Renaissance humanists rejected Christian thought in favor of earlier pagan ideas.

The Christian stream continued through writings of the Protestant Calvinists and the Spanish Dominicans who linked natural rights to "the laws of nature and God."[40] Over the centuries, the Dominicans, in particular, advocated the principle of inalienable liberty by insisting that "men were not . . . in general free to enslave themselves, and they could not rightfully be traded as slaves if the grounds for their servitude were unclear" because liberty "was given by the law of God."[41]

The humanists, however, insisted that all rights were state created, not God given.[42] The humanist preoccupation with civil convention and state power limited their ability to think in terms of rights. Humanists were unsympathetic to the view of rights held by America's founders. To the humanists, one only has rights in society and then only the rights that the society recognizes, grants, or permits. It is, therefore, erroneous to trace early American law-of-nature and inalienable-rights theory to the Renaissance humanists, since the humanists rejected that entire perspective.

The humanists were true naturalists in the secular sense. They saw nature as impersonal and amoral. Thus, whatever occurred in nature was natural. For the humanist, no law of nature could constrain humans. Law was whatever a particular society determined law to be. They did not believe that there was a transcendent moral order that binds human laws.

The humanist approach and the Christian approach then stand in complete distinction from each other. Francois Connan (1540s) limited natural right only to humans in a state of nature. Humanity has meaningful rights only under civil law. Salamonio explained social compact as simply the outgrowth of arrangements among humans for the fostering of convenience and civilization. Thus, the theistic and moral base was entirely removed.

As Tuck points out, these Quattrocento ideas led easily to absolutism in Bude, Piccolomini, More, and others. There was no natural *dominium* and no place for natural rights of any kind. Tuck says, "all rights were thus civil rights": but by saying this, the humanist lawyers immediately diverted attention from the right to the remedy, the civil action that actually secured his objective for the possessor of a right.[43] The Renaissance concept (of property) belonged to a theory in which the natural life of humans was rightless and therefore propertyless, while the Thomists believed that by nature humans did possess certain limited rights.[44]

A quick survey of other leading writers of the period between the Renaissance and the Declaration reveals that to the extent one was committed to an Aristotelian—Renaissance—model rather than to the Bible, one leaned toward absolutism, positivism, and the alienability of all rights. Tuck mentions such names as Louis Le Roy (1579) of England, and Johannes Felden of Germany, noting that "Aristotelians . . . were themselves absolutists."[45] He points to Robert Filmer as a defender of absolutism owing to his Renaissance beliefs (and it should be noted that John Locke wrote to refute Filmer).[46]

Turning to England and the development of natural-law and natural-rights theories there, we find that John Selden's partial commitment to Renaissance thinking caused him to tend toward absolutism; although he "accepted a non-humanist account of *dominium*."[47] This explains Selden's Erastianism—the belief that the government should control the church.

Tuck deals specifically with the Tew Circle writers, a group of British humanist intellectuals in the Renaissance stream who followed along the lines of Selden's thought. They wrote specifically to refute the widespread belief that the law of nature provides for the rights of self-defense in a people and for military resistance against a tyrannical king.[48] This inalienable right of revolution traced clearly back to earlier Protestant and Catholic thought. It linked the laws of nature and inalienable rights precisely in the same way as found in the Declaration of Independence, but this way of thinking was rejected by Renaissance-oriented intellectuals.

THE BIBLICAL PARADIGM FOR RIGHTS

A survey of the biblical materials from which the medieval scholars worked is necessary to understand how they developed the Western theories of rights. As pointed out above, their starting point in treatise after treatise and debate after debate was Genesis chapters 1 and 2.

God the Creator

In Genesis 1 and 2, we find that in the beginning God created the universe. As Creator or Author, God has the inherent right to decide or dispose of all that He has created. He is sovereign. He is lord of all, and He governs all. Of Him and through Him and to Him are all things. The created universe is entirely subject to Him and dependent on Him in everything. We also find in Genesis 1 that God created humanity. Humanity is entirely subordinate to God and dependent on Him for all things. Humanity is God's creature and servant.

Man Endowed with God's Image

Genesis 1 teaches that God created humans in His own image. God gave humans certain faculties, abilities, and capacities that put them in a unique class of beings. These faculties represent the image of God in four ways. First, humanity is rational, "able to form concepts, think thoughts, carry through trains of reasoning, make and execute plans, live for goals, distinguish right from wrong and beautiful from ugly, and relate to other intelligent beings. This rationality is what makes us moral beings, and it is the basis for all other dimensions of Godlikeness."

Second, God made us subcreators under Him, "able and needing to find fulfillment in the creativity of art, science, technology, construction, scholarship, and the bringing of order out of various sorts of chaos."

Third, we are stewards, vice-regents, lords with a small *l,* to have dominion over God's estate, which is His world.

Fourth, we were at one time naturally and spontaneously righteous, actively responding to God by doing what God loves and commands and by avoiding what God hates and forbids.[49]

Humanity Endowed with Authority from God

Not only did God create us in His own image, thus endowing us with certain faculties and abilities, according to Genesis 1:28–29 God gave us a decree, a "creation mandate." God commanded us to be fruitful, multiply, fill the earth, and take dominion over the earth and all its resources—the land, the plants, and the animals. God's command immediately endowed us with both the duty and authority to live for God. Endowed with God's image and also with God-given authority, we became lords (small *l*) over God's earth.

The idea that we are created in God's image and have lordship over the earth is the key to the modern notion of subjective rights. Subjective rights are those that are inherent in the individual person as such; they are inseparably part of the human personality. Being made in God's image makes us beings of enormous value and inherent worth. This notion was foreign to all ancient systems of thought and accounts for the lack of any strong concept of subjective rights outside ancient Israel or in non-Christian cultures.

The English word *dominion* used in Genesis 1:28 translates the Hebrew word *rādâ*, meaning to reign or to rule. The word *dominion* derives from the Vulgate Latin verb *dominamini* (*dominari*), from *dominus* meaning lord, or ruler. It shares the stem of the Latin noun *dominium* meaning property or lordship over possessions and lands. Translators used the word *dominion* in part because it accurately reflects the biblical idea that property, an attribute of lordship, was given to humanity before the fall into sin and is part of the original law of nature.

In Genesis 1, therefore, we find that God reserves ultimate sovereignty to Himself but has created us in His own image and has endowed us with authority and dominion. Every human is under an absolute, inalienable duty to live life for God, to cultivate the image of God in himself or herself, and to be a steward, taking dominion over the resources of the earth, which God has subjected to us. The image of God in us and our possession of the creation mandate with its twin aspects of duty and authority are the starting point for the biblical model of rights.

Humans share that image and authority in common. Thus, all people are created equal. In human terms, no one person is higher or better than any other person. No one is lord over any other. No one may insert himself or herself between God and another person. No one may interfere with another person's righteous effort to fulfill his or her duty to live out the image of God and take dominion over the earth.

Biblically speaking, every person's duty to God gives rise to rights between persons. We have a duty to respect and honor the image of God in other people and the duty to refrain from interfering with another person's righteous efforts to take dominion over the earth. These parallel duties are not passive but active. Our duties to God are rights toward other people. We are under a complete duty to God as stewards, and God forbids idolatry. No one is permitted to allow another person to usurp God's control or lordship in his or her life. Every person has a duty to God to resist other people's attempts to degrade the image of God or to interfere with dominion activity, except when he or she chooses to suffer for the Gospel's sake. When one person degrades the image of God in another by murder or other crimes to the person and interferes with dominion activity by theft or other trespasses, that person tries to take the place of God and makes himself or herself an idol. Likewise, people commit idolatry when they allow another person to take the place of God in their lives.

Humanity's inalienable duties toward God translate into inalienable rights among humans. God gave and commands life, liberty, property, and a life of blessedness or happiness for people. Each person is a steward under an absolute duty to God for these things. As a steward, trustee, and protector under God, a person may resist other people's unlawful interference with the performance of that duty. This is the historical analysis and starting point of the church's doctrine of the right of self-defense and of rights generally.

The Language of Rights and the Linguistics of Scripture

The word for rights in the Hebrew Old Testament is *mishpat*. It is the ordinary Hebrew word for justice and occurs about 410 times in the Old Testament. *Mishpat* is often used in connection with another Hebrew word, *ṣedeq*, which means both justice and righteousness. A study of all the places these words occur in Scripture provides enormous insight into what God has established about justice and rights. The biblical model of rights cannot be separated from the biblical teaching about justice.[50]

First of all, God is the God of *mishpat*, or justice and right (Isa. 30:18). Justice is the essence of His nature and being. He is all-righteous. The character of God himself is the standard of justice. And God has explained Himself to us, making clear the principles of justice and righteousness in human terms. Justice is what He requires as the norm of all human interaction. Justice is that which is "right" (Gen. 18:25, Isa. 32:7). Hence, the term *rights*, because biblical rights are based on a belief about rectitude and normativity. Justice is something we "do" because justice is active rather than passive (Gen. 18:19, Ps. 119:121). This leads eventually to the notion that rights are active, not merely passive.[51] God's justice is a standard or law that binds all men (Ex. 15:25; Deut. 1:17; Isa. 26:9–10). God's justice is the standard of fairness and equity to which all human statutes, ordinances, and judicial sentences must conform (Ex. 21:1; Deut. 16:18; 17:8–9; Prov. 1:3; Isa. 10:1–2; 11:4). Justice can also be reflected in custom (Ps. 119:132). True justice always conforms to the manner in which God has created all things and agrees with His purposes and plans for each part of his creation (Ex. 21:9; Rom. 1:26, 27; 1 Cor. 11:4). Because justice is a norm imposed by God and required of us, it must not be perverted by us (Ex. 23:6; Prov. 17:23). It binds all equally and demands equal treatment of all before the law (Lev. 24:22; Deut. 1:17; Prov. 24:23). We must judge by principles rather than by expediency or appearances (Isa. 11:3–4). The *mishpat* is the Lord's (Deut. 1:17). God is the source of all original authority, rights, and justice.[52]

The word *mishpat* is translated as a "cause" or legal case in Numbers 27:5; 2 Samuel 15:4; 2 Chronicles 6:35, 39; Job 13:18; 23:4; 31:13; and Isaiah 50:8. It is translated as a "right" in Deuteronomy 21:17; 1 Kings 8:45, 49; Job 34:6; 36:6; Psalms 9:4; 140:12; Jeremiah 5:28; 32:7–8; Lamentations 3:35; and Ezekiel 21:27. The justice and rights spoken of in these Scriptures are not simply the distributive justice of Aristotle nor the right of nature of the Stoics.[53] They include rightly ordered relationships and a moral order imposed on those relationships. They also include the power to act on one's inherent God-given authority and to make demands of others based on an objectively revealed moral order. These rights are active claims rather than passive hopes. Thus, they are both objective (regulated by law) and subjective (annexed to human nature), whereas in the classical model, rights are almost entirely objective.[54]

The biblical uses of the word *mishpat* can be divided into two broad meanings. First, *mishpat* is justice, an objectively ordered relationship between God and man, and between man and man, including a body of legal and moral precepts and the right order itself.[55] Second, *mishpat* is a subjective personal right inherent in one's being, part of what it means to be a person since we are created in God's image.[56] Thus, the Bible provides for an objectively revealed moral law from which flows objectively ordered relationships for individual rights.

For example, God has ordained justice and given the law. He had the right to do this because of who and what He is. He has the authority or right to act in certain ways toward humanity and creation. The nature of His rights is defined by what kind of being He is. His sovereignty or divine right is part of what it means for Him to be God. Conceptually His rights are separate from His justice, but they cannot be separated from His nature.

We, created in God's image, have been given similar rights, appropriate to our created nature and inherent in that nature by the decree of the Creator. To deny these rights is tantamount to denying what it means to be a human being.

According to the Old Testament, God relates to men in a judicial way and in legal terms. Numerous Scriptures speak of God's lawsuit against humans in which God pleads His case and vindicates His just claims on us (Isa. 41:21).[57] According to biblical teaching and usage of the word *mishpat*, God has rights that are active as well as passive, and that are claim-rights—God has the right to demand our service and obedience.[58]

The Hebrew Scriptures use the same terminology and legal framework of justice, authority, and rights when speaking about humanity. The only difference is that whatever authority and rights we have are given by God, and we are bound by God's standards of justice. But we do have rights—claim rights—and we receive justice when those rights are protected.

The verb *shaphat* makes this clear in the numerous instances where it is translated *plead*, meaning to argue, advocate, or pursue. Rights can be pleaded or prosecuted according to the biblical model. Other Old Testament words that support this analysis are *deen*, meaning judge, plea, and cause; and *yakah*, meaning to reason, rebuke, reprove, plead, or argue your case.

The New Testament continues this paradigm of rights that we find in the Old Testament, using the Greek words *exousia* and *dikaion*, ordinarily translated authority and right.[59]

THE RIGHTS DEBATE CIRCA 1776

Prior to the seventeenth century, the home of rights theory was clearly with the church. Rights theory was born and nurtured first within the Catholic Church. Later the Protestant church embraced the principles without major revision. Beginning in the late eleventh century, Catholic Scholastics developed both the theoretical concepts as well as the technical language for a modern rights theory. One of the little-known facts of history is that it was Christian theologians who first articulated the concept of inalienable rights. And the even more startling fact is that secular intellectual leaders opposed the principles of rights theories and opposed the principle of inalienability for centuries.

In the fertile era of the seventeenth century, the choices between available options in rights theory became crystal clear. To the extent that intellectuals adopted a Greco-Roman or Aristotelian view of society and government, they rejected the Christian theory of rights, and particularly the notion of inalienable rights. As mentioned earlier, humanist intellectuals of the Enlightenment did not accept the notion of inalienable rights. Where there was a mixture between the Christian and Aristotelian worldviews, rights theory suffered.

Hugo Grotius—A Detremental Synthesis

Hugo Grotius, for example, was primarily a Christian theorist. He was a vocal advocate for much of the traditional Christian theory of rights. He specifically spoke in favor of the notion of inalienable rights, but he attempted to reach a compromise between Aristotelian thought and biblical thought. In the process, he departed from the Scholastic stream by making liberty an alienable right and by insisting that a people give up the right of resistance when they enter into a compact of government with a king.[60] By making such rights alienable, Grotius's theory played into the hands of the Dutch slave traders who were largely responsible for starting the race problem that still exists in America. By mixing Christian rights principles with Aristotelian principles, the principle of inalienability was lost, and it became acceptable to practice slavery or to silently acquiesce to its practice.

The Declaration of Independence, however, makes liberty an inalienable right under the laws of nature and God and argues primarily for the right of a people to resist a tyrannical king. Jefferson's colleagues back home in Williamsburg explicitly rejected the Grotian, humanist model when they wrote Article 1 of the Virginia Constitution of June 12, 1776.[61] There they insisted that humans cannot by compact or constitution give away certain rights, including liberty.[62] That Jefferson shared these views with George Mason and other Virginians is questioned by no one. Sadly, however, the Aristotelian justification for slavery was accepted by a sufficient number of people in early America that the institution of slavery remained intrenched in American culture despite the Declaration and the Revolutionary War.

The Posture of the Debate

It is important to understand that the rights debate was clearly defined in 1776 when the Declaration of Independence was written. There had been an enormous amount of writing and debating about the basic concepts and terms at stake where rights were concerned. The clearest lines were drawn between the Christian theory that promoted inalienable rights and the humanist theory that denied the principle of inalienability outright. In between the two extremes there were varying degrees of syncretistic theories that tried to reconcile these contradictory positions. These compromise theories were widely known, and their key terms were common knowledge.[63]

That is why, when one looks at the rights theory and rights language chosen by Jefferson and the framers of the Declaration of Independence, it is outrageous for someone to claim that the source of that theory was humanism and Enlightenment rationalism. The humanists and Enlightenment rationalists viewed the concept of inalienable rights with scorn. They decried the notion that God endowed us with sacred and immutable characteristics that civil government must respect and never transgress.

CONCLUSION

There were alternative theories and other terminology available to Jefferson and the framers. Had they wanted to make a conscious endorsement of secularism, they could have done so. Had Jefferson wanted to take a stand against Christian-derived ideas of rights, he could have done so. He could have chosen the language of the Aristotelians and humanists or of Deists and rationalists. Yet, he chose instead to use rights concepts and terminology that was squarely within the mainstream Christian philosophy and theory of rights. And it is impossible that he was ignorant of the significance of his choice of rights theories and rights terminology in the Declaration.

That is one reason why it is clearly appropriate to speak of the influence of Christian principles on the Declaration of Independence despite the fact that Jefferson did not believe in the deity of Christ. Remarkably, it is the Thomist-Dominican view of rights as refined by the English common law and the Protestant Reformation that we find in the Declaration of Independence. We do not find the nonbilibical or antibiblical influences of rationalism, deism, and humanism as so many suggest.

APPENDIX A

Code of Virginia
Title-57.
Religious and Charitable Matters

Section 57–1. Act for religious freedom recited.—The General Assembly, on January 16, 1786, passed an act in the following words:

Whereas, Almighty God hath created the mind free;

That all attempts to influence it by temporal punishment, or burthens, or by civil incapacitations, then only to beget habits of hypocrisy and meanness, and are a departure from the plan of the Holy Author of our religion, who, being Lord both of body and mind, yet chose not to propagate it by coercions on either, as was in his Almighty power to do;

That the impious presumption of legislators and rulers, civil as well as ecclesiastical, who, being themselves but fallible and uninspired men, have assumed dominion over the faith of others, setting up their own opinions and modes of thinking as the only true and infallible, and as such endeavoring to impose them on others, have established and maintained false religions over the greatest part of the world, and through all time;

That to compel a man to furnish contributions of money for the propagation of opinions which he disbelieves, is sinful and tyrannical, and even the forcing him to support this or that teacher of his own religious persuasion, is depriving him of the comfortable liberty of giving his contributions to the particular pastor whose morals he would make his pattern, and whose powers he feels most persuasive to righteousness, and is withdrawing from the ministry those temporary rewards which, proceeding from an approbation of their personal conduct, are an additional incitement to earnest and unremitting labors, for the instruction of mankind;

That our civil rights have no dependence on our religious opinions any more than our opinions in physics or geometry;

That therefore the proscribing any citizen as unworthy the public confidence by laying on him an incapacity of being called to offices of trust and emolument, unless he profess or renounce this or that religious opinion, is depriving him injuriously of those privileges and advantages to which, in common with his fellow citizens, he has a natural right; that it tends only to corrupt the principles of that religion it is meant to encourage, by bribing, with a monopoly of worldly honors and emoluments, those who will externally profess and conform to it;

That though, indeed, those are criminal who do not withstand such temptation, yet, neither are those innocent who lay the bait in their way;

That to suffer the civil magistrate to intrude his powers into the field of opinion, and to restrain the profession or propagation of principles on supposition of their ill tendency, is a dangerous fallacy, which at once destroys all religious liberty, because he, being of course judge of that tendency, will make his opinions the rules of judgment, and approve or condemn the sentiments of others only as they shall square with or differ from his own;

That it is time enough for the rightful purposes of civil government, for its officers to interfere, when principles break out into overt acts against peace and good order; and finally,

That truth is great and will prevail, if left to herself;

That she is the proper and sufficient antagonist to error, and has nothing to fear from the conflict, unless by human interposition disarmed of her natural weapons, free argument and debate; errors ceasing to be dangerous when it is permuted freely to contradict them;

Be it enacted by the General Assembly,

That no man shall be compelled to frequent or support any religious worship, place or ministry whatsoever, nor shall be enforced, restrained, molested or burthened, in his body or goods, nor shall otherwise suffer on account of his religious opinions or belief; but that all men shall be free to profess, and by argument to maintain, their opinions in matters of religion, and that the same shall in no wise diminish, enlarge or affect their civil capacities.

And though we well know that this Assembly, elected by the people for the ordinary purposes of legislation only, have no power to restrain the acts of succeeding assemblies constituted with powers equal to our own, and that therefore, to declare this act to be irrevocable would be of no effect in law; yet we are free to declare, and do declare, that the rights hereby asserted are of the natural rights of mankind; and that if any act shall be hereafter passsed to repeal the present, or to narrow its operation, such act will be an infringement of natural right. (Originally drafted by Thomas Jefferson in 1779 as An Act for Establishing Religious Freedom.)

APPENDIX B

Constitution of Virginia
June 12, 1776
Bill of Rights

A declaration of rights made by the representatives of the good people of Virginia, assembled in full and free convention; which rights do pertain to them and their posterity, as the basis and foundation of government.

SECTION 1. That all men are by nature equally free and independent, and have certain inherent rights, of which, when they enter into a state of society, they cannot, by any compact, deprive or divest their posterity; namely, the enjoyment of life and liberty, with the means of acquiring and possessing property, and pursuing and obtaining happiness and safety.

SECTION 2. That all power is vested in, and consequently derived from, the people; that magistrates are their trustees and servants, and at all times amenable to them.

SECTION 3. That government is, or ought to be, instituted for the common benefit, protection, and security of the people, nation, or community; of all the various modes and forms of government, that is best which is capable of producing the greatest degree of happiness and safety, and is most effectually secured against the danger of maladministration; and that, when any government shall be found inadquate or contrary to these purposes, a majority of the community hath an indubitable, inalienable, and indefeasible right to reform, alter, or abolish it; in such manner as shall be judged most conducive to the public weal.

SECTION 4. That no man, or set of men, are entitled to exclusive or separate emoluments or privileges from the community, but in consideration of public services; . . .

SECTION 15. That no free government, or the blessings of liberty, can be preserved to any people, but by a firm adherence to justice, moderation, temperance, frugality, and virtue, and by frequent recurrence to fundamental principles.

SECTION 16. That religion, or the duty which owe to our Creator, and the manner of discharging it, can be directed only by reason and conviction, not by force or violence; and therefore all men are equally entitled to the free exercise of religion, according to the dictates of conscience; and that it is the mutual duty of all to practise Christian forbearance, love, and charity towards each other.

APPENDIX C

Excerpt
James Madison
A Memorial and Remonstrance on the Religious Rights of Man
1784

Because we hold it for a "fundamental and undeniable truth," that religion, or the duty which we owe to our creator, and the manner of discharging it, can be directed only by reason and conviction, not by force or violence. The religion, then, of every man, must be left to the conviction and conscience of every man; and it is the right of every man to exercise it as these may dictate. That right is, in its nature, an unalienable right. It is unalienable, because the opinions of men, depending only on the evidences contemplated in their own minds, cannot follow the dictates of other men; it is unalienable, also, because what is here a right towards men, is a duty towards the creator. It is the duty of every man to render the creator such homage, and such only, as he believes to be acceptable to him; this duty is precedent, both in order of time and degree of obligation, to the claims of civil society. Before any man can be considered as a member of civil society, he must be considered as a subject of the governor of the universe, and if a member of civil society, who enters into any subordinate association, must always do it with a reservation of his duty to the general authority, much more must every man who becomes a member of any particular civil society do it with the saving allegiance to the universal sovereign.

NOTES

1. For a more thorough treatment of this thesis see my book *Defending the Declaration* (Brentwood, Tenn.: Wolgemuth & Hyatt, 1989).
2. My analysis of MacPherson is borrowed from the writings of Richard Tuck. I am tremendously indebted to Richard Tuck for the major outlines

of my treatment of this subject. I consider his book, *Natural Rights Theories: Their Origin and Development* (London: Cambridge University Press, 1979), indispensable to a proper understanding of the development of rights theories from the medieval to the modern era.

3. For my earlier treatment of Becker see, *Defending the Declaration*, 51.

4. See generally, Wilson Smith, ed., *Essays in American Intellectual History* (Hinsdale, Ill.: Dryden Press, 1975), and Cushing Strout, ed., *Intellectual History in America: From Darwin to Niebuhr*, vol. 2, (New York: Harper & Row, 1968).

5. For a review and critique of Villey's work see, Tuck, *Natural Rights Theories*, 7; and, Brian Tierney, "Villey, Ockham, and the Origin of Individual Rights," in *The Weightier Matters of the Law: Essays on Law and Religion*, ed. John Witte and Frank S. Alexander Jr. (Atlanta: Scholars Press, 1988), 1–31 [hereafter, Tierney, *Origin of Rights*].

6. For purposes of this paper, I will use "Western-rights theory" and "modern-rights theory" as synonyms. By them I mean the kind of rights theory that is found in the Declaration of Independence. They are to be distinguished from the denatured positivistic approaches to rights theories in the other half of the twentieth century.

7. See for example, Tuck, *Natural Rights Theories*, 14–15.

8. The passive-right, active-right distinction, introduced by David Lyons and adopted by Richard Tuck, has been roundly criticized by Brian Tierney. I agree with Tierney's conclusions that the notion of active rights occurs centuries earlier in medieval thinking than Tuck suggests. See, Brian Tierney, "Tuck On Rights: Some Medieval Problems," *History of Political Thought* 4, no. 3 (winter 1983): 432–35 [hereafter, Tierney, *Medieval Rights Problems*].

9. See generally, Tiemey, *Medieval Rights Problems*.

10. See, Michael Bertram Crowe, *The Changing Profile of the Natural Law* (The Hague: Martinus Nijhoff, 1977), 33–34.

11. For an excellent survey of the Greek worldview as contrasted with a biblical worldview see, *Theological Dictionary of the New Testament* [hereafter *TDNT*], 2:284–317, see also *dunamai* by Walter Grundman; see also *theos* by Hermann Kleinlsnect, Gottfried Quell, Ethelbert Stauffer, and Karl Georg Kuhn, *TDNT*, 3:65–123.

12. *TDNT*, 9:251, see also *phusis*, in *TDNT*, by Helmut Foster.

13. Leo Strauss, *Natural Right and History* (Chicago: University of Chicago Press, 1953), 93.

14. *TDNT*, 2:179–80.

15. Strauss, *Natural Right and History*, 133.

16. Ibid.

17. Ibid., 134.

18. Ibid., 135.
19. Tuck, *Natural Rights Theories*, 7. Tierney cautions that Tuck's book is "marred by inaccurancies and methodological flaws." Tierney, *Origin of Rights*, 1n.1.
20. Tuck, *Natural Rights Theories*, 7. "To have a passive right is to have a right to be given or allowed something by someone else, while to have an active right is to have the right to do something oneself." Ibid, 6. For Tierney's criticisms of Tuck's passive-right, active-right analysis, see Tierney, *Medieval Rights Problems*, 432–35.
21. Tuck, *Natural Rights Theories*, 8.
22. Strauss, *Natural Right and History*, 147.
23. Tuck, *Natural Rights Theories*, 14.
24. Ibid., 12.
25. Strauss, *Natural Right and History*, 144.
26. Ibid.
27. Harold J. Berman, *Law and Revolution: The Formation of the Western Legal Tradition* (Cambridge: Harvard University Press, 1983).
28. Ibid., 2.
29. Tuck, *Natural Rights Theories*, 13.
30. Ibid.
31. See Amos, *Defending the Declaration*, 116.
32. Tuck, *Natural Rights Theories*, 24.
33. Ibid., chap. 2, 32–57.
34. Ibid., 35.
35. Ibid., 33.
36. Ibid.
37. Ibid.
38. Ibid., 40.
39. Ibid., 40–41.
40. Ibid., 43, 48.
41. Ibid., 49.
42. For the Greek roots see, *TDNT*, 2:179–85.
43. Tuck, *Natural Rights Theories*, 40.
44. Ibid., 48.
45. Ibid., 44, 75.
46. Ibid., 76.
47. Ibid., 86. Selden was close to the Dominican position when he said, "I cannot fancy to myself what the law of nature means, but the law of God." Quoted in Tuck, *Natural Rights Theories*, 92.
48. Tuck, *Natural Rights Theories*, 102.
49. J. I. Packer, "A Christian View of Man," in *The Christian Vision: Man in Society*, ed. Lynne Morris (Hillsdale, Mich.: Hillsdale College Press, 1984), 111–12.

50. The English reader can study these words by consulting George Wigram, *The Englishman's Hebrew and Chaldee Concordance of the Old Testament: Numerically Coded to Strong's Exhaustive Concordance* (Grand Rapids: Baker, 1980), 776–78, 1062–64; and R. Laird Harris, Gleason L. Archer, Bruce K. Waltke, eds., *Theological Wordbook of the Old Testament*, 2 vols. (Chicago: Moody Press, 1980), 2:752–55, 947–49 [hereafter, *Theological Wordbook*].

51. A passive right is a right to expect someone else to act in a certain way toward the holder of the right. I have a right to goods I have paid for. The person who received money for the goods has a duty to give them to me. My right is passive in that it is fulfilled by the action of another, not by my own action.

52. *Theological Wordbook*, 2:949, sec. 7.

53. On the Greek views of justice and *iustitia distributiva* see, Gerhard Kittel and Gerhard Friedrich, eds., *TDNT*, also see *dike* by Gottfried Quell and Gottlob Schrenk, *TDNT*, 2:174–93, esp., 183–85 and 193.

54. The biblical model of justice has a three-fold nature: justice is the payment due to us for the works of our hands; justice is proportional to our actions (Ezek. 7:27); justice is receiving no more and no less than we deserve based on what we have done, whether good or evil (Jer. 26:11). In the sense that justice is payment due for a deed done, justice is retributive (Latin *retribuere*, to repay).

Retribution does not mean retaliation or revenge. It is not morally right to hate criminals. Retribution does not mean that the community can satisfy its outrage by heaping abuse on the criminal. Justice is the Lord's, not ours.

Since justice belongs to God, there is something sacred about justice. Justice is inseparable from righteousness, making justice a holy thing. When man acts as though there is no divinely given standard of justice, he awakens God's displeasure, and God must vindicate the law of justice that man has sought to nullify. So justice is also vindicatory. And the form of vindication is by some "sanction" (from the Latin *sanctus*, meaning sacred). *Theological Wordbook*, 2:948, see also *shephet*.

Justice also restores the wrongdoer, the victim, and the community to the condition of peace, harmony, and wholeness that existed before the wrong was committed, Ibid., 2:930–31, sec. 2401. So justice is restitutionary. The Hebrew Bible uses the word *shelem*, which is translated into English as "to complete" (*TWOT*, 2:932). The word *shalam* means to "restore to the covenant of peace." Ibid., sec. 2401C. In biblical terms there is a social compact, or "covenant of peace" among all the members of a community whether people know it or not. Justice restores the criminal to the covenant of peace by causing him to make payment for the wrong done. Justice restores the victim by awarding him a proper compensation for the loss or injury suffered. Justice restores the community by bringing its members into right relationship again.

55. This is true because God has posited the law, *TDNT*, 2:176, sec (2). Therefore, one should not conclude that such a definition is inherently platonistic.

56. "Individual men, as created by God, have inalienable *mishpatim* (rights)," *Theological Wordbook*, 2:949, sec. 7, see also *mishpat*.

57. *Theological Wordbook*, 1:376–77; 2:949.

58. The passive-right, active-right distinction, introduced by David Lyons and adopted by Richard Tuck, has been roundly criticized by Brian Tierney. I agree with Tierney's conclusions that the notion of active-rights occurs centuries earlier in medieval thinking than Tuck suggests. See Tierney, "Tuck On Rights."

59. For *exousia* see George V. Wigram, Ralph D. Winter, eds., *The Word Study Concordance* (1978; reprint, Wheaton, Ill.: Tyndale House Publishers), 269–70; and *TDNT*, 2:560–75. For *dikaion* see *Word Study Concordance*, 155–57; *TDNT*, 44:174–225.

60. Tuck, 78.

61. That is why T. Robert Ingram's analysis of the rights language in the Virginia Constitution is fatally flawed. He represents the Virginia Bill of Rights as "a repudiation of Christendom," contrary to the belief in rights as founded on divine law, because the Virginians supposedly wanted to set up a government with "no recognition of God." "(T)he Virginia declaration. . . . is a blind alley search for principles . . . The direction taken by the Virginia declaration has no other way to go but toward, at the very least, holding God to have no place in temporal government. . . . (C)olonial Virginians . . . were introducing a change, a radical one . . . (of) no recongition of the role of God in government. . . . The Virginia Declaration marks a decisive departure from such often proposed evolutionary ancestors as the Mayflower Compact or documents of the Massachusetts and Connecticut colonies." T. Robert Ingram, "What's Wrong With Human Rights," in *The Theology of Christian Resistance*, ed. Gary North (Tyler, Tex.: Geneva Divinity School Press, 1983), 134–37, 144. Ingram not only misrepresents the meaning of the terms of the Virginia Constitution, he has missed the Founders' point entirely.

62. Perry, *Sources of Our Liberties*, 311: "SECTION I. That all men are by nature equally free and independent, and have certain inherent rights, of which, when they enter into a state of society, they cannot, by any compact deprive or divest their posterity; namely the

enjoyment of life and liberty, with the means of acquiring and
possessing property, and pursuing and obtaining happiness and safety."

63. For an exposition of the terminology, particularly the inalienable
right to "life, liberty, and the pursuit of happiness," see Amos,
Defending the Declaration (Walgemuth & Hyatt, 1989), 115–21.

THREE

Operation Josiah: Rediscovering the Biblical Roots of the American Constitutional Republic

John Eidsmoe

THE YEAR WAS 621 B.C. After a "dark age" in which King Manasseh and King Amon had led Judea into paganism and immorality, eight-year-old Josiah had become king of Judea in 640 B.C. Through the Lord's providence, young Josiah had godly advisors to lead him in the right paths. As he grew toward adulthood, he began to "seek after the God of David his father" (2 Chron. 34:3).

In the eighteenth year of his reign (621 B.C.) he directed that the temple be repaired. During the renovation process, somewhere in the back shelves of the temple archives, Hilkiah, the priest, discovered a copy of the Law of Moses. He delivered it to King Josiah, who directed that it be read, was convicted of his sin and his people's sin by what was read in the Law, and instituted reforms accordingly (2 Kings 22; 2 Chron. 34).

Why did the Law of Moses have to be rediscovered in, of all places, Judea? Probably because the apostate kings who preceded Josiah, together with their apostate priests, had destroyed all the copies of the Law that they could find. What is the significance of this account for today? It demonstrates that in the course of one or two generations, a nation's foundational heritage can be almost completely wiped from memory.

The same has happened in twentieth-century America. Either by telling falsehoods or by selectively telling only part of the truth, our history books have eliminated most of our biblical heritage. So completely have these foundations been eradicated from the modern memory that secular historians can often say without fear of contradiction that the United States Constitution is purely a secular document and those who drafted it were Deists and skeptics.

In the tradition of Josiah and Hilkiah, then, let us reexplore and rediscover the biblical foundations of our nation.

All agree that the fifty-five delegates to the Constitutional Convention of 1787 did not formulate their ideas out of thin air. They came to the Convention with a certain worldview and certain basic moral values. They learned this worldview and these values from sources they had read or heard. But what sources?

To answer this question, two political-science professors, Donald Lutz and Charles Hyneman, conducted a detailed study of political writings from the founding period of American history, 1760–1805. They reviewed an estimated 15,000 writings from the period—pamphlets, newspaper articles, and monographs with explicitly political content. They then reduced the study to 916 items, and they studied these closely for the purpose of identifying quotations. Their desire was to find out which authorities the framers quoted, which authorities they respected, and from where they derived their ideas.

Lutz and Hyneman identified 3,154 references to other sources, and the source cited far more than any other—34 percent—was the Bible. Interestingly, the book of the Bible the framers cited most often was Deuteronomy, the restatement of the Law. Excluding the Bible, the authorities cited most often were Baron Montesquieu of France, a Roman Catholic, and Sir William Blackstone of England, an Anglican. In third place was John Locke, a professing Christian with a few unorthodox ideas. The framers were familiar with the anti-Christian writers of their time, such as Thomas Hobbes, David Hume, Francois Voltaire, and Jean-Jacques Rousseau; but these authorities were cited far less often and frequently in a negative or critical manner.[1]

That the framers relied on the Bible should not be surprising. Most of them were raised on the Bible. It was read in the home and expounded in church; and when they learned to read, the Bible and the thoroughly Christian *New England Primer* were their primary texts. It should not be surprising that the Bible was a major formative influence on their ideas. When they became adults, most of them were actively affiliated with Christian churches where they regularly listened to lengthy Bible-based sermons. At election time the clergy of that period commonly preached "election sermons," in which they explained the biblical view of civil government and the responsibilities of Christian citizenship, and discussed the issues of the day from a biblical perspective.

This sounds strange to our ears today, because we have been told over and over that the Founding Fathers were Deists and skeptics. Those who make this claim seldom produce proof for the assertion. Frequently they cite no sources at all. If they do, they usually cite only twentieth-century authorities. If they go back to original sources at all, they commonly take an isolated statement of Thomas Jefferson or Benjamin Franklin, cite those statements out of context or with undue regard to their importance, and present them as though they were typical of the framers as a whole.

But while Deism, the belief in a "clockmaker god" who created the universe and established certain natural and moral laws for its operation but who has now separated himself from creation and lets it run according to these natural laws,[2] was popular in eighteenth-century France, it had little influence in England and less in America. The late Dr. M. E. Bradford of the University of Dallas undertook a detailed study of the fifty-five delegates to the Convention and concluded that at most only three or four of them were Deists. The vast majority were professing Christians and actively affiliated with Christian churches—twenty-eight Episcopalians, eight Presbyterians, seven Congregationalists, two Reformed, two Lutherans, two Methodists, two Roman Catholics, one whose religious preference is unknown, and at most three Deists.[3]

The formative influence of the Bible, and particularly the law code of the Old Testament, is noted in Max I. Dimont's *Jews, God and History:*

> The Mosaic Code . . . was the first truly judicial, written code, and eclipsed previously known laws with its all-encompassing humanism, its passion for justice, its love of democracy. It also helped to established a new Jewish character and directed Jewish thinking into new paths which tended to set the Jews further apart from their neighbors.
>
> The ideological content of the Mosaic Laws is of great interest. Here we find the Jewish concept of the state and philosophy of law. These laws were essentially divided into three categories: those dealing with man's relation to man, those dealing with man's relation to the state, and those dealing with man's relation to God.
>
> . . . The lofty framework of these laws permitted the emergence of a democratic form of government virile enough to last eight hundred years until the Prophets in turn renovated them. . . .
>
> The Mosaic Code laid down the first principles for a separation of church and state, a concept not encountered again in world history until three thousand years later, during the Enlightenment in the eighteenth century of our era. In the Mosaic Code the civil authority was independent of the priesthood. Though it is true that the priesthood had the

right to settle cases not specifically covered by Mosaic law (Deuteronomy 17: 8–12), that did not place it above the civil government. The priesthood was charged with the responsibility of keeping this government within the framework of Mosaic law, just as the United States Supreme Court is not above the federal government but is, nevertheless, charged with the responsibility of keeping it within the framework of the Constitution. Moses also laid the foundation for another separation, which has since become indispensable to any democracy. He created an independent judiciary.

There is a curious resemblance between the philosophic outlook of American constitutional law and that of Mosaic law. The federal government has only the powers specifically granted to it by the Constitution. The individual states can do anything not specifically denied to them. In essence, the Mosaic law also established the principle that the Jews could do anything not specifically denied to them. Instead of saying "Do such and such a thing," the laws of Moses usually say "Don't do this or that." Even where the Mosaic law makes a positive statement, it is often either an amendment to a negative commandment or else hemmed in by a negative admonition, saying, in effect, "When you do this, then don't do that." The Ten Commandments, for instance, list only three dos but seven don'ts. The three positive commandments are "I am the Lord thy God"; observe the Sabbath; and honor your parents. The seven don'ts leave little doubt as to what one is not supposed to do. By fencing in only the negative, Moses left an open field for positive action. This allowed the Jews great flexibility. As long as they did not do anything specifically prohibited, they could, like the individual American states, do anything they wanted to do. This type of thinking led Jewish philosophers into stating their maxims in negations.

We can see this gulf in thinking interestingly illustrated in a maxim attributed by Christians to Jesus and by Jews to Hillel, one of the great teachers of Judaism. According to the Christians, Jesus said, "Do unto others what you want others to do unto you." According to the Jews, Hillel, who lived 100 years before Jesus, said, "Do not do to others what you don't want others to do unto you." There is a world of difference between these two expressions, and the reader is invited to ponder on them and reason out why he would prefer one to the other as applied to himself.[4]

Most Americans today are unaware that there is any unique Jewish concept of the state and philosophy of law. Not so our Founding Fathers! President John Adams wrote, "As much as I love, esteem and admire the Greeks, I believe the Hebrews have done more to enlighten and civilize the world. Moses did more than all of their legislators and philosophers."[5]

But while some of the principles of our legal system came directly from the Bible, others came more indirectly. As the Roman legions came conquering into western Europe, they brought the *pax Romana* (Roman peace) and the rule of Roman law. But after the Empire embraced Christianity, the Roman Law of the Twelve Tables underwent three major revisions: the Constantinian Code of the fourth century, the Theodosian Code of the fifth century, and the Justinian Code of the sixth century. Each was designed to bring Roman law into harmony with the teachings of the Christian religion. But meanwhile, beset by internal decay and barbarians at the gates, Rome abruptly withdrew its legions from England and western Europe in the fifth century. As the legions withdrew, so did most vestiges of Roman civilization and Roman law. In the chaos that followed, the church, by default, became the light of civilization, learning, order, and law. Disputes were commonly resolved by the only courts available—the church courts governed by canon law. As Houlbrooke says, "The law of the church courts was the common law of Christendom, much of it supplemented by local custom or reinforced by local legislation."[6] As law professor John C. H. Wu of Seton Hall says, "holy and learned clerics like Lanfanc, St. Thomas à Becket, John of Salisbury, and many others continued to infuse natural-law principles into the common law. It may be said that canon law was the nurse and tutor of the common law. The very name 'common law' was derived from the *ius commune* of the canonists."[7]

The two greatest rulers of medieval Europe, Charlemagne of the Franks (A.D. 742–814) and Alfred the Great of England (A.D. 849–899), both established legal systems based on biblical law. A devout Christian, Charlemagne had committed great portions of the Old Testament to memory and was conversant in Latin and Greek. Strongly influenced by the writings of St. Augustine, he established a system of law that, according to the *Dictionary of Christian Biography*, was "drawn much more from the theocracy of the Old Testament than from the despotism of the Roman Empire."[8]

Also a devout Christian, Alfred codified biblical law in his kingdom. He inherited a system of law drafted by King Ethelbert (also known as St. Ethelbert [A.D. 556–616]) titled the "Ninety Dooms (Commands) of Ethelbert," which followed many of the Old

Testament criminal provisions, normally prescribing restitution as the penalty and providing special protection for the Church.[9] But these lacked structure. As John Canning says, Alfred

> set to work to codify the laws of England, which had been a chaos of local rules and customs. He sought to revise and combine these with regulations borrowed from Mosaic laws and Christian principles. His Book of Dooms (law) formed the basis for administration of justice in the Courts of the Shires and Hundreds, and with additions and modifications became the ancestor of our Common Law of today.[10]

Harvard law professor Harold Berman writes,

> The Laws of Alfred (about A.D. 890) start with a recitation of the Ten Commandments and excerpts from the Mosaic Law; and in restating and revising the native Anglo-Saxon laws. Alfred includes such great principles as: "doom (i.e., judge) very evenly; doom not one doom to the rich, another to the poor, nor doom one to your friend, another to your foe."[11] (cf. Exodus 23:1–3; Deuteronomy 1:16–18)

Jewish commercial law also influenced the development of the common law. During much of the medieval period the church prohibited money-lending based on its interpretation of various passages of Scripture. But the Jews interpreted these passages differently, and as a result they were a main source of lending capital. Outstanding Jewish scholars, such as Rabbi Moses Ben Maimon (Maimonides, A.D. 1135–1204) developed much of the commercial code for medieval Europe, basing it in large part on Old Testament law.[12]

Pollock and Maitland describe the court of King Henry II (A.D. 1154–1189) and King Richard the Lionhearted (A.D. 1189–1199) as a fusion of ecclesiastics and laymen:

> English law was administered by the ablest, the best educated, men in the realm; not only that, it was administered by the selfsame men who were "the judges ordinal" of the church's courts, men who were bound to be, at least in some measure, learned in the canon law. At one moment Henry had three bishops for archjusticiars. The climax is reached in Richard's reign. We can then see the king's court as it sits day by day. Often enough it was composed of the archbishop of

Canterbury, two other bishops, two or three archdeacons, two or three ordained clerks who were going to be bishops, and but two or three laymen.[13]

English common law, then, is based on a combination of sources: the Bible-based laws adopted by Anglo-Saxon kings, the canon law of the church, and the Jewish commercial law. During the thirteenth century when Henricus Bracton began the serious systematization of the common law, *De Legis et Cay Anglia (Of the Laws and Customs of England)*, he used the organizational structure of Roman law—not the old Law of the Twelve Tables but the Christianized Justinian Code. He also drew on his knowledge of the canon law of the church, using Gratian's Decretum and the Decretals of Pope Gregory IX.[14]

Sir William Blackstone, the English judge and Oxford law professor whose *Commentaries on the Laws of England* (1765–1769) were standard fare for American judges, lawyers, and law students, stressed that to find the basis for common law we must look not so much to the Roman law but more to the laws of Alfred the Great. He then spoke of three categories of law: (1) revealed law; (2) law of nature; and (3) municipal law. Of the revealed law he says:

> Revealed Law. This has given manifold occasion for the interposition of divine providence; which in compassion to the frailty, the imperfection, and the blindness been pleased, at sundry times and in divers manners, to discover and enforce its laws by an immediate and direct revelation. The doctrines thus delivered we call the revealed or divine law, and they are to be found only in the Holy Scriptures.[15]

Blackstone wrote concerning the law of nature:

> Law of Nature. This will of [man's] Maker is called the law of nature. . . . When He created man, and endued him with free will to conduct himself in all parts of life, He laid down certain immutable laws of human nature, whereby that free will is in some degree regulated and restrained, and gave him also the faculty of reason to discover the purport of those laws. . . .
>
> This law of nature, being coeval with mankind and dictated by God Himself, is of course superior in obligation to any other. It is binding over all the globe in all countries, and at all times: no human laws are of any validity, if contrary to this.[16]

Municipal or human law, Blackstone said, was man's attempt to understand and apply the revealed law and the law of nature in parliaments, legislatures, and city councils. But municipal law depends for its validity on the higher revealed law and law of nature. As Blackstone said, "On these two foundations, the law of nature and the law of revelation, depend all human laws; that is to say, no human law should be suffered to contradict these."[17]

While others besides Blackstone had a hand in the development of English common law, it was Blackstone more than any other who systematized the common law into the form that was used in the legal systems of early America.

Even before the days of Blackstone, the colonists generally followed the English common law, but they often altered it to more specifically embody the legal precepts of the Bible. In the year 1636, the general court (legislature) of Massachusetts established a council to draft a body of laws "agreeable to the word of God." Until such laws were drafted and adopted at the next session of the general court, magistrates were to follow such laws as were already adopted—and where no statute governed—to decide cases "as near to the law of God as they can."[18]

In 1641, the Massachusetts general court adopted the Massachusetts Body of Liberties that had been drafted by Nathaniel Ward, a minister who had some legal training. The Body of Liberties enacted into statute many provisions of the Old Testament law and stated that no man's life was to be taken unless by some express law established by the general court, or by the Word of God. It further provided that "in all criminal offenses where the law hath prescribed no certain penalty, the judges have power to inflict penalties according to the rule of God's Word."[19]

At times, the strict adherence to biblical law worked to the benefit of the accused. In one case involving several defendants, Governor John Winthrop remarked that "the only reason that saved their lives was that the sin was not capital by any express law of God, nor was it made capital by any of our own."[20]

The Connecticut code of 1642 was copied from that of Massachusetts.[21] Criminals were to be punished "according to the mind of God revealed in his word:"[22]

> In the fundamental agreement all freemen assent that the Scriptures hold forth a perfect rule for the direction and government of all men in all duties. The Scriptural laws of inheritance, dividing allotments, and all things of like nature are adopted, thus very clearly founding the entire system of

civil and criminal law on the word of God. This principle is reenacted in similar language in 1644.[23]

Some of the other colonies were less explicit than those of New England in their recognition of Scripture as law, but they commonly referred to God and His law as the source of all governmental authority.

The Declaration of Independence of 1776 was drafted by a congressional committee consisting of Thomas Jefferson, Benjamin Franklin, Roger Sherman, John Adams, and Robert Livingstone. The Declaration clearly states that the united colonies are entitled to independence by the "Laws of Nature and of Nature's God." They further declared that "all men are created equal," and that they are endowed "by their Creator" with certain inalienable rights. They closed by appealing to the "Supreme Judge of the world for the rectitude of [their] intentions," declaring their "firm reliance on the protection of Divine Providence," and pledged their lives, their fortunes, and their sacred honor. The "Creator" God they trusted was more than the impersonal and uninvolved god of the Deists; the term *Providence* implies a God who continually provides for the human race. And the reference to the laws of nature and of nature's God reflects their belief in the law of nature and the revealed law described by Blackstone.

It is impossible to properly understand the Constitution apart from the Declaration of Independence. The Declaration may be found at the beginning of the *United States Code Annotated*, along with the Constitution, the Articles of Confederation, and the Northwest Ordinance, as part of the organic law of our nation. The Declaration sets forth the basic ideals on which the nation is founded, but the Declaration is silent as to the precise form of government our nation is to adopt. It declares that governments are legitimate so long as they further certain basic principles such as government by consent of the governed, the preservation of God-given rights, and human equality; but it does not specify what form of government is necessary to further these principles. The Constitution goes a step beyond the Declaration in that it sets forth a practical form of government by which the ideals of the Declaration are to be realized. It might be said that the Declaration is the founding document that establishes our *nation;* the Constitution is the founding document that establishes our *government*. The nation is older than the government; note that the Constitution closes with the words, "Done in Convention by the Unanimous Consent of the States present the Seventeenth Day of September in the Year of our Lord one thousand seven hundred and eighty seven and of the Independence of the United States of America the Twelfth." In a very real sense the Declaration is the true preamble to the Constitution.

To secure their independence from Britain, the American colonists had to fight a protracted war. The treaty by which Britain, in 1783, recognized American independence begins with the following words: "In the name of the Most Holy and Undivided Trinity. It having pleased the Divine Providence to dispose the hearts. . . ."[24] The independence of the United States of America was thus not only founded on, but also recognized by, documents reflecting the God of the Bible.

The Constitution was framed with that view in mind. As the Convention opened, George Washington was unanimously elected President of the Convention. As he took the chair he declared, "Let us raise the standard to which the wise and honest can repair; the event is in hands of God."[25]

And as noted above, the Convention closed the wording of the Constitution with the phrase, "in the Year of Our Lord one thousand seven hundred eighty seven." Unlike the antireligionists who fomented their French Revolution and changed the calendar to date events before and after the revolution, the framers of American independence were perfectly willing to recognize the birth of our Lord Jesus Christ as the central event of human history.

During the Convention itself, the delegates did not regularly quote Scripture in the floor debates. They were not a theological debating society; they were practical men gathered for a practical purpose—the drafting of a constitution to create a civil government. But the principles that underlie their discussions and the Constitution they created are clearly based on their Christian worldview found in the Bible. As noted earlier, the vast majority of the delegates were active churchmen who were raised on the Bible and who turned to the Bible as their primary source of thought and inspiration. Probably all of them had read Blackstone, and at least one (General Charles Cotesworth Pinckney of South Carolina) had studied law personally under Blackstone in England. At least nine of them had studied under the Rev. John Witherspoon at the College of New Jersey (now Princeton). It is only natural, then, that the Constitution they drafted reflects their biblical worldview.

Detractors note that Benjamin Franklin's motion to have a clergyman come to the Convention every morning for daily prayer was never adopted. But we need to explore the reasons. According to Madison's *Notes of Debates in the Federal Convention of 1787*, Franklin made this motion amid severe discord on 28 June 1787. Since, of all the delegates, Franklin was perhaps the least orthodox in his religious beliefs, his words are worthy of note:

> In the beginning of the Contest with G. Britain, when we were sensible of danger we had daily prayer in this room for the divine protection.—Our prayers, Sir, were heard, & they were graciously answered. . . . I have lived, Sir, a long time, and the longer I live, the more convincing proofs I see of this truth—that *God Governs in the affairs of men*. And if a sparrow cannot fall to the ground without his notice, is it probable that an empire can rise without his aid? We have been assured, Sir, in the sacred writings, that "except the Lord build the House they labour in vain that build it." I firmly believe this; and I also believe that without his concurring aid we shall succeed in this political building no better than the Builders of Babel.[26] (emphasis original)

The delegates' reaction is interesting to note:

> Mr. SHARMON seconded the motion.
>
> Mr. HAMILTON & several others expressed their apprehensions that however proper such a resolution might have been at the beginning of the convention, it might at this late day, 1. bring on it some disagreeable animadversions. & 2. lead the public to believe that the embarrassments and dissensions within the Convention, had suggested this measure. It was answered by Docr. F. Mr. SHERMAN & others, that the past omission of a duty could not justify a further omission—that the rejection of such a proposition would expose the Convention to more unpleasant animadversions than the adoption of it: and that the alarm out of doors that might be excited for the state of things within, would at least be as likely to do good as ill.
>
> Mr. WILLIAMSON, observed that the true cause of the omission could not be mistaken. The Convention had no funds.
>
> Mr. RANDOLPH proposed in order to give a favorable aspect to ye measure, that a sermon be preached at the request of the convention on 4th of July, the anniversary of Independence; & thenceforward prayers be used in ye Convention every morning. Dr. FRANKLIN 2ded this motion. After several unsuccessful attempts for silently postponing the matter by adjourning, the adjournment was at length carried, without any vote on the motion.[27]

The fact that the delegates did not vote on Franklin's motion did not reflect any irreverence on their part. Rather it stemmed in part from concern that bringing in an outside clergyman at this time might cause rumors that the Convention (the proceedings of which had been kept secret) was facing difficulty, and most especially the fact that the Convention was without funds to pay a clergyman. Remember that the motion was to bring in an outside clergyman to lead in prayer. This was a regular custom in colonial legislatures and in the Continental Congress, and they regularly paid the clergyman for his services.[28] In those days the lines between clergy and laity were more fixed than today, and believing as they did that "the labourer is worthy of his hire" (Luke 10:7; 1 Tim. 5:18 KJV), it was unthinkable that they would ask a clergyman to come to the Convention and lead in prayer without paying him for his services.

The Convention debates largely centered on practical questions of government because the delegates mostly shared the same basic theological and philosophical assumptions. But the practical provisions of the Constitution reflect the Christian worldview of the delegates. It is possible to go through the Constitution phrase by phrase and find parallels with Scripture, but instead it must suffice to examine some of the more basic premises of the Declaration and the Constitution.

HIGHER LAW

In keeping with Blackstone, Montesquieu, Locke, and others, the framers believed that to be valid, human law must conform to the higher law of God, often called the law of revelation and the Law of Nature, or sometimes the Laws of Nature and of nature's God. Consider just a few statements from leading Americans of the time:

> The smiles of Heaven can never be expected on a nation that disregards the eternal rules of order and right, which Heaven itself has ordained (George Washington).[29]

> Good and wise men, in all ages . . . have supposed that the Deity, from the relations we stand in to Himself, and to each other, has constituted an eternal and immutable law, which is indispensably obligatory on all mankind, prior to any human institutions whatever (Alexander Hamilton).[30]

> [Moral or natural law was] . . . given by the Sovereign of the universe to all mankind. . . . Being founded by infinite wisdom and goodness on essential right, which never varies, it can require no amendment or alteration (John Jay).[31]

The transcendent law of nature and of nature's God, which declares that the safety and happiness of society are the objects at which all political institutions aim, and to which all such institutions must be sacrificed (James Madison).[32]

The Rights of Colonists as Christians . . . may be best understood by reading—and carefully studying—the institutes of the great Lawgiver and head of the Christian Church: which are to be found clearly written and promulgated in the New Testament (Samuel Adams).[33]

(The) gallant Struggle in America, is founded in Principles so indisputable, in the moral Law, in the revealed Law of God, in the true Constitution of Great Britain, and in the most apparent Welfare of the Nation as well as the People of America, that I must confess it rejoices my very Soul (John Adams).[34]

. . . the great command of nature and nature's God (Benjamin Franklin).[35]

That law, which God has made for man in his present state; that law, which is communicated to us by reason and conscience, the divine monitors within us, and by the sacred oracles, the divine monitors without us . . .

As promulgated by reason and the moral sense it has been called natural; as promulgated by the holy scriptures, it has been called revealed law.

As addressed to men, it has been denominated the law of nature: as addressed to political societies, it has been denominated the law of nations.

But it should always be remembered, that this law, natural or revealed, made for men or for nations, flows from the same divine source; it is the law of God. . . .

Human law must rest its authority, ultimately, on the authority of that law, which is divine (James Wilson).[36]

It pleased God to write his law on the heart of man at first. . . .

Such authority hath natural conscience still in man that it
renders those . . . inexcusable in the sight of God (Romans
1:20–2:14) (John Witherspoon).[37]

The Founding Fathers expressly wrote the concept of God-given
law and God-given rights into the Declaration of Independence,
stating that the colonies are entitled to independence by the laws of
nature and of nature's God and that all men are endowed by their
Creator with certain inalienable rights. The concept is less explicit
in the Constitution, but the framers assumed that the Constitution
would be interpreted according to a natural-law framework as reflected
in the Declaration; because they assumed the continuation of a
Christian order. And the phrase, laws of nature and of nature's God
finds further expression in Article 1, Section 8, Clause 10, which
authorizes Congress to define and punish "Offences against the Law
of Nations." The term, Law of Nations, as used for centuries by
Grotius, Pufendorf, Vattel, and others, was based on the belief in a
higher law that came from God.

The concept of the higher law of God was both an empowering
factor and a limiting factor in the framers' view of human government.
On the one hand, God's law gave divine authority to human
government. On the other hand, God's law placed limits on human
government, for no human laws are of any validity if contrary to the
higher law of God. This provided the basis for the framers' belief that
governmental power is to be severely limited, and for the belief that
when government goes beyond its appointed limits it becomes
illegitimate and tyrannical, and it becomes the duty of the Christian
citizen to resist.

GOD-GIVEN RIGHTS

Closely related to the concept of God-given higher law is that of
God-given rights. In fact, the framers saw natural rights as part of the
law of nature. Here are a few representations:

The sacred rights of mankind are not to be rummaged for
among old parchments or musty records. They are written,
as with a sunbeam, in the whole volume of human nature, by
the hand of the Divinity itself, and can never be erased or
obscured by mortal power (Alexander Hamilton).[38]

He wrote an essay titled "The Rights of the Colonists as
Christians" in which he said:

These may be best understood by reading—and carefully studying the institutes of the great Lawgiver and head of the Christian Church: which are to be found clearly written and promulgated in the New Testament—

. . . Magna Charta itself is in substance but a constrained Declaration, or proclamation in the name of the King, Lord, and Commons of the sense the latter had of their original inherent, indefeasible natural Rights, and also those of free Citizens equally perdurable with the other (Samuel Adams).[39]

The God who gave us life gave us liberty at the same time; the hand of force may destroy but cannot disjoin them (Thomas Jefferson).[40]

Can the liberties of a nation be thought secure when we have removed their only firm basis, a conviction in the minds of the people that these liberties are . . . the gift of God. That they are not to be violated but with His wrath? (Thomas Jefferson).[41]

This belief in God-given rights found expression in the Declaration of Independence, which states as a self-evident truth that all men "are endowed by their Creator with certain unalienable Rights, that among these are Life, Liberty and the pursuit of Happiness." It finds further expression in the various rights secured throughout the Constitution, most notably Article I, Section 10, and the Bill of Rights.

The concept that human rights are ordained of God is an important limit on state power and essential to human freedom. It provides the only firm basis for lasting limits on the state's power over the individual person. If there are no God-ordained human rights, the state can do to people whatever it wants. If the state is the source of human rights, then they are not inalienable rights at all but rather negotiable privileges: The State giveth; the State taketh away; blessed be the name of the State.

A LOW VIEW OF HUMAN NATURE

Unlike the French Revolutionists who believed that man is basically good or that human nature is perfectible, the framers of the American Republic knew that man is as the Bible describes him: sinful, self-interested, ambitious, corruptible.

Take mankind in general, they are vicious—their passions may be operated on (Alexander Hamilton).[42]

The depravity which mankind inherited from their first parents, introduced wickedness into the world. That wickedness rendered human government necessary to restrain the violence and injustice resulting from it. To facilitate the establishment and administration of government, the human race became, in the course of Providence, divided into separate and distinct nations. Every nation instituted a government, with authority and power to protect it against domestic and foreign aggressions (John Jay).[43]

Show me that age and country where the rights and liberties were placed on the sole chance of their rulers being good men, without a consequent loss of liberty (Patrick Henry).[44]

Few in public affairs act from a mere view of the good of their country, whatever they may pretend; and, though their actings bring real good to their country, yet men primarily considered that their own and their country's interest was united, and did not act from a principle of benevolence. That fewer still, in public affairs, act with a view to the good of mankind.(Benjamin Franklin).[45]

[Universalism is] very erroneous and if believed will tend to relax the restraints on vice arising from the threatenings of the divine law against impenitent sinners. . . . I think we are as much bound to believe the threatenings as the promises of the gospel (Roger Sherman).[46]

The evil of sin appears from every page of the sacred oracles. . . . The history of the world is little else than the history of human guilt. . . . Nothing is more plain from scripture, or better supported by daily experience, than that man by nature is in fact incapable of recovery without the power of God specially interposed (John Witherspoon).[47]

Let me ask you very seriously, my friend, where are now in 1813 the perfection and perfectibility in human nature? Where is now the progress of the human mind? Where is the amelioration of society? Where the augmentation of human comforts? Where the diminution of human pains and miseries? (John Adams).[48]

Even Thomas Jefferson, who earlier in life had probably held a higher view of human nature than did most of the framers, declared after seeing firsthand the abuse of power in the French Revolution, "In questions of power, then, let no more be said of confidence in man, but bind him down with the chains of the Constitution."[49]

Holding this view of human nature, the framers knew that government was necessary to check the sinful impulses of humanity. Humans cannot live in a state of anarchy. But knowing that those who hold public office—kings, presidents, governors, legislators, sheriffs, prosecutors, judges—have the same sinful nature as everyone else, likewise caused the framers to fear excessive governmental power in the hands of sinful rulers, for they knew that government officials can be corrupted by power and are likely to misuse it and become tyrannical, corrupt, and oppressive. James Madison expressed this dilemma in his classic passage of *Federalist No. 51*:

> Ambition must be made to counteract ambition. The interest of the man must be connected with the constitutional rights of the place. It may be a reflection on human nature, that such devices should be necessary to control the abuses of government. But what is government itself, but the greatest of all reflections on human nature? If men were angels, no government would be necessary. If angels were to govern men, neither external nor internal controls on government would be necessary. In framing a government which is to be administered by men over men, the great difficulty lies in this: you must first enable the government to control the governed; and in the next place oblige it to control itself.[50]

To keep government within its God-appointed limits, and to keep government from becoming tyrannical and corrupt while at the same time giving government sufficient power to control the governed, the Framers drafted a Constitution based on what can be called the "Founding Fathers' five-fold formula for freedom:"

Government of Limited, Delegated Powers. Government has only such power as we, the people, have delegated to it through the Constitution, and no other. This concept was assumed by the Framers, but, to make it clear, they cast it in concrete in the Tenth Amendment: "The powers not delegated to the United States by the Constitution, nor prohibited by it to the States, are reserved to the States respectively, or to the people."

While often ignored by the courts today, the concept of limited government embodied in the Tenth Amendment is a cornerstone of freedom. Speaking through Moses, God likewise ordained limited government for Israel in Deuteronomy 17:14–20 (KJV), in stark contrast with the pagan nations around Israel who practiced emperor-worship and totalitarian government:

> When thou art come unto the land which the LORD thy God giveth thee, and shalt possess it, and shalt dwell therein, and shalt say, I will set a king over me, like as all the nations that are about me,
>
> Thou shalt in any wise set him king over thee, whom the LORD thy God shall choose: one from among thy brethren shalt thou set king over thee: thou mayest not set a stranger over thee, which is not thy brother.
>
> But he shall not multiply horses to himself, nor cause the people to return to Egypt, to the end that he should multiply horses: forasmuch as the LORD hath said unto you,
>
> Ye shall henceforth return no more that way. Neither shall he multiply wives to himself, that his heart turn not away: neither shall he greatly multiply to himself silver and gold.
>
> And it shall be, when he sitteth on the throne of his kingdom, that he shall write him a copy of this law in a book out of that which is before the priests the Levites: And it shall be with him, and he shall read therein all the days of his life: that he may learn to fear the LORD his God, to keep all the words of this law and these statutes, to do them:
>
> That his heart be not lifted up above his brethren, and that he turn not aside from the commandment, to the right hand, or to the left: to the end that he may prolong his days in his kingdom, he, and his children, in the midst of Israel.

Vertical Division of Powers. Just as Jethro had advised Moses in Exodus 18:13, 27, the framers divided the powers among the various levels of government. Certain powers were delegated to the national government; others were reserved to the states; still others were to be exercised at the local level. In this way no one level of government became too powerful.

Horizontal Separation of Powers. Likewise the power delegated to each level of government is diffused among three branches: legislative, executive, and judicial.

Checks and Balances. Each level and each branch of government is not entirely independent of the others. Each interacts with the others, and each checks and balances the powers of the others. For example, Congress passes laws subject to the veto of the president, which in turn can be overridden by two-thirds of both houses of Congress. The Supreme Court can strike down congressional acts as unconstitutional, but there are checks on the Court: The Justices are appointed by the President with the advice and consent of the Senate; Congress can limit the Court's appellate jurisdiction, and Congress sets the Court's budget. Under the original formula, states had a powerful check on the federal government in that each state's United States senators were not popularly elected but rather were selected by the legislature of each state. This check on federal power was eliminated by the Seventeenth Amendment (1915), which established popular election of Senators.

Reserved Individual Rights. Representative government means that the people select their leaders, who generally make policy decisions for the nation. But a constitutional republic places limits even on the will of the majority, for a majority can ride roughshod over the rights of the minority if left unchecked. As Madison said in *Federalist No. 51*, "A dependence on the people is, no doubt, the primary control on the government; but experience has taught mankind the necessity of auxiliary precautions."[51] Thus, the framers provided that certain God-given rights shall be considered inviolate, and even the majority cannot take these rights away (except by amending the Constitution, which takes far more than a simple majority). The protection of minority rights—often an unpopular task—falls especially on the courts.

These are the basic underlying principles of the American Republic as established by the framers in the late eighteenth century, and they have their roots in the Bible. Many other provisions of the Constitution are likewise based on biblical principles. The belief that "all men are created equal" is based on belief in a creator God and is rooted in the Old Testament concept that judges were to treat everyone equally and fairly under the law (Ex. 23:6) and the New Testament concept that "God is no respecter of persons" (Acts 10:34) and that in Christ "there is neither Jew nor Greek" (Gal. 3:28). While the framers did not practice true equality, at least they planted the seeds of equality in a world where slavery had been almost universally practiced for thousands of years.

The belief, so eloquently expressed in the Declaration, "that to secure these rights, Governments are instituted among Men, deriving their just powers from the consent of the governed," is rooted in the Hebrew republic. Unlike the surrounding pagan nations that practiced state worship and emperor worship, the Jews understood that God gives power to human rulers through the people (Judg. 8:22; 9:6; 2 Sam. 16:18; 2 Kings 14:21; Deut. 5:1; 6:18). Drawing on the biblical view directly in some cases, and indirectly in others, through the social-compact theory of John Locke or the covenant views of the Puritans, the framers of the Constitution recognized that all government authority flows upward from the people through the Constitution; thus they began the Preamble with the words, "We the People." This did not necessarily mean that the people chose their leaders through democratic elections, but it does mean that in some way they establish their government and give it authority and legitimacy.

Other parallels abound. The rights of criminal defendants as guaranteed in Article 1, Section 10 and in the Bill of Rights parallel in many respects the rights of criminal defendants under the Law of Moses that went further than any ancient system toward protecting the rights of the accused, recognizing that even the suspected criminal was created in the image of God. Among these are the requirement that no one may be convicted of treason except on the testimony of two witnesses or confession in open court (Article III, Section 3, Clause 1; cf. Deut. 17:6; 19:5; Num. 35:30; Mark 14:55–59), and that no conviction of treason shall work "corruption of blood" or a legal taint on the convicted person's descendants (Article III, Section 3, Clause 2; cf. Deut. 24:16).

As Max Dimont noted, the Old Testament also laid the foundation for the concept of separation of church and state[52]—not the absolute separation of government from God or from biblical values, but rather the belief that church and state are to be separate institutions, each established by God for a different purpose, one to teach righteousness through Jesus Christ, the other to preserve order by restraining the exercise of sin. In Israel, the kings always came from one tribe (Judah) while the priests always came from a different tribe (Levi). But both institutions were ordained by God and both were subject to biblical law. Without entering the issue of whether the command to honor the Sabbath applies to this age and whether today's Sabbath is Saturday or Sunday, note that the principle of sabbath rest is explicitly recognized in Article 1, Section 7, Clause 2 of the Constitution, which provides concerning the president's veto power that

> If any bill shall not be returned by the President within ten days (Sundays excepted) after it shall have been presented to him, the Same shall be a Law, in like Manner as if he had signed it. . . .

The question is often asked, "is the United States a Christian nation?" The answer must be, "It depends on how the term is defined."

If by *Christian nation* one means a nation in which everyone is a Christian, or in which only Christians are welcome, or in which non-Christians are second-class citizens, then in that sense the United States is not a Christian nation.

But every nation is founded on certain basic principles or values, and those values have their source in religious belief. If by the term *Christian nation* one means a nation that was founded on biblical values that were brought to the nation by mostly professing Christians, then in that sense the United States may truly be called a Christian nation.

NOTES

1. Donald S. Lutz, "The Relative Influence of European Writers on Late Eighteenth Century American Political Thought," *American Political Science Review* 189 (1984): 189–97. cf. Charles S. Hyneman and Donald S. Lutz, *American Political Writing During the Founding Era 1760–1805*, vols. 1 and 2 (Indianapolis: Liberty Fund Press, 1983).

2. *Encyclopedia Britannica*, 1986, s.v. Deism. While the above definition of Deism as the belief in a God who created the universe and established basic laws for its operation but who does not actively intervene in His creation anymore, is the classic and common definition of Deism, the term is also used sometimes in a wider sense to denote the philosophy of anyone who believes that God is known through human reason rather than divine revelation. In the former sense almost none of the leading framers were Deists; Thomas Paine might have been a Deist in this sense, but he could not be called a leading framer since he never held public office, was denounced by many of the leading framers, and in the end renounced his American citizenship and went to France. In the latter sense of the term, a few like Jefferson might be considered Deists, but they were a small minority. The overwhelming majority were Christians, and most of these came out of a Calvinist background.

3. M. E. Bradford, *A Worthy Company: Brief Lives of the Framers of the United States Constitution* (Marlborough, N.H.: Plymouth Rock Foundation, 1982), iv–v.

4. Max I. Dimont, *Jews, God and History* (1962), quoted in Law: A *Treasury of Art and Literature*, ed. Sara Robbins (New York: MacMillan, 1990), 27–29.

5. John Adams, handwritten comments on his copy of a book by the Marquis de Condorcet, *Outlines of an Historical View of the Progress of the Human Mind*, reprinted in Zoltan Haraszti, *John Adams and the Prophets of Progress* (Cambridge: Harvard University Press, 1952), 246.

6. Ralph Houlbrooke, *Church Courts and the People During the English Reformation 1520–1570* (Oxford: Oxford University Press, 1979), 8.

7. John C. H. Wu, *Fountain of Justice* (London: 1959), 64–66.

8. *New Catholic Encyclopedia* , s.v. Charlemagne.

9. Wu, *Fountain of Justice*, 64–66.

10. John Caning, ed., *100 Great Kings, Queens and Rulers of the World* (New York: Taplinger, 1968), 211, 214.

11. Harold J. Berman, *The Interaction of Law and Religion* (Nashville: Parthenon Press, 1974), 55.

12. Rousas J. Rushdoony, *The Institutes of Biblical Law*, vol. I (Nutley, N.J.: Craig Press, 1978), 788–89.

13. Frederick Powell and Frederick Maitland, quoted by Wu, *Fountain of Justice*, 64–66.

14. Wu, *Fountain of Justice*, 64–66.

15. Sir William Blackstone, *Commentaries on the Laws of England*, quoted by Verna M. Halt, *The Christian History of the Constitution of America: Christian the United States of America and Self-Government with Union* (San Francisco: Foundation for American Christian Education, 1969), 140–46.

16. Ibid.

17. Ibid.

18. Paul S. Reinsch, *English Common Law in the Early American Colonies* (Madison, Wis.: Da Capo Press), 11.

19. Ibid., 13.

20. John Winthrop, quoted by Reinsch, "English Common Law," 15.

21. Reinsch, "English Common Law," 25.

22. Ibid, 26.

23. Ibid.

24. "Treaty of Paris," in *Select Documents Illustrative of the History of the United States, 1776–1861*, ed. William McDonald (New York: MacMillan, 1898).

25. Elizabeth Bryant Johnston, *George Washington, Day by Day, 1894*, 70, quoted by William J. Johnson, *George Washington the Christian* (Euclid, Ill.: Christian Liberty Press, 1919), 152.

26. James Madison, *Notes of Debates in the Federal Convention of 1787* (Athens, Ohio: Ohio University Press, 1984), 209–10.

27. Ibid., 210–11.

28. *Marsh v. Chambers*, 463 U.S. 783, 103 S.Ct. 3330 (1983).

29. Johnston, *George Washington*, 68.

30. Alexander Hamilton, "The Farmer Refuted," 1775 quoted by Saul K. Padover, *The Mind of Alexander Hamilton* (New York: Harper, 1958), 430.

31. John Jay, to John Murray, 15 April 1818, in, *"In God We Trust:" The*

Religious Beliefs and Ideas of the American Founding Fathers, ed. Norman Cousins (New York: Harper & Brothers, 1958), 365–73.

32. James Madison, *The Federalist Essay* No. 43 (Springfield, Va.: Global Affairs, 1987), 238.
33. Samuel Adams, *The Writings of Samuel Adams,* vol. 2, ed. Harry Alonzo Cushing (New York: Octagon Books, 1968), II: 355–56.
34. John Adams, to *Boston Gazette,* 20 January 1766 in *Diary and Autobiography of John Adams,* vol. 1, ed. L. H. Butterfield (Cambridge, Mass: Belknap Press, 1962), 275–76.
35. Benjamin Franklin, "The Speech of Polly Baker," *Gentleman's Magazine,* April 1747, quoted by Carl Van Doren, *Benjamin Franklin,* (New York: Viking Press, 1938), 154.
36. James Wilson, quoted by James Dewitt Andres, *Works of Wilson, vol.1* (Chicago, 1896): 91–93; quoted by Charles Page Smith, *James Wilson: Founding Father* (Chapel Hill: University of North Carolina Press, 1956), 329.
37. John Witherspoon, quoted by Roger Schultz, "Covenanting in America: The Political Theology of John Witherspoon" (master's thesis, Trinity Evangelical Divinity School, Deerfield, Illinois, 1985), 96.
38. Alexander Hamilton, "The Farmer Refuted," 1775; quoted by Nathan Schachner, *Alexander Hamilton* (New York: Barnes & Co., 1961), 38.
39. Samuel Adams, "The Rights of the Colonists as Christians," quoted by Samuel Eliot Morison, *The Struggle over the Adoption of the Constitution of Massachusetts, Massachusetts Historical Society Proceedings,* L (1917), 317, 379.
40. Thomas Jefferson, "Summary View of the Rights of British America," 1774; quoted by M. Richard Maxfield, K. DeLynn Cook, and W. Cleon Skousen, *The Real Thomas Jefferson,* 2d ed. (Washington, D.C.: National Center for Constitutional Studies, 1983), 523.
41. Thomas Jefferson, "Notes on Virginia," 1781, 1782; quoted by Maxfield, Cook, and Skousen, *The Real Thomas Jefferson,* 523.
42. Alexander Hamilton, "Remarks to Constitutional Convention," 22 June 1787, quoted by Padover, *The Mind of Alexander Hamilton,* 80.
43. John Jay, to John Murray, 365–73.
44. Patrick Henry, "Remarks," Virginia Ratifying Convention Debates, 1789, quoted by Moses Coit Tyler, *Patrick Henry* (New York: Frederick Ungar Publishing Company, 1966), 328.
45. Benjamin Franklin, 1788, quoted by Albert Henry Smyth, ed., *The Writings of Benjamin Franklin,* vol. 1 (New York: MacMillan, 1905–1907), 339.
46. Roger Sherman, to David Austin, 1 March 1790 in *Roger Sherman's*

Connecticut, ed. Christopher Collier (Middletown, Conn.: Wesleyan University Press, 1971), 327.

47. John Witherspoon, quoted by Schultz, "Covenanting in America," 137.

48. John Adams, to Thomas Jefferson, 15 July 1813, quoted by Page Smith, *John Adams*, vol. 2 (Garden City, N.Y.: Doubleday, 1962, 1963), 1112.

49. Thomas Jefferson, Kentucky Resolutions of 1798, quoted by Madeld, 200.

50. James Madison, *The Federalist*, Essay No. 51, 281.

51. Ibid.

52. Dimont, *Jews, God and History*, 28; see also E. C. Wines, *The Hebrew Republic* (Cambridge, Massachusetts: American Presbyterian Press, 1980); Martin Diamond, "The Declaration and the Constitution: Liberty, Democracy, and the Founders," *The Public Interest* no. 41 (fall 1975), 50.

PART TWO

How Christians Should Relate to American Law

FOUR

Civil Authority and the Bible

Harold O. J. Brown

"The question," said Humpty, "is who is to be master."
Lewis Carrol, *Alice in Wonderland*

THE QUESTION OF THE relationship between church and state, between divine law (revealed law) and natural law is both a theoretical and a practical question. On the highest theoretical level, the question is easily answered. Peter told the high priest and the Jewish council, "We ought to obey God rather than men" (Acts 5:29),[1] expressing a general principle with which every Christian probably agrees. The issue becomes more difficult, even on the theoretical level, as soon as one plunges into details. More often than not, when conflicts arise, it is not altogether plain how the general commandments of God relate to the usually far more detailed laws and regulations of men. Human regulations and the conditions of contemporary human society create a sociocultural system in which the relevance and applicability of God's commandments are often far less than self-evident. In addition, it may be the case that a whole system—social functions, regulations, and conditions—is inconsistent with the fundamental principles of the Law and the justice of God, so that it is not possible to say in a specific case, "This human regulation is contrary to the divine law," but instead it would appear necessary, in order to conform to principles of divine justice, totally to change the system.

Events in the early 1990s in New York City, Texas, and Florida appear to have raised, in the eyes of CBS News, for example, the question of whether religion as such is incompatible with good social order. "Religion," or at least strongly held religious views, is said to cause terrorism, shootouts, and murder. Secular thinkers, and perhaps the state itself, have appeared to question the legitimacy of religion in general; outrages perpetrated by some of the more extreme examples of religious fanaticism may come to be laid to the charge of all religion. At the same time, serious Christians—and no doubt serious Jews as well—may be asking whether or to what extent the state has forfeited the right to the kind of obedience and loyalty specified, for example, by Paul in Romans 13. We are entering a kind of crisis of legitimacy in which both state and church question each other's authenticity.

THE STATE AND THE BIBLE

This topic could perhaps be dealt with in only a minute or two, especially if we called it "the state and the Bible." One could simply say, the Bible has nothing to say about the state. The state as we know it did not exist in biblical times. The idea of the state is a fairly late concept, dating at the earliest from the Renaissance. Prior to then, in the Middle Ages as well as in classical antiquity, there were rulers and ruled, there were governors and governments; but the concept of the State had not been developed, at least not in its modern, abstract, bureaucratic-institutional, impersonal sense. The monarchies, principalities, and chiefdoms of antiquity were highly personal. Authority, as Hannah Arendt points out, was vested in persons, and, "its hallmark is unquestioning recognition by those who are asked to obey." "Power," she observes, "is never the property of an individual, it belongs to a group and remains in existence only as long as the group keeps together."[2] The strength of even the strongest individual can be overpowered by a group, which will respond in obedience and respect only if that individual possess authority: "To remain in authority requires respect for the person or the office."[3] Sovereignty in antiquity goes with the authority to command voluntary obedience—when an individual is strong enough to compel obedience on the part of the group that he would have to support him.

The term *sovereign* is traditionally used with respect to a person; *national sovereignty* became a concept after the break-up of Roman imperial power and the fading of the imperial idea of the Holy Roman Empire; because individuals—kings, dukes, electors, and the like—individually possessed the authority to exercise enough power to make them independent of two greatest authorities, emperor and pope. The national sovereignty of the United States began when the sovereign, King George III, lost the authority necessary to secure the unquestioning recognition of the colonists.

Ancient Egypt, the first highly organized social structure about which we know much, was a kind of theocratic monarchy. The story of Joseph and the Pharaoh who made him prime minister reflects the highly personal nature of ancient government. The church, that is, Egyptian religion, and civil society really constituted a sort of organic whole. It was not necessary to argue the divine right of kings, as in seventeenth-century England, for it was taken for granted that the aura of divinity surrounded the ruler, the Pharaoh.

The household of Pharaoh and the government were closely intertwined. Likewise, in the days of the Old Testament when the Hebrew Scriptures were being written, there is no mention of the state, or even of government as an institution.

There is virtually no talk of institutions in the Bible, or at least not of the kind that we associate with government and with other aspects of modern society. There are no corporations, no legal persons. Natural persons and personal relationships dominate. We have marriages, parents and children, brothers and sisters, fathers-in-law and mothers-in-law, chiefs and followers, kings and subjects but not unions, trade associations, or chambers of deputies. Both in the Bible and in extrabiblical literature, high officials frequently bear names that indicate personal service to the monarch, personal service actually performed, or at least symbolically expressed by the official's title, such as cupbearer, a post held by Nehemiah.

INSTITUTIONS IN THE BIBLE

When we speak of church and state, it is important to recognize that as far as *institutions* go, the earliest and primary human social institution, or rather social structure, is the family. The family is a simple society and does not need to be organized on a formalized, legally structured basis. The only commandment in the Decalogue that relates to what we might call the exercise of government is a family rule: "Honor thy father and thy mother."

Examples of simple governmental institutions do exist in the Hebrew Scriptures, but the duties of the individual toward civil government are not spelled out as they are, at least in principle, in the New Testament. Perhaps the explanation is the fact that from the age of the patriarchs to the Exile, authority remained primarily personal and familial. In the early chapters of the Bible, family, society, and congregation are interwoven. Religious leaders are civil leaders: Moses himself is the prime example. Both the family and the church *antedate* the state.

Specific instructions relating to the duties of the individual over against civil government come from the era of the New Testament and are addressed to people, the Christians, who were outsiders as far as the civil authorities were concerned (although governmental persecution of Christians as Christians came later) and who, therefore, could not be expected to have the rather natural affinities to those in authority that could have been expected of the Hebrews under the Davidic monarchy.

The New Testament word for church is *ekklesia,* which means "the called out," i.e. "the assembly." In Old Testament times, the religious and civil assemblies were identical. By the time of the New Testament, against the background of the more highly structured political systems of Greece and Rome, there was clearly a difference between the political assembly *(ekklesia)* and the religious one (also *ekklesia),* but the term *ekklesia* had not yet become a technical expression for what we now know as church (Latin *ecclesia).* However, when it is used in a religious context, the word takes on a special significance.

For the centuries during which the highly structured authority and administrative system of the Roman Empire were being overrun in the west by Germanic barbarians, it is a commonplace wisdom to say that the church began to replace the empire. The evolution of the church followed a similar pattern to that of the empire. The Roman republic began as a city-state with authority residing in an assembly and with the people, symbolically expressed by the political tetragrammaton SPQR, *Senatus Populusque Romanorum,* "the Senate and the People of the Romans," but as its reach (das Reich) spread across the Mediterranean world, it was symbolized as the *dominium* (lordship) of a single man, the emperor. The Roman Republic became the Roman Empire as a result of the recognition of the principate, the personal authority of an individual man symbolized by the use of personal and family names, Augustus and Caesar, from which are derived the modern words *Kaiser* and *czar.* It was the influence of the first Caesars and Augusti that really took the collection of cities and towns, territories and provinces under Roman rule and made them into the empire, into the *oikumene,* into an "ecumenical" or universal society. The medieval revival of the imperial idea in the Holy Roman Empire did not require an imperial capital city, as Rome had been; but the center of authority traveled with the person of the *Kaiser* whose court accompanied him as he circulated about his empire.

One might even be tempted to suppose that the American president, Mr. Clinton, is unconsciously attempting, by his incessant itineration about his domain and his frequent recourse to the illusory omnipresence of television, even of MTV, to draw the center of authority away from the institutions of the government and to his person, thus in a sense to become a modern Caesar. It is significant that the first Caesar, Julius, rose to power—not quite to the status of Emperor—in the wake of dramatic internal crises of the republic, while Mr. Clinton has not ceased to point to the crises of the American republic, as though to say, like the late General Charles de Gaulle, *"C'est moi ou le chaos!"* ("It's me or chaos!").

THE CHURCH

To return to our central topic, the church, we know that the church in principle was intended by Jesus to be ecumenical. However, under the conditions of suppression and persecution by the imperial power, the church was in its early reality the local congregations, the individual *ekklesiai*. It could not truly become an *oikumene* until the empire became first more tolerant, then weaker, and finally ceased to exist. (It is significant that in the lands where the political empire survived, in the Byzantine east, the church never came under the personal leadership of the spiritual successor to the Roman Caesars, the pope.)

The local congregations became the church in the context of the world-wide expansion and acknowledgment of the personal authority of the Lord, the *kurios*. It is therefore interesting that when the religious concept of the *ekklesia* comes over into the Germanic languages, it is not merely transliterated (Latin *ecclesia*, French *eglise*), but a new word takes its place: it becomes church, kirk, *kirche*, *kerk*, and the like. What is the derivation of this family of words? It seems to be derived from the Greek *kuriakos*, meaning "pertaining to the kurios," to the Lord. The important thing to note here is that the church is intimately associated with a *person*, specifically, with the person of the Lord of the church, Jesus Christ. The church is spoken of as "the bride of Christ" and as "the body of Christ," two metaphors that stress the intensely personal dimension of the church, in contrast to a purely institutional concept. Thus, we may say that the church in the West did not simply take over the Roman concept of institution, which had become less and less personal and more and more bureaucratic with time; but additionally it specifically reaffirmed the *personal* relationship of the church to her Founder and suggested that in the church we are dealing with a structure held together by ties akin to personal and family loyalties (faith, fidelity, German *treue*) rather than by organizational ties. The fact that the institutional church in the West revolved around a single human person, the pope, reflects the fact that its spiritual reality was made universal by revolving about the divine Person of its Lord, Christ.

HOW OLD IS THE CHURCH?

The concept of church is thus older than the concept of state, as far as the Bible is concerned (although by the time the Bible speaks of either the ancient Hebrew congregation, the *q'ahal*, or of the church, it was already describing secular institutions of civil authority that were older). The Bible reports events that predate the establishment of secular governments and tells of personal leaders who gathered a people around themselves: Noah and his little group of flood survivors, Joseph and the family he invited to join him in Egypt, Moses and the people of the Exodus, Nehemiah and those who returned from captivity. Joseph, however, did not gather his people in an unpopulated region of earth, but in the midst of a highly developed culture where civil and religious authority were interwoven, centering on the person of the Pharaoh. Even among the nations outside of Israel, civil authority was, in the initial stages, primarily personal.

Looking ahead for a moment, we observe that the institutions of the modern state are in general no longer personal, but intensely impersonal and anonymous. The personal totalitarian dictatorships of the middle of our century, those of Mussolini and Hitler, Stalin and Mao Tse-tung, only apparently represent an exception, a continuation of the concept of personal authority, because beyond the immediate circle of the dictator's intimates, there was no unquestioning recognition, no obedience to authority in Arendt's sense. Compliance was enforced by the exercise of power.

In his 1965 work, *The Secular City*, theologian Harvey Cox characterizes the Exodus as the exhibition of God's intention to "desacralize" government. While it is more straightforward to view the Exodus primarily as the liberation of the Hebrews from the house of bondage, there is no doubt that in the encounter between Moses and Pharaoh, any claims of the Egyptian monarchy to divine right were set aside. From the stories of Exodus and the Exile, we see that the people of God are to be distinguished in important respects from civil society, to be, in Peter's expression, "a peculiar people." Except for a brief time under the monarchy of David, a critical distinction between the religious and the civil society is always evident, even though neither was fully structured; and neither the state nor the church had yet come into being in the form that they would subsequently take.

It is really first with the Gentile monarchs of Persia that we encounter something resembling a state with its working apparatus, a bureaucracy (see the accounts in Daniel). Nevertheless, what we call government remained intensely personal. The Roman Empire, which ruled over scores of peoples and nations in the entire Mediterranean basin and much of Europe and Asia Minor, was only able to accomplish this feat by means of disciplined, organized structures, and generally by a reliable administrative and military bureaucracy.

Nevertheless, even ancient Rome was highly personalistic. The emperors were called "divine Augusti"; they dwelt in the "sacred palace"; and the imperial treasurer was the "Count of the Sacred

Largesses." After the conversion of Emperor Constantine, the emperors no longer claimed the title of Pontifex Maximus, Supreme Pontiff; but the quasisacral association of government power with the person of the emperor continued. The East Roman, or Byzantine, emperors wanted to be considered as the successors of David, occupying a role not quite messianic but bordering on it. Like David, they were anointed and were thought to possess a priestly as well as a civil status. The English skeptic Thomas Hobbes (1588–1677) was perhaps the first to conceive of the state as an impersonal *Leviathan.* From his day onward the state has not ceased to grow and to expand, until in our own era it has attained immense proportions. In seventeenth-century France, the "Sun King" Louis XIV boasted, "L'état, c'est moi" ("The state is me"), but the twentieth-century Fifth Republic has far more involvement in and influence on the day-to-day life of the average Frenchman than the monarchy of Louis could have imagined. Modern means of communication and administration have magnified the power of the state to reach down into the lives of individuals even before the advent of the computer. The computer has made cradle-to-grave, virtually round-the-clock surveillance and supervision not merely possible but increasingly a matter of course for every citizen of a modern state. Under the spell of what Jacques Ellul calls "the political illusion" in a book of that name,[4] modern societies think that all problems are essentially political in nature; and, therefore, that all solutions will be political as well. This leads to the proliferation of administrative and regulatory bureaucracy everywhere; for, as Ellul points out, bureaucracy is the arms and legs of the state; and when government is expected to do everything and to change everything, this can only be accomplished by means of a great and constantly expanding bureaucratic apparat.[5]

A preliminary conclusion, then, is that the development of the societies we know from biblical days into the modern states of the present inevitably will present us with serious conflicts of conviction, conduct, and competence between church and state. The church, in order to be obedient to her calling to influence Christians, cannot but be in tension with the increasingly total state in its determination to direct all society and to guide all social development. Any effort on our part to set forth principles and practical suggestions for the guidance of Christians today will lead us to deal with this present and growing tension.

LEGITIMACY AND LIMITS

The original family in the Bible was established by the Creator, who brought the first woman to the first man (Gen. 2:22). The first civil society, the first city, by contrast was founded by the first murderer, Cain (Gen. 4:8, 17). Once the principle of violence has entered human society, an organized social structure, the city, becomes necessary to make human life possible. The law, as Paul points out, exists to restrain the lawless and disobedient. (1 Tim. 1:9, Paul is speaking here of the law of God, but the same principle applies to human laws.) Where there is no civil authority, no "king in Israel," every man does that which is right in his own eyes (Judg. 21:25).

In view of the inevitable tension between the authority of Christ and that of the Caesars of this world, a tension that often becomes violent in the persecution and suppression of Christianity, or, less frequently, in Christian rebellion against civil authority, it is necessary to affirm and reaffirm the legitimacy of human civil authority in the plan of God. Calvin warns against considering "the whole nature of government a thing polluted, which has nothing to do with Christian men."[6] The temptation to dismiss civil government as representing the power of evil was widespread among Christians in America during the antiwar protests of the 1960s and early 1970s; and it may reappear in the context of current government endorsement of policies perceived as morally evil, such as the promotion of abortion and the elevation of homosexual conduct to the same level of acceptability as normal heterosexuality.

Paul makes the legitimacy of government plain in Romans 13:1: "The powers that be are ordained of God." In the confrontation with Pilate, when the Roman procurator warned Jesus that he had the power to put Him to death, Jesus acknowledged that that power had been given to Pilate "from above," not by Emperor Tiberius, but by God. In his appeal to Caesar, Paul also acknowledged the lawful authority of the government to put him to death (Acts 25:11).

THE *CLAUSULA PETRI*

At other times and under other circumstances when it seems that civil government is on the point of claiming itself to be the source of all moral and legal authority, it is necessary for Christians to reaffirm the *limits* of human civil authority. The first of these limits is quite clearly expressed in Scripture and is universally accepted by Christians and, to some extent, even respected by the civil laws of secular states: We may not do that which God's law prohibits, even when the secular authority commands it (Dan. 3:4–6), and we must do what God's law requires, even when secular (or religious) authorities prohibit it (Dan. 6:7–12; Acts 4:18; 5:28). Both the incidents in Daniel and those in Acts involve commanded or prohibited *religious* acts, namely, worship and witness. Some Christians might assume that the conflict between spiritual and civil authority arises only when the secular authorities interfere in religion (or vice versa). This was the assumption that persuaded most of the Protestants in Germany that they should not agitate against Hitler's anti-Semitic measures, which were supposedly civil matters, not religious ones. Parallels to the incidents in Daniel and Acts are uncommon in an open society such as the United States, although the increasingly vigorous banning of all that is religious from every secular area including those where presence is quasimandatory, such as public schools, may be beginning to resemble them. It is seldom that government appears to command things that are direct violations of the moral or religious laws of the Christian and Scriptures, to forbid those activities—specifically, prayer, worship, and witness—that are commanded there. Consequently, government in the United States can let the limitation of the *clausula Petri* stand without great risk to its own authority (Peter's exception, "We ought to obey God rather than men"). The other two limitations are more significant, namely the limitation from God's prior claim, and the limitation from the nature of God's mandate to government.

GOD'S PRIOR CLAIM

God's prior claim is expressed by two concepts: the "first fruits," or tithe, and the sabbath. "The earth is the Lord's, and the fullness thereof " (Ps. 24:1). God neither needs nor demands "thousands of rams or ten thousand rivers of oil" (Mic. 6:7), but he does have a prior claim on the produce of the earth as well as on us those of us who live on it: the firstlings of the flocks, the firstborn sons, the first fruits are the Lord's. Payment of the firstfruits, of the tithe, is a symbolic acknowledgment of the final and ultimate sovereignty of God, from whom every good and perfect gift comes (James 1:17). The king and his successor, the modern state, have a lawful claim on a portion of the wealth and energy of their subjects or citizens, but not on the first fruits, the tithe. Both the first fruit regulations and the sabbath legislation (of which more will be said) are intended to honor the sovereignty of God. Failure on the part of the state, even of the secular state where separation reigns, to show God a measure of honor and thankfulness will expose the society and its people to vanity, foolishness, and degradation (Rom. 1:21–24.). When well-meaning Christians, cognizant of the increasingly secular, increasingly multicultural nature of our American society, agree to the removal of all vestiges of reverence from secular institutions, they make a dangerous mistake. Neglect of nominal reverence and thankfulness to God will be punished by nation-wide folly that will penalize those Christians who still worship privately as well as the secularists who dishonor God publicly. The tithe, or specifically, the tax exemption granted to churches and synagogues and the deductions allowed for religious contributions does not represent state support of religion, so-called tax expenditures, because not all that we have and produce in the secular state belongs by right to the state. The prior claim is God's, expressed symbolically in terms of the tithe or the firstfruits. When Christians agree that a secular society need not grant tax exemption to churches and religious works, they implicitly join in the great offertory prayer of the divinized state: "All things come of thee, O State, and of thine own have we given thee." The fact that God has a prior claim on the firstfruits does not require an unlimited tax exemption or tax deduction: If an individual should want to give one hundred percent of his or her income to the church, it would not be a violation of the prior claim of God for the government to tax a portion of it—provided that the principle of the firstfruits be allowed to stand. For the state to demand, by contrast, that its portion must be taken *first*, and God's share paid by believers out of the remainder, is symbolically to deny the sovereignty of God.

In like manner, the sabbath-rest commandments of Exodus and Deuteronomy—the world's first labor laws—reserve a part of each person's productive ability for purposes chosen by God—rest and restoration, but also worship. Neither the individual employer nor the state may *fully* exploit human strength, energy, and time—not his own, nor that of his children, nor of his employees, nor even that of his work animals. The abolition of Sunday closing laws in the name of the separation of church and state, which has taken place not only in the United States but also in Canada in recent decades, means that there is no time in the week when people are protected from being fully exploited, even to the point of exhaustion of their physical and mental resources, whether it is self-exploitation or exploitation by employers. Sabbath legislation, like the tithe, sets a symbolic limit on both individual selfishness and the power of the state. In a society such as ours where different sabbaths are observed by substantial population groups, it might be possible to permit some variety but nevertheless to ensure that every commercial operation provide at least *some* sabbath in terms of a six-day week and a time of rest and restoration for its workers.

The tax exemptions and deductions granted to churches by the state should not be interpreted as state support for religion, and thus a putative violation of the First Amendment to the United States Constitution. Of course tax privileges for religious groups can be justified from a secular perspective, like tax exemption and tax deductibility for charitable, educational, and other nonprofit institutions. It is reasonable for Christians to support tax privileges not only for their own institutions, but also for similar activities of other religions and other socially valuable undertakings.

When tax privileges are granted to religious organizations, there is always the chance that fraudulent groups will be organized solely to profit from such privileges. Advocates of the separation of church and state have argued under such circumstances that the First Amendment forbids the government to pass judgment on the legitimacy of a religious organization; hence it cannot identify some religious groups as legitimate and deserving of tax privileges and call others illegitimate and undeserving. In consequence, so the thinking goes, inasmuch as government cannot plausibly grant tax exemption to everyone who can think up a specious religious reason to claim it, it must refuse it to all religious groups. Against this line of arguing it is necessary to acknowledge that at least some discretion must be allowed to government to distinguish between *bona fide* and fraudulent religious claims. If government is not allowed to make any such judgment, then all religions will be equally harmed.

GOD'S MANDATE TO THE POWERS
THAT BE (ROMANS 13:1–4)

The third biblical limitation on government is derived from the biblical mandate that legitimatizes the powers that be, found in Romans 13:3–4. This legitimacy might seem to extend to almost every form and institution of civil authority, and indeed Christians at some times and in some places have interpreted it as effectively requiring them to submit to and to obey every government, no matter how tyrannical and perverse that government might be. Paul wrote these lines under the capricious, mentally unstable tyrant Nero and it would be easy to jump to the conclusion that if Paul could approve Nero's government, there is hardly any kind of civil government that should not be dutifully obeyed by Christians. There is one important potential qualification: Paul describes civil government as God's servant. It is to administer justice, to reward the good, to punish evildoers, and thus to establish domestic peace and harmony within the society that it governs. Even in Paul's day when Nero was emperor, the government as a general rule provided national (i.e., imperial) security, a good measure of domestic peace, and sought to promote social welfare. Thus, in general, it did seek to fulfill what Paul describes in verses 3 and 4 as its God-given purpose.

One reason that the Roman administration could and did so function even under the tyrant Nero lay precisely in the personal nature of the Caesar's rule. The elaborate Roman administrative machinery that spanned the Mediterranean basin and took in a good portion of western Europe, northern Africa, and Asia Minor operated under its own momentum and did not immediately reflect and implement arbitrary, malicious, and cruel attitudes on the part of the monarch. Modern governments, however, are much more directly and promptly in touch with their rulers, whoever those may be, and in addition are much more ideological. Modern means of propaganda, surveillance, and control make what we call totalitarianism possible, a thing that was not even conceivable until the twentieth century. Administrative regulations and executive orders can effectively overturn traditional priorities and moral standards that have been in place for centuries.

Is it conceivable that a government could so pervert its divine mandate that it no longer *is* a lawful government in God's sight and that disobedience, opposition, and even rebellion become acceptable? If a government begins systematically to punish the good and to reward the evildoers, can it forfeit its claim to legitimacy so that Christians are no longer required, under God, to submit to its every ordinance? Under such circumstances, when lawful protests and opposition prove fruitless, civil disobedience and, ultimately resistance, to such tyranny may become justified. Among classical theologians, Calvin is one of the firmest in his declarations of the duty of Christians to respect and obey government. Yet even he recognizes that a time may come when it becomes incumbent on some "to withstand, in accordance with their duty, the fierce licentiousness of kings."[7] Calvin's commitment to lawful civil authority was such that he was unwilling to allow individuals to take such resistance into their own hands: it was the duty of lesser magistrates to fulfill their duty to God by resisting a tyrant who was perverting his mandate. Thus according to Calvin's theory, the American War of Independence (or Revolution) and Yeltsin's divestment of Gorbachev and break-up of the USSR can be justified, but not the French or the Bolshevik revolutions. Do we have examples from recent history of governments that so violate the divine purpose of civil government that they have forfeited their right to obedience? Nero was an individual tyrant and certainly rewarded evildoers who pleased him while punishing many of those who sought to do good—notably his former tutor, the greatest of Roman philosophers, Seneca, whom he forced to commit suicide— but this degree of depravity was not characteristic of Roman government as a whole. Indeed, inasmuch as Roman government like premodern governments in general, was not ideological and lacked the technological tools of totalitarian control, it would have been impossible for one tyrant, even for a Nero, totally to change the character of the government that he headed. Today this has become far easier. Certainly the Nazi government of Adolf Hitler qualified as a government that had begun, as a matter of policy, to punish the innocent and to reward the guilty. The resistance movement against Hitler, although ultimately unsuccessful, was justifiable according to Calvin's standards in that it was the resistance of lesser magistrates— government officials and military officers whose civic duty obliged them to promote the welfare of their people, and thus to resist the fierce licentiousness of Hitler. What about contemporary world governments? Without a detailed knowledge of the behavior of the tyranny of Saddam Hussein in Iraq, one is still tempted to suggest that the current Iraqi government may have forfeited its claim to biblical legitimacy. But what of governments closer to home? Has any government in Christendom begun to forfeit its claims to legitimacy? This is not to suggest that we have in any nominally Christian nation a government worse than that of Nero's Rome. Nevertheless, there are trends here and elsewhere that if carried to their logical conclusions, can render any government, even our own, to be a government unworthy of a Christian's obedience. Hitler's slaughter of the innocents has at least a partial parallel in developments in the United States. The Austrian Christian sociologist Hans Millendorfer says, "Euthanasia, like abortion, is a method in which killing represents a solution."[8] Abortion is now the law of the land in the United States, and euthanasia is finding increasing acceptance. But abortion, a state-endorsed and increasingly state-supported practice of killing as a solution, is far from the only example of such a procedure. Euthanasia is coming increasingly to the fore. University of Chicago political philosopher, Milton Rosenberg, is not alone in thinking that an inescapable consequence of current governmental health-care projects will be government-promoted euthanasia of the old, expensive, and useless. And of course the government is far from alone in resorting to this solution. Crimes against women and children, murder, rape, armed robbery, and criminal assault are becoming daily fare across the entire country. When a situation arises in which government can no longer protect the innocent and reward the good, and seems not merely unable but actually unwilling to do so, the command of Romans 13 may have become inapplicable.

Confronted with such developments, Christian responses have varied all the way from mere hand wringing sometimes accompanied by polyannaish prayers for "our leaders," through letter writing, marches, and political campaigns; to the more vigorous—but still nonviolent—tactics of Operation Rescue; and finally, in one extreme case, to killing as a solution.

Operation Rescue clearly disobeys instructions of the powers that be, and many noted Christians have taken a stand against its civil disobedience. At this point it may be pertinent to observe that the actions of protest groups such as Operation Rescue violate no divine commandment and no fundamental principle of the natural law. They do not murder; they do not steal; they do not bear false witness. Thus, they do not violate any basic principle or statute of secular criminal law. They violate relatively minor regulations against trespass, loitering, picketing, and the like in an effort to prevent the killing of developing children, which indeed *does* violate both the law of God and natural law. Just as one would unhesitatingly disregard a "No Trespassing" sign to rescue children from a burning building, so the "Rescuers" argue that they disregard minor regulations in order to forestall terrible deeds and to save helpless, endangered lives. Indeed, one could argue for *more* than what Operation Rescue does, namely, for the right or even the duty to resist with violence, rather than merely nonviolently. Would one be justified in assaulting, even killing, an arsonist about to set fire to a kindergarten or an ax wielder about to dismember a child? The extremely repressive measures that police have taken against Rescuers, the physical abuse and beatings—which in numbers of cases result in physical harm to the victims—the use of so-called Racketeer Influenced and Corrupt Organizations (RICO) laws, and a national "free access to clinics" law show the degree to which the government is now committed to defending the legitimacy of its program of killing as a solution. The consequences of this government violation of the principles of Romans 13:3–4 are likely to be with us for a long time.

FROM NONVIOLENCE TO COUNTERVIOLENCE

Once a government legalizes killing as a solution instead of treating it as a crime, the practice will spread across the general population. A bizarre example may illustrate the point: When an antiabortionist murdered an abortionist in front of his Florida clinic in 1993, some abortion opponents sought to rationalize the criminal act by drawing a parallel between the gunshot killing perpetrated on the abortionist and the far more numerous "medical-killings" that he perpetrated on developing children. The two kinds of killing are not morally equivalent. It was not morally defensible to frustrate Dr. Gunn's purpose of taking developing lives "safely and legally" by taking his. In addition to robbing Dr. Gunn of life, the crime has brought personal disaster on the murderer and great suffering on his family in addition to bringing the antiabortion cause into disrepute. Lest there be any misunderstanding, let it be plainly stated that the murder of the abortionist is not defensible and cannot be condoned. Nevertheless, the question of legality—abortion is legal, murder is not—is not the only difference between the crime of the murderer and the abortions of Dr. Gunn. For example, Dr. Gunn would still be alive if he had limited his obstetrics to the delivery of babies and had eschewed the practice of destroying them in the womb. The developing children have no way of avoiding the death intended for them. For a variety of reasons we do not wish to suggest moral equivalency between the murder of an unsuspecting, unarmed abortionist and the aspect of the "full range of medical services" that he was on the point of providing to eleven pregnant women that would have "terminated" the lives of eleven unsuspecting, unarmed developing children. However, the fact that lawfully constituted government calls one legal and the other a capital crime is precisely the sort of thing that causes people to think of their government in the way against which Calvin warns, and to call it "a thing polluted."

A CONTRADICTION IN TERMS?

The late Austrian legal theorist Hans Kelsen stated that an unjust law is a contradiction in terms, because it is law itself that sets the standard for what is just. Indeed, although Kelsen was Jewish, the anti-Semite Hitler availed himself of Kelsen's arguments in setting up his totalitarian system. We would not want to compare Hitler to any ruler in Christendom today, yet it cannot be denied that when government begins to follow Kelsen in this regard, it may eventually find itself in the company of Hitler. If Kelsen is right, then Romans 13:1–2 is an absolute command with no exceptions; and verses 3 and 4 can be disregarded. Then the proabortionists are right; there are indeed two fundamentally different kinds of killing—killing at three months in the womb is the legal kind while killing at forty-seven years on the streets is the illegal kind. The illegal kind is wrong, but the legal kind is just and right.

FROM THE ATOM TO CAESAR

As Hannah Arendt shows in *The Origins of Totalitarianism*[9] the rise of totalitarianism depends on the creation of what she calls an "atomistic mass," the elimination of intermediate structures and the establishment of a dependency of every individual directly on the central government. Consciously or unconsciously, our present American government is in the process of systematically disqualifying society's most significant intermediate structures and rendering them impotent. Within a few days of his inauguration in 1993, President Clinton had effectively attacked the effectiveness of both the majority

Christian churches and the military: the exaltation of abortion on demand to a protected, government-endorsed and promoted national policy stalemates much of the religious community and continues the ongoing weakening of the family and marriage; government endorsement of open homosexuality in the military preoccupies and weakens the military leadership, itself an important intermediate structure, and virtually eliminates government support for the ideals of marriage and the family. His proposals for health-care reform systematically excluded the guild of physicians from deliberation and planning. Defense Department cutbacks and closures will continue to force hundreds of thousands, perhaps millions onto the streets as unemployed, where they will be picked up by government aid and retraining programs. The longer-term implications of total government health care inevitably point, as Professor Rosenberg says, in the direction of euthanasia. The intermediate structures of government are to some extent bypassed as the president and his ministers traversed the country taking their proposals for vast restructuring of government directly to the people in situations and surroundings where, due to the disparity of power of the participants, no true deliberation or debate is possible, only acclamation. These rather sober perspectives may be more apocalyptic than realistic, yet they are not entirely without plausibility. In times of social chaos and anarchy, it is vitally important to emphasize the *legitimacy* of government.

Today, it is rapidly becoming more important to emphasize its *limitations*, lest Christians, too, join the "atomistic mass" that makes totalitarianism practically inevitable if not logically necessary.

NOTES

1. All Scripture in this chapter is from the King James Version of the Bible.
2. Hannah Arendt, *On Violence* (New York: Harcourt, Brace, and World, 1970), 45.
3. Ibid., 44, 46.
4. Jacques Ellul, *L'illusion politique* (Paris: Robert Laffont, 1965).
5. This subheading is borrowed from the title of Jacque Ellul's book of the same name (Grand Rapids: Eerdmans, 1972) translated from *Politique de Dieu, politique de l'homme* (Paris: Editions Universtaires, 1966).
6. John Calvin, *Institutes of the Christian Religion*, ed. John T. McNeill, trans. Ford Lewis Battles (Philadelphia: Westminster, 1960); 4.20.2.
7. Ibid., 4.20.31.
8. According to the Alan Guttmacher Institute, a research center of

the Planned Parenthood Federation, only about 2,500 physicians are currently engaged in the practice of abortion in this country, or an average of 640 abortions annually per abortionist.

9. Hannah Arendt, *The Origins of Totalitarianism* (New York: Harcourt, Brace, and Company, 1951).

FIVE

The Biblical View of Submission to Constituted Authority

R. C. Sproul

THE PROTESTANT REFORMATION was in some respects a revolt against authority. Though its chief architects, Martin Luther and John Calvin, did not consider themselves revolutionaries but reformers, there remained an element of revolt in their labor. They revolted against both ecclesiastical and civil authority. Luther's burning of the Papal Bull, *Ex Surge Domine,* was a public revolt against the highest authority in the church. His refusal to recant at the Diet of Worms was a revolt against the civil magistrates as well as ecclesiastical authority.

The reformers, however, eschewed the label of revolutionary because they held a high view of the order of both civil and ecclesiastical authority. They sought reform, not revolution, so that the supreme authority of God would be recognized and honored by both state and church. They saw their historical "revolt" as justified, nay, demanded by their allegiance to the supreme authority of God and His Word.

Though scrupulous in their views of civil obedience, both Calvin and Luther faced the same dilemma the apostles faced when they were forbidden by the magistrate of Israel, the Sanhedrin, to preach the Gospel. They asked a question that they tacitly understood as rhetorical:

> But so that it spreads no further among the people, let us severely threaten them, that from now on they speak to no man in this name. So they called them and commanded them not to speak at all nor teach in the name of Jesus (Acts 4:17–18 NKJV).

The apostles responded rhetorically:

> Whether it is right in the sight of God to listen to you more than to God, you judge (v. 19).

We note the content of the authorities' decree. They forbad the apostles from speaking or teaching in the name of Jesus. The time frame for this limitation was unambiguous; it was to be immediate and perpetual, "from now on."

It is hardly hyperbole to suggest that no magisterial decision in human history was so flagrantly and frequently violated by Christians. From that "now on" the apostles did little else besides speak and teach in the name of Jesus.

Had the apostles obeyed the command not to speak or teach in Jesus' name from that moment onward, there would be no church and possibly no American republic to wrestle over issues of church and state.

The apostles were driven to continue their ministry by an overarching ethical imperative. What words they couched in a gossamer veil of the rhetorical in Acts 4, they proclaimed "without horns" in chapter 5: "We ought to obey God rather than men" (v. 29). This ethical imperative, resting on an obligatory oughtness, is structured in a comparative form. The operative word in the comparison is "rather." It is not a universal license for revolt against all human authority. The Bible, as we shall endeavor to show, imposes solemn obligations upon us to honor, respect, submit to, and obey human authority. The "rather" comes into play only when there is conflict between the lesser and greater magistrate. The principle is always and ever prior obligation to the higher authority. Since God's authority clearly transcends human authority when there is conflict between the two, God's authority not only *may*, but *must* be obeyed.

The apostolic dilemma was centered on diverse and contradictory orders. They had one command from Christ, and the opposite and opposing command from the Sanhedrin. Given the comparative ethical imperative, their moral choice was an easy one to discern but a costly one to live out.

Conflict between obedience to God or to men has been a moral struggle from that day on. But the conflict was not born in first century Jerusalem. The roots of the conflict predate that encounter by centuries and are documented on numerous occasions in the pages of the Old Testament.

The very formation of the nation Israel in the redemptive-historical event of the Exodus was rooted in civil disobedience. Before Moses was even able to resist the authority of Pharaoh, it was necessary for him to exist. For him to exist in this world as a leader, he had to first be born, an event occasioned by a heroic act of civil disobedience:

> Then the king of Egypt spoke to the Hebrew midwives, of
> whom the name of one was Shiphrah and the name of the
> other Puah; and he said, "When you do the duties of a midwife
> for the Hebrew women, and see them on the birthstools, if it
> is a son, then you shall kill him; but if it is a daughter, then
> she shall live" (Ex. 1:15–16).

The response of the midwives to the royal decree was both blatant
disobedience and an attempt to cover up their disobedience by
deception. They disobeyed the king, and they lied to him. Both actions
were rewarded by God:

> But the midwives feared God, and did not do as the king
> commanded them, but saved the male children alive (1:17).

This act of disobedience was further buttressed by a lie:

> And the midwives said to Pharaoh, "Because the Hebrew
> women are not like the Egyptian women; for they are lively
> and give birth before the midwives come to them" (v. 19).

The following verses indicate God's sanctioning of the midwives'
behavior:

> Therefore God dealt well with the midwives and the people
> multiplied and grew very mighty. And so it was, because the
> midwives feared God, that He provided households for them
> (vv. 20–21).

In this episode we see that God not only sanctions certain kinds of
civil disobedience but even specific occasions of lying. Though the
scriptural ethic places a premium on the sanctity of truth, the
obligation to tell the truth has limits. One frequent principle discussed
in the history of the ethics of truth-telling (as for example in Aquinas)
is the principle of telling the truth *to whom truth is due.* Here truth is
linked to justice in a way that allows for the righteous and honorable
to lie when to tell the truth involves aiding and abetting injustice.
(See Rahab's "lie" as another illustration of this principle.)

Similar episodes in the Old Testament further illustrate the
legitimate occasions for civil disobedience, such as the refusal of
Shadrach, Meshack, and Abednego. These men answered
Nebuchadnezzar by saying:

Our God whom we serve is able to deliver us from the burning fiery furnace, and He will deliver us from your hand, O king. But if not, let it be known to you, O king, that we do not serve your gods, nor will we worship the gold image which you have set up (Dan. 3:17–18).

Daniel's refusal to defile himself by eating the king's food or by obeying the decree of Darius led him ultimately into the lion's den. His rescue from certain death is interpreted as an act of God's vindication of him:

My God sent His angel and shut the lions' mouths, so that they have not hurt me, because I was found innocent before Him; and also, O king, I have done no wrong before you (6:22).

Mordecai's resistance to the decree of King Ahasuerus coupled with Esther's courageous intervention are other examples of biblically sanctioned acts of civil disobedience.

The *locus classicus* of biblical teaching regarding the believers' responsibility to the civil magistrate is found in Paul's letter to the Romans, chapter 13. What follows is an exposition of this text leaning heavily, though not exclusively, on the interpretation rendered by Luther and Calvin.

Chapter 13 begins with a general exhortation, "Let every soul be subject to the governing authorities."

The phrase "every soul" (*pasa psyche*) is generally understood as a verbal equivalent to "every person." It is emphatic, all-inclusive designation. That Paul speaks of every "soul" rather than every "man" was understood by Luther to be a thinly veiled reference to the spiritual dimension of this universal obligation. He saw it as a tacit appeal to a kind of submission that is sincere and comes from the heart.

The "governing authorities" can also be rendered "higher powers." The powers or authorities (*exousia*) in view are not restricted to the supreme office of king or emperor but are applied to anyone who is in authority over us. In 1 Peter 2:13 reference is made to the king who is supreme, but in this text no single class of magistrates is compared with another. Our obligation is submission to all who hold magisterial authority over us. These are encompassed by the word *higher* (*hoperechon*).

The word *exousia* is sometimes translated as "power" and sometimes "authority." When Jesus was said to speak as "One having authority," exousia is used. The word derives from the prefix *ek* (out of or from) and the root *ousia*. The root is the participial form of the verb "to be." It is variously translated "being," "essence," or "substance." (This root had a crucial role in church history, especially in the church's formulation of the Trinity and of the dual nature of Christ. The controversy over Christ's essential divine nature culminated in the *homo-ousios* formula of the Nicene Creed.)

Etymologically, *exousia* is a power or authority that is "out of substance." The word can mean authoritative power, or powerful authority. It is not to be confused with raw or naked power or force. Jesus' "authority" was not vacuous. It was substantive. This is important for our consideration in that the authority invested in magistrates is not empty or titular. It is substantive and real. Delegated authority has the real power to impose obligation upon us.

> *For there is no authority except* from God, and the authorities
> that exist are appointed by God (Rom. 13:1, paraphrased).

This passage is the foundation stone for the biblical call to the respect for civil authority. The civil magistrate has authority that is delegated. It is an authority that is from God *(hupo theou)* and appointed by God. God is at the apex of all authority. He alone possesses intrinsic authority; all lesser authority is extrinsic and derived from Him.

Since all authority is rooted in God, obedience to authority is an intensely theological matter. The Bible may give some warrant to distinctive *spheres* of authority between church and state but never allows for an autonomous view of civil authority. In biblical terms, no concept of separation of church and state can justly yield the notion of separation of state and God. Every civil authority receives its authority from God and is in turn accountable to God for the exercise of that authority.

A few years ago I was asked to address the inaugural prayer breakfast for an incoming governor of the State of Florida. On that occasion I likened the event to the ordination of a minister to the service of the church. The governor's inauguration was his ordination to service to God in the sphere of the State. I reminded the governor that his newly invested authority was *jure divino*.

> Therefore whoever resists the authority resists the ordinance
> of God, and those who resist will bring judgment on
> themselves (Rom. 13:2).

The authority of which Paul speaks are is authorities that exist; they are the authorities in place or the "powers that be" (*ousai exousia*). The radical character of this exhortation is that our obligation to submission is not limited to *good* magistrates but to whatever magistrates happen to be in office. The reason, of course, is that they do not simply "happen" to be in place. Their existence at any given time is a matter of providential ordination. It is the *de facto* government that is to be regarded as, at least for the time being, ordained of God. It is significant that Paul's words were penned when his own nation was under the rule of an oppressive tyranny, a regime that would ultimately execute the apostle himself. It was the same government that imposed the legal necessity upon Mary and Joseph to make the arduous and vexing journey to Bethlehem in order to enroll in the census, by which Providence so ordered as to have the Scripture fulfilled regarding the birthplace of the Messiah. Hodge remarks:

> It was to Paul a matter of little importance whether the assumption of the imperial authority by Caesar was just or unjust, or whether his successors had a legitimate claim to the throne or not. It was his object to lay down the simple principle, that magistrates are to be obeyed. The extent of this obedience is to be determined from the nature of the case. They are to be obeyed as magistrates, in the exercise of their lawful authority.[1]

Hodge seems to be hedging his bets a bit here. On the one hand he labors the point that we are to submit to the powers that be regardless of how they came into power, yet seems to limit the "extent" of this obedience to when *lawful authority* is exercised. Calvin said that "dictatorships and unjust authorities are not ordained governments." These qualifiers have been regarded in times past as loopholes by which revolutions against existing governments may sometimes be justified.

The scope of this essay is not to penetrate the vexing question of justifiable revolutions but to explore foundational requirements of civil obedience. Whatever the verdict is on that question we must take seriously the ominous warnings the apostle gives to those who resist the powers that be: To resist that authority is to resist the ordinance of God and to incur judgment. It seems that the risk of judgment in view here (*krima*, sometimes rendered "damnation" or "sentence") is not merely the judgment of the human magistrate, but the judgment of God. Calvin remarks:

For since it pleases God thus to govern the world, he who attempts to invert the order of God, and thus to resist God himself, despises his power; since to despise the providence of him who is the founder of civil power, is to carry on war with him.[2]

That resistance to earthly authority risks resistance to God's authority and is linked to the entire matter of delegated authority. Authority does not exist in a vacuum. There is a complex of authority in which a chain of command exists. This is borne out by the numerous conflicts Jesus encountered, especially with the Pharisees regarding Jesus' own authority. He argued that to reject His authority was to reject the authority of the Father who sent Him. By extension, the same issue existed and continues to exist with respect to apostolic authority. When the delegated authority is resisted, the Supreme authority is by extension likewise resisted.

This complex of authority is suggested by Peter: "Therefore submit yourselves to every ordinance of man for the Lord's sake" (1 Peter 2:13).

The striking aspect of this injunction is the phrase, "for the Lord's sake." In what sense is obedience to human ordinances for the Lord's sake? In the broader complex of obedience, we bear witness to the lordship of Christ on every occasion that we are under obedience and service to His delegated authorities. We honor Him by honoring them. We render our obedience as to the Lord.

The great cosmic issue that provokes God's plan of redemption is the issue of obedience. The fall of mankind originally was a fall from obedience to the authority of the Creator. The very essence of sin is disobedience. It is an exercise in lawlessness. When we break the law of man unjustly, we side with evil. We become partners with the man of lawlessness; we join forces with the antichrist. It is this broader complex of lawful obedience that gives weight to the simple command to obey lesser authorities.

The qualifications regarding obedience and submission are limited to what is allowed via our highest obligation to obey God. We infer from this a basic and primary ethical principle. We must always and ever obey the authorities over us *unless* they command us to do what God forbids or forbid us to do what God commands.

The assertion of this principle is an easy matter. The application of it to complex and concrete situations may be excruciatingly difficult. The point is, however, that mere disagreement with human authorities is no justification for civil disobedience. Neither is being inconvenienced or even oppressed by corrupt rulers a license to disobey them. We may in the providence of God be called upon to suffer greatly at their hands, which sufferings we patiently endure for the Lord's sake. Yet let the authority require us to sin and, like the midwives of Israel, we must disobey. This refusal to submit exposes us to no danger from the judgment of God. Indeed, we would risk that judgment if we did obey. Surely this is what was in view with Calvin in his comment regarding the lawful exercise of the magistrate's authority. No magistrate ever has the right to command his subjects to disobey God.

The apostle continues:

> For rulers are not a terror to good works, but to evil. Do you want to be unafraid of the authority? Do what is good, and you will have praise from the same (Rom. 13:3).

Unless we interpret this text as being somewhat elliptical (which is characteristic of Paul), we will seek in vain to make any sense of it. What is more obvious than the record of a host of rulers who indeed have been a terror to good works? Adolf Hitler was not given to heaping praise upon those who did what was good.

Paul is not giving us an exact, comprehensive, universal prophecy or analysis of the behavior of human magistrates. Verse 3 must be read in light of what is taught in verse 1. That is, the tacit assumption is that rulers are acting according to the function they are designed to have by God. It is the divine purpose of human authorities to be God's instrument of restraint of evil. Just rulers reward the righteous and punish the wicked. They are called to order society in behalf of righteousness and justice. That is their office and their duty under God.

Even in corrupt societies, benefits accrue to the good and penalties are incurred by the wicked and the criminal. Both Augustine and Aquinas saw the link of government to evil, though they looked at it differently. Augustine saw human government not so much as a necessary evil but as necessary *because* of evil. Government is an instrument of divine grace for restraining evil and making life and society possible in a fallen world. Aquinas agreed in the matter of the grace afforded by governmental restraint but argued that some measure of government might have been necessary even without the Fall to order the division of labor established by God in creation.

Calvin saw grace even in the presence of wicked rulers. This was not only because wicked government was deemed preferable to no government (anarchy); but because in His providence, God is wont to use wicked rulers as instruments in discipling His own people, as the Old Testament clearly indicates. Calvin says:

> For since a wicked prince is the Lord's scourge to punish the sins of the people, let us remember, that it happens through our fault that this excellent blessing of God is turned into a curse.[3]

Again, Calvin is sanguine in his appraisal of the function of even unjust governments:

> . . . princes do never so far abuse their power, by harassing the good and innocent, that they do not retain in their tyranny some kind of just government: there can then be no tyranny which does not in some respects assist in consolidating the society of men.[4]

Paul continues:

> For he is God's minister to you for good. But if you do evil, be afraid; for he does not bear the sword in vain; for he is God's minister, an avenger to execute wrath on him who practices evil (Rom. 13:4).

In this passage Paul refers to the civil magistrate twice as a minister and once an avenger. Here Paul is concerned with two concepts: justice and law-enforcement. The two are related. The function of government is to promote justice via law and to enforce justice by enforcing the law. Justice involves the vindication of the innocent and the punishment of the guilty.

To accomplish this purpose, God has given the power of the sword to the civil magistrate. The word "sword" (*machaira*) does not refer to the dagger worn by Roman emperors as a sign of their office but to the ancient symbol of authority to uphold the law by force. The sword goes beyond the whip; it is an instrument of capital punishment. A common method of execution for capital crimes in the ancient world was by decapitation; the tool employed was the sword.

That the sword is not borne in vain means that its use is not merely symbolic. It is not an instrument of futility; it is an instrument of force, a tool of coercion.

The essence of civil authority is the right to coercion. We may call government "legal force." This simply acknowledges that laws enacted by civil magistrates are not suggestions but legal obligations. The power of the sword gives the right to government to *force* compliance to the law. Calvin notes:

It is another part of the office of magistrates, that they ought
forcibly to repress the waywardness of evil men, who do not
willingly suffer themselves to be governed by laws, and to inflict
such punishment on their offences as God's judgment requires.[5]

A question arises with respect to the magistrate's role as "avenger
of wrath" *(ekdikos eis)*. The concept of vengeance is related to the
root of the word that is derived from the word for "justice."

There is a tendency for Christians to see vengeance as an evil
thing, that is, an *intrinsic* evil. This tendency undoubtedly rests on
inferences drawn from strict biblical prohibitions against the
individual's seeking for revenge. Leviticus 19:18 amplifies the Great
Commandment:

> You shall not take vengeance, nor bear any grudge against
> the children of your people, but you shall love your neighbor
> as yourself: I am the LORD.

What is prohibited to man, however, is promised by God:

> Behold, your God will come with vengeance, with the
> recompense of God; He will come and save you (Isa. 35:4b).

Here vengeance is set in parallel terms with God's salvific action.
What is wrong for a private individual who acts in vigilante fashion
is right and just for God to assume for Himself and to His delegated
authorities.

Paul summarizes this principle earlier in his letter to the Roman
Christians:

> Beloved, do not avenge yourselves, but rather give place to
> wrath; for it is written, "Vengeance is Mine, I will repay,"
> says the Lord (12:19).

It is not difficult to speculate about the reason why vengeance is
prohibited to the individual. The modern aphorism, "Don't get mad,
get even" expresses the destructive attitude that is proscribed here.
The aphorism itself is misleading. Few people are satisfied with a tie.
They want to get one-up. When the subjective emotions hold the
injured party in their grasp, it is difficult to seek a balancing of the
scales of justice. The desire for retaliation can escalate to repayments
that are more severe than the crime.

Vengeance belongs properly to God. It is an expression of His perfect justice. He promises to "repay," to redress the harm done to people by the evildoer. This promise for repayment is both proximate and ultimate. Proximate justice is to be meted out by God's delegated authorities who are given the role of ministers of justice. Provisions for appeals to justice are found in the legal institutions established in Scripture both in the sphere of the state and in the sphere of the church. The individual has recourse to the "gates" of the civil magistrate in civil affairs and to church courts in ecclesiastical affairs.

That proximate justice is imperfect and not always just calls for the ultimate tribunal that God promises at the final judgment, where justice will be meted out in perfection. God's justice is to serve as the model for the execution of justice by earthly authorities.

The parable of the unjust judge derives its poignancy from the reality that people encounter with corrupt human institutions. What is often heralded as "social justice" in this world may at times actually be an exercise in injustice. In the parable we meet a judge who is described by Jesus as a judge who "did not fear God nor regard man" (Luke 18:2). The widow who pursued her case with this corrupt official asked, "Avenge me of mine adversary" (v. 3 KJV). Christ uses this parable to make a promise of ultimate justice:

> And shall God not avenge His own elect who cry out day and night to Him, though He bears long with them? I tell you that He will avenge them speedily (vv. 7–8).

There is some ambiguity in this text. Some translations favor the English word "vindicate" over the word "avenge" to translate *ekdikesin*. This is the same root word Paul uses in Romans 13 and in Romans 12:19.

In English there is a subtle difference between avenge and vindicate. To vindicate is usually used in ordinary language to mean "show that one is innocent of charges or slanderings against him." It conveys the idea of exonerating the innocent from false charges and to show that a person was "in the right." The word "avenge" is somewhat stronger. It suggests further punishment meted out to the evildoer for doing wrong to the innocent.

In this sense one can be vindicated (shown to be right) without necessarily being avenged. When the wrong-doer is punished, both vindication and avenging take place.

That Paul has in view the stronger meaning of *ekdikesin* in Romans 12 and 13 is made clear by the context. The promise of repayment (*antapodoso*) followed by the reference to heaping coals of fire on the heads of the wicked indicate more than mere vindication. Likewise the linkage of avenging with the power of the sword indicates punishment for the guilty. The role of the avenger is to execute wrath on the evildoer.

Paul continues his teaching regarding the role of civil authorities and the delegations imposed upon us:

> Therefore you must be subject, not only because of wrath but also for conscience' sake (13:5).

Civil obedience does not rest merely upon a "scare theology." The motive of the Christian to render obedience to civil magistrates is not to be a mere fear of punishment or the quest for a ticket out of jail. It is to be a scrupulous matter of conscience. Civil obedience, wherever possible, is a religious duty. It is to be rendered out of regard for and reverence for God. Both Luther and Calvin stressed that the conscience is to be bound by the Word of God. In Luther's words at Worms it was the captivity of his conscience to Scripture that impelled him to take his historic stand. Calvin says:

> Though then the magistrate were disarmed, so that we could with impunity provoke and despise him, yet such a thing ought to be no more attempted than if we were to see punishment suspended over us; for it belongs not to a private individual to take away authority from him whom the Lord has in power set over us.[6]

Hodge reminds us that Paul elsewhere enjoins the enforcement of all relative and social duties on the same religious grounds, including the submission of children to parental authority, servants to masters.[7]

Conscience is also linked to the ensuing passages of Romans 13 in which Paul commands Christians to pay their taxes:

> For because of this you also pay taxes, for they are God's ministers attending continually to this very thing. Render therefore to all their due: taxes to whom taxes are due, customs to whom customs, fear to whom fear, honor to whom honor (vv. 6–7).

This list is representative and not all inclusive. The basic principle is that we are, as a matter of conscience, duty bound to God to render to every person whatever is due them. We must "pay our dues."

Aristotle defined justice itself as a rendering to persons what is due them. If Aristotle was correct, then giving people what is due to them is simply an exercise in justice. It is to fulfill the biblical mandate to *do justly*. This is the Lord's requirement of us (Mic. 6:8).

Finally, we consider briefly the question of the church's role in her relationship to the state. Since this is a major issue in its own right, this essay will address one aspect of it only—the church's role of rendering not only honor, obedience, and the like, but the rendering of prophetic criticism.

In biblical history, the prophets of the Old Testament served as the conscience of Israel. The prophets did not wield the sword. They did use the voice and the pen to call rulers to repentance when they abused their offices and became instruments of injustice. We think of Elijah's rebuke of King Ahab in the matter of Naboth's vineyard (1 Kings 21:18) and of John the Baptist's criticism of Herod regarding his illicit marriage. Examples could be multiplied almost endlessly.

In our day, much purple rhetoric has been spewed out and much vitriolic ink spilled against the church for speaking out on social or political ethical issues. Nowhere has this been more evident than in the controversy over abortion. When the church criticizes the civil magistrates on this matter, people cry "Foul!" Such criticism is viewed as an unwarranted intrusion into the affairs of the state by the church, a violation of "sphere sovereignty." It is deemed as an attempt by the church to make the state an instrument or service of the church, threatening the autonomy of the state.

In these matters of prophetic criticism, nothing could be further from the truth. The church is not asking the state to be the church or to perform the church's ministry for her. Nor is the church grasping for possession of the sword. Rather, the church is simply calling the state to be the state. It is reminding the state that no civil authority is autonomous. The state and the church exist side by side in a heteronomous cosmos. Both are under God and His sovereignty; both are to be ministers of justice and righteousness. When the state acts unjustly, it is not only the right but the duty of the church to call the state to obedience to the One who invests the state with whatever authority it enjoys.

NOTES

1. Charles Hodge, *Commentary on the Epistle to the Romans* (Grand Rapids: Wm. B. Eerdmans Publishing Company, 1950), 407.
2. John Calvin, *Commentaries on the Epistle of Paul the Apostle to the Romans,* trans. John Owen (Grand Rapids: Baker Book House, 1979), 479.
3. Ibid., 480.
4. Ibid.
5. Ibid., 481.
6. Ibid., 482.
7. Hodge, 408.

SIX

The Christian's Duty of Civil Disobedience to the Government: Contemporary Struggles Between Christians and the State

H. Wayne House

IT IS A BRISK OCTOBER morning. Even though it is a weekday and not yet six A.M., faithful Christians have gathered at their small, modest church for prayer and worship. Naturally, one is amazed at this dedication and wonders what has motivated such a gathering. Suspicions are confirmed when one learns that indeed these believers are facing many trials. The government has already closed the church's small school and is threatening to close the church itself. Moreover, the authorities have jailed the pastor of the church for his attempts to defend the school and ensure its continued operation.

Thus this group of Christians, along with pastors from other towns who have come to support them, have assembled to pray for the release of the church's pastor from jail, as well as to petition God to prohibit the state's closure of their church and its school. Suddenly, this fervent stream of prayers is interrupted; it is shortly past six. Armed intruders file into the church. As these men close in on the assembly, the Christians notice that these men are in fact local and regional police, a combined force filling fifteen cars. One by one, the worshipers are forcibly dragged or carried to the rear of the church by the police. Then the police remove each person from the church to the sidewalk. Finally, the police raid is complete as the doors of the church are padlocked and the congregation is left in the street.

This incident actually happened. However, it did not occur in the Soviet Union or some other totalitarian state. It happened in the United States of America. The time: October 18, 1982. The place: the small town of Louisville in Cass County, Nebraska. The church was Faith Baptist Church; the law enforcement officials were the

Sheriff of Cass County and his deputies along with a contingent of Nebraska State Patrol Troopers.[1]

This incredible incident serves to illustrate the increasing tension and conflict in our country between Christians and the state. The history of this conflict is as old as the institutions of church and state and has always existed on an international scale. Yet developments in recent years have brought this conflict into even sharper relief. Few would have thought prior to 1982 that such a blatant denial of religious liberty would be possible in the United States. Yet the Faith Baptist Church incident is not isolated. Many other churches have found themselves facing battles with states over licensure of church schools, struggles with the I.R.S. and other agencies over taxes, and conflicts with local authorities over such issues as zoning.[2]

The individual Christian and Christian parents who would be faithful to their calling from God in various areas find themselves at odds with the state. Pastors must defend themselves against lawsuits. Christian parents who choose to homeschool their children find it necessary to defend their right to do so, especially in states like North Dakota, which is generally hostile to homeschooling.

Nowhere is the intersection between the faithful Christian and the state so clearly and visibly pronounced today than the case of Operation Rescue. The 1973 Supreme Court case *Roe v. Wade* has given women virtually unlimited access to abortion. This controversial decision has since prompted various responses of protest from Christian and secular groups alike. Apart from a few isolated cases of abortion clinic bombings (and these are not necessarily connected with the pro-life movement), these protests have been peaceful and legal.

The mid-1980s witnessed a new response of some in the pro-life movement with an old tactic—civil disobedience. Under the leadership of Randall Terry, a movement called Operation Rescue began. Operation Rescue involved organized attempts by "rescuers" to stop abortions by actually blocking the entrance to abortion clinics with their own bodies. These rescuers were guilty of trespassing and usually arrested for such. Even then, rescuers, while not actively resisting arrest, would still refuse to cooperate with police by going limp when arrested. Operation Rescue participants, as well as others in the pro-life movement who are influenced by its philosophy and method, insist that they are actually saving lives and that it is entirely appropriate to do so even when violating trespassing laws. Terry writes, "But far more importantly, rescues are a physical attempt to save the lives of innocent children about to be murdered."[3] Terry uses Proverbs 24:11–12 to support the activities of Operation Rescue: "Rescue those being led away to . . . slaughter. If you say, 'But we knew nothing about this,' does not he who weighs the heart perceive it? Does not he who guards your life know it? Will he not repay each person according to what he has done?"

The reaction to Operation Rescue among evangelical and pro-life leaders has been mixed. Jerry Falwell, D. James Kennedy, and James Dobson are all ardent supporters. Supporters claim that Operation Rescue is the only response appropriate to the severe crisis of legalized genocide in our country. Others, such as Norman Geisler and Charles Stanley, are opposed to Operation Rescue. The mainstream pro-life movement, represented by the National Right to Life Committee, is also opposed to Operation Rescue. They claim that such radical methods could result in a backlash of support for legalized abortion by previously apathetic citizens and politicians.

Operation Rescue raises the central issues regarding the intersection of conflicting claims of church and state. Its controversial mission has already polarized the evangelical community and will continue to do so. Operation Rescue forces Christians to reexamine their views of the Christian's relation to the state and the appropriateness of civil disobedience, and this has caused a division among clergy and laity alike. This difference of opinion is not new; there has been division on this matter for hundreds of years. Since the Reformation, religious and secular thinkers, among whom are Martin Luther, Thomas Hobbes, and Edmund Burke, have argued against most forms of disobedience, while civil disobedience has been championed by persons like John Locke, Samuel Rutherford, Henry David Thoreau, Mahatma Ghandi, and Martin Luther King Jr.[4]

Though the rescue movement may focus our attention on civil disobedience, the struggle between church and state will continue as long as either institution claims a sphere of authority or jurisdiction that is seen as excluding all other institutions. All would agree that the church should not tax, or provide for defense against hostile nations. Neither should the state assume the role of the church by dictating specific religious practices. Yet there are other issues that are not so easily decided. Who is responsible for education of children—the state, the church, or the family? Do the church and individual Christians have a duty to intervene to protect innocent life that is threatened by the state? Is civil disobedience an appropriate response of the church and the individuals and families who comprise the church?

These tough questions necessitate that we examine the biblical and theological bases for disobedience to government. In doing that, we must investigate the biblical view of the Christian's duty to lawful authority; next, the nature of civil disobedience; and finally, the reason for Christian resistance[5] to unlawful authority and how that resistance is to occur. A final question regards whether or not Christians may be involved in forceful resistance, as contrasted with non-violent civil disobedience. Furthermore, specific guidelines will be offered regarding the Christian and disobedience to the state.

THE BIBLICAL BASIS FOR CIVIL DISOBEDIENCE

The Lordship of Christ

Scripture teaches that Jesus Christ is Lord of all (Phil. 2:11). No person or institution stands outside the sphere of His lordship, including government. Scripture also says that government is a God-ordained instrument of justice and order (Rom. 13:1–2). The state has authority to punish crime, support and encourage public good, promote social order, collect taxes, and demand military service (Rom. 13:1–7; 1 Peter 2:13–14). It is not authorized to demand God's rightful place. Caesar's authority is limited (Luke 20:19–26). When the state tries to make its citizens violate a commitment to God, it oversteps its bounds. The Bible is full of examples of God's people responding faithfully to His law when government attempted to usurp the Lord's place. These are the general parameters that set the stage for a discussion of Christian obedience and disobedience to the secular government.

The Nature of the Secular State

A Pagan View of the State

The Jewish philosopher Philo records a meeting between a delegation of Alexandrian Jews and the Roman Emperor Gaius. The Jews denied charges that they failed to give thanksgiving offerings for the emperor's recovery during an illness early in his reign. They swore that they often sacrificed on Gaius' behalf, claiming that they "had offered twice daily for the emperor since the time of Augustus." The emperor replied, "What is the use of that? You offered sacrifices for me, it is true; but you offered none to me." He then called them "pitiable fools" because they did not recognize his "divine nature."[6]

The story of Gaius and the Jews illustrates a view of the state that has profoundly influenced events in the twentieth century. In ideologies like Nazism and Marxism, the state embodies all virtue and truth, with references to God or a god only used to meet some end of the state's goals. These systems deny the reality of a personal, infinite God; thus humanity in the form of the state becomes the center of all things. The individual's worth is negligible compared to the value of the mass of humanity represented by the state.

It is ironic that Marxist-Leninist theory predicts the state will wither away. Once a truly communist society evolves, the theory goes, no coercive government is needed. Everyone will share in the products of everyone's toil, and there will be plenty and prosperity for all.[7] Marxism fails to understand the basic nature of fallen man.

Friedrich Georg Hegel, an important influence on Marx, wrote that the state is "god walking on earth."[8] State-worship generally accompanies emperor-worship. Even as the state embodies its people, so a revered and emulated leader (or group of leaders) embodies the state. Lenin, Stalin, Hitler, Mao Tse Tung, Castro, or Quddafi all emerged as unquestioned leaders, the will of the people incarnate.

When the state abandons its divine commission, it usurps God's authority and replaces Him in the life of a nation. Neither it nor its leaders answer any longer to God but proclaim themselves as lords of the citizenry. This becomes applicable in the life of the United States today. As the United States drifts from its Judeo-Christian heritage and as the state becomes ever more pervasive in American life, government could ultimately insist on full allegiance from the people, an allegiance belonging only to God. American government seems to have begun viewing itself as master, not servant. Agencies, without any reference to God's laws, are seeking to regulate more and more spheres of public and private life; files of data on its citizens are expanding; and bureaucracy increasingly asserts its authority. While these trends may have begun with good intentions, they reflect a dangerous tendency to deny deity to the Creator and claim it for Uncle Sam.

A Biblical View of the State

Government Is a Divine Institution (Rom. 13:1-5)

Rather than the state being a god, for Paul the state was God's servant, established by Him to do His will. The state is a servant, not a sovereign. It is a minister of God for human benefit. When government fails to acknowledge its proper source of authority and seeks to become a law unto itself, it makes man the absolute standard of right and wrong, and so relativizes law.[9]

Why has God appointed the state His minister and servant (Rom. 13:4–6)? Why should government exist? Much of the answer to these previous questions is found in Romans 13:1–7, the major New Testament passage on the believer's relationship to government. Unlike the statements on government made by Jesus in the Gospels (especially

Matt. 22:15–22 and parallels Mark 12:13–17 and Luke 20:20–26), this passage occurs in a letter giving instruction to a local church. It is more extensive than the passages in 1 Peter 2:13–17; 1 Timothy 2:1–2; or Titus 3:1, and goes into more detail regarding the nature of government, the function of government, and the Christian's response to it. Like all passages of Scripture containing vital teaching directly applicable to contemporary life, Romans 13 must be understood in its context. Notice that Paul deals with this subject following his call to present our bodies as a living sacrifice (12:1) and not to be conformed to this age (12:2). This means that a proper attitude toward government is part of the believer's priestly service to God. In addition, a Christian's attitude toward government will be distinct from that of unbelievers under the authority of Satan (cf. Eph. 2:2).

In Romans 12:17 the apostle discusses the Christian's relationship to those outside the church (notice the "all" in vv. 17–18 RSV). He discourages an attitude of revenge and encourages believers as far as possible to seek peace and harmonious relations with everyone, summing up with "do not be conquered by the evil, but conquer the evil with the good." After these admonitions, Paul, in Romans 3:1–7, immediately begins to discuss the relationship of the Christian to government. This discussion is not an abrupt change of subject, but leads from chapter 12 without any distinct break. Paul uses some of the same terminology as in 12:17–21. Notice especially the words "evil," "good" (12:17, 21; 13:3–4 NASB); "pay" (or "repay," 12:17, 19; 13:7); "revenge" (or "revenger," 12:19; 13:4 NASB); and "wrath" (12:19; 13:4–5).

The state's fundamental role is to provide for good social order. Romans 13:1–7 emphasizes that government prevents social collapse and enforces social justice. Thus, the bedrock responsibility of government is the prevention of anarchy. How can government fulfill its mandate? According to Romans 13, it can be done by punishment of "the wrongdoer" (v. 4), so that the one who pursues good conduct has nothing to fear. With all this in mind, I offer this definition of the proper purpose of government: *God ordains human government to uphold social order by promoting social justice and freedom.* This definition limits government's role in society.

One of the problems in interpreting the Pauline view of government in Romans 13:1–7 is whether its teaching may be directly applied to modern government. Most commentators refer the passage to the Roman Empire, citing the phrase "the [authorities] which exist" (13:1b). The peculiar thing is that the same commentators (e.g., Murray, Cranfield, Newman, and Nida) exposit the passage as if it were universally applicable: "The apostle is . . . [not writing an essay on casuistic theology but] . . . setting forth the cardinal principles pertaining to the institution of government and regulating the behavior of Christians."[10] It is likely that the entire passage deals with government in general while the phrase "the authorities that exist" (v. 1) is used by Paul to apply these general principles to his readers and their situation within the Roman Empire. While not obvious in the translations, the first two references of authority in verse 1 are indefinite, while the third is definite. This can be seen in a stiff English translation: "Everyone must submit himself to governing authorities, since authority does not exist apart from God. Yet *the* authorities which do exist have been appointed by God." Romans 13:1–7 should therefore be understood as spelling out *the principles* of government in general and the believer's relation to it.

These *principles* are the concern of this section. When one understands the reasons for government, a determination can be made as to whether it is faithfully carrying out its God-given mission. Government can foster a just and free society in two primary ways: by punishing criminals and by promoting public good and political freedom. This is the "essence of good government."[11]

The Punishment of Criminals

Romans 13:4 declares that the state "bear[s] the sword" as "God's servant, an agent of wrath to bring punishment on the wrongdoer." The apostle Peter says much the same when he writes that governmental authorities are sent by God "to punish those who do wrong and to commend those who do right" (1 Peter 2:14). Thus, force is legitimate for maintaining law and order.[12]

It must be emphasized that crime is not only personal, but societal. If an intruder illegally enters a person's home and steals valuables, he or she has committed a criminal act. A just government will punish that act. But criminal activity may occur in the suprapersonal level. If a corporation knowingly pollutes a river with toxic waste, destroying aquatic life and making the river unsafe to drink, this too may be criminal. If a farmer withholds just wages from his laborers or if a shopkeeper subjects his employees to dangerous work conditions, he or she may also be guilty of wrongdoing. Governments are also obliged to protect their citizens from the attacks of international criminals. Although the Bible does not authorize governments to crusade against *anyone* they dislike, it does direct them to protect their own lands. "At root," George Ladd comments, "it makes little difference whether this force is exercised through local police punishing wrongdoers within the community, or in international terms through armies enforcing justice among nations."[13]

Still, the state is not commanded to punish *all* evil. It has no right to punish someone for an unkind thought or wrong attitude. It must be concerned with punishing evil that endangers the existence of an organized society. Only actions that damage the social structure are punishable. The German theologian Helmut Thielicke writes that "the state, when it restrains evil, is not aiming at sin itself . . . but simply contesting the excesses of selfishness. It resists the selfishness which is inimical to order."[14] The state executes God's wrath on that sin which disrupts social order. In doing so, it deters crime and punishes criminals.[15] An obvious corollary is the upholding of justice. The government punishes criminals because it is unjust for them to harm either individuals or society. The promotion of justice, then, is the underlying theme of Romans 13:4.

The Promotion of Public Good and Political Freedom

Paul says, "Do what is right, and he [the magistrate] will commend you." The apostle does not so much speak of obtaining specific reward—a letter of commendation, financial gifts, etc.—but of social approval. "The idea of reward is not implicit in the term," writes Murray.[16] The phrase could be expressed by saying that good behavior secures good standing in the state, a status to be cherished and cultivated."[17] The law-abiding citizen has nothing to fear from his government; the government will allow him to live in peace and freedom.[18]

BIBLICAL AUTHORITY PATTERN

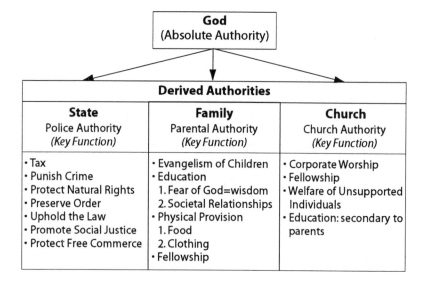

God (Absolute Authority)		
Derived Authorities		
State Police Authority *(Key Function)*	**Family** Parental Authority *(Key Function)*	**Church** Church Authority *(Key Function)*
• Tax • Punish Crime • Protect Natural Rights • Preserve Order • Uphold the Law • Promote Social Justice • Protect Free Commerce	• Evangelism of Children • Education 1. Fear of God=wisdom 2. Societal Relationships • Physical Provision 1. Food 2. Clothing • Fellowship	• Corporate Worship • Fellowship • Welfare of Unsupported Individuals • Education: secondary to parents

Many commentators point out that Paul does not discuss whether an evil government may encourage evil actions. "The presentation seems to take no account of the possibility that government may be tyrannical and may reward evil and suppress good,"[19] notes Everett Harrison. Why? Paul's silence probably means he is dealing with the "norm," with the state that fulfills the ideal for government.[20] But recognize one thing: Paul does not call for absolute obedience to everything the state demands, or for a willingness to comply at any cost for the sake of security. He deals instead with the mandate God gives to government and with the way a government *should* function. This is supported by Romans 13:6b: "for they are God's servants, attending to this very thing." "This very thing" probably does not refer to collection of taxes but goes back to verse 4, "he is God's servant to you for [the] good." Putting this together with the fact that the participle "attending" can be understood as meaning "if " or "when," the phrase may be translated "when they do what they should do."[21] This would mean that the state is God's servant provided it acts in accordance with God's law. The statement in verse 3b ("do [the] good, and you will have praise from it [the authority]") implies a state acting as it should, namely, in accord with God's law.

The responsibility of the state to act in harmony with God's law creates a difficult biblical/political problem. The problem is: How can a state which is pagan (as in the ancient world) or "pluralistic" (as in modern Western society) be expected to uphold the law of God? This problem is further complicated by the fact that the New Testament does not set down a code of civil law for the state. The role of the state is expressed in Romans 13 and other passages in the broad terms of good and evil. Paul's definition of these terms must be based on the law of God as revealed in the Old Testament. This immediately raises another question: How could a pagan state know, or a pluralistic state enforce, Old Testament law? A quotation from Calvin may bring the issue into sharper focus: "The law of the Lord forbids killing; but, that murders may not go unpunished, the Lawgiver himself puts into the hand of his ministers a sword drawn against all murder."[22]

Virtually all societies have enforced, and still do enforce, civil sanctions against murder. (Surely such aberrations as cannibalism, genocide, and abortion do not negate this general principle.) Why is it that pagan and pluralistic societies enforce "the law of the Lord" when they either do not have the Bible or reject it as a basis for law? The apostle Paul gives a clue to this in Romans 2:14–15: "For even the Gentiles who do not have the Law do naturally the things contained in the Law, they have become a law to themselves (not having the Law), who demonstrate the work of the Law written on their hearts." It is only because of this "law written on their hearts" (presumably the human conscience) that civil authorities do good and punish evil apart from a conscious policy of applying biblical law in the civil sphere. To rely on the secular conscience for the framing and enforcing of just laws, however, is a risky proposition. Not only is it possible, as Paul says, for the conscience to be "seared" (1 Tim. 4:2) and therefore insensitive to the law written on the heart, but in fact the unbelieving world in general is under the control of Satan (Eph. 2:1–3). It seems better, when possible, for society as a whole to be under the restraining influence of God's moral law.

Israel, the Church, and Civil Law

This leads to two other important questions. Is not Old Testament law a unique code of regulations given to Israel to observe as a witness to God's character? And is not this law done away with in Christ? Granted that the ceremonial code governing priesthood, sacrifices, etc., was fulfilled in Christ. In addition, the general and specific laws governing Israel's relationship to God (generally called the first table of the Law) cannot and should not be enforced by a government in a democratic and pluralistic society that quite properly avoids restricting the free exercise of religion. This leads to the second table of the Law, dealing with interrelationships between humans created in God's image. The objection to using this part of the Old Testament as the basis for civil law today may take the following form: God dealt with Israel as a religio-civil state. Israel was an earthly nation even though Israel was more than a nation. The church on the other hand is the mystical body of Christ with a fully spiritual and heavenly calling. Israel as a state was given a body of civil law to enforce. The church was given the law of love.

While this is good biblical theology for private relationships, as a basis for civil law it is a cop-out. It will not do for Christians to leave the secular state to base its laws solely on the non-Christian conscience, whether determined by elected leaders or the whims of a fifty-one percent majority. What is more, to argue that because we live in a "pluralistic society" Christians ought to argue *against* biblical standards as a basis for civil law, or even maintain neutrality, is downright ludicrous! This is *not* to suggest that the state should overtly push unique and specific Christian laws and theology. So then, when Old Testament Scriptures, principles, and illustrations are used here, I am attempting to apply creatively biblical standards to the mutual responsibilities of the established state and Christian citizens within the state.

Nothing in the New Testament would specifically say that the government is to provide religious freedom, but there are implications of this truth. Believers in Christ should pray "for kings and all those in authority, that we may live peaceful and quiet lives in all godliness and holiness" (1 Tim. 2:2). We should pray for our leaders so that we can practice our faith unmolested. This implies that freedom of religion—and by inference, a variety of other freedoms (e.g., speech, assembly)—should be guaranteed by the government. So then by implication, government ought to promote political freedom (1 Tim. 2:2; cf. Jer. 34:13, 17; Lev. 25:10). Man, like God, is capable of making free choices within the context of his character. To prohibit responsible exercise of this ability is to dehumanize God's creation. It is therefore a logical, Scriptural inference that government should allow citizens to make morally and socially responsible choices. I am not advocating "total" freedom, which results in anarchy. Instead, I would advocate the exercise of freedom within the confines of Judeo-Christian ethics—the type of freedom promoted by the United States Constitution. Supporting this is a vital function of civil government.

The State's Authority Is Not Absolute

It is precisely because the state is a *divine* institution that its authority is not absolute. Biblically speaking, government does not derive its authority from the consent of those it governs.[23] Constitutional democracies, as the United States, are preferable forms of government in my opinion, but one must realize that it is God who gives government legitimacy. That a government does not *need* to be such a liberal form may be seen in the Roman state, as known by Paul when he wrote Romans 13. Rome, then, was "an antidemocratic theory of power."[24]

God has given authority to the state (Rom. 13:1; Dan. 2:21), but this authority derives from a higher power and hence is subordinate and non-absolute. But "when power becomes an end in itself and seeks its own glorification, transgressing the divinely appointed bounds of good order, it becomes demonic."[25]

Government has legitimate areas of authority. Criminal justice (both personal and corporate), military defense, and the promotion of freedom, order, and justice are all delegated by the Bible to government. It follows that governmental authority is limited by biblical revelation. Once government oversteps those bounds—when it interferes with the life of the church or demands compliance with unjust laws, for example—it exceeds its God-ordained boundaries.

CULTURAL AUTHORITY PATTERN

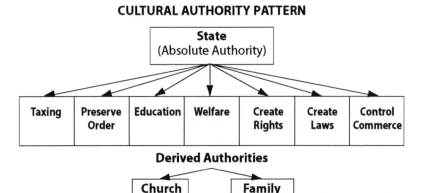

Jesus said to "give Caesar what is Caesar's, and to God what is God's" (Luke 20:25). Caesar must be rendered some very specific things: Government has particular areas of jurisdiction, but there *are* limits. What does Scripture say about those limits?

First, as we have seen, the state is under God and is responsible to Him for its activities. When the state behaves unjustly, inefficiently, or oversteps its biblical role, it rebels against its divine Sovereign.

Second, civil government should not regulate the church. This is not to say there are not legitimate interests the government may have that affect the activities of the church. These are primarily neutral interests such as safety, health, and broader police powers. But the state cannot legitimately dictate to the church its functions as a church, even in the name of the need to regulate (for example, times of meeting, biblical counseling).

Third, since the state and church are different institutions of God and have different responsibilities under God, the church should not formally regulate the state. The church's mission is not to govern the world, but to evangelize it and help meet its needs. To help accomplish this, the government should act biblically and responsibly. However, I am not saying that the state should not support Judeo-Christian values, fulfill its own biblical mandate, or admit its dependence on God. The Bible does not directly argue the issue of separation of church and state. In the Old Testament, at least from the time of Moses down to the Babylonian captivity, Israel was God's constituted nation. They were to be holy as a nation in order to be a witness of the Lord's character to the pagan nations. This necessitated a natural connection between the state and the ceremonial functions of religious life. Indeed, to speak of "church" and "state" as if they were separate entities may well have confused the Old Testament believer for whom no real analogy to such a distinction existed. It is surprising then in this context to note that a definite "no trespassing" policy was enforced between civil and religious leadership. Note that in 1 Samuel 13, Saul, growing impatient in his wait for Samuel, decided to offer sacrifices himself. That impetuous act earned him the wrath of God. In trying to fulfill a role designated for a religious leader, Saul overstepped his sphere of authority and was judged; God deposed him.

On the other hand, we read in 1 Chronicles 26:20 that the Levites had specific charge over the treasury of the temple and over the gifts devoted to God. Their sphere was religious, and they were not to control government.

After the Babylonian captivity the situation was different. The civil authority under which Israel then lived was accustomed to enforcing the establishment of pagan religion. This led to a *de facto* separation of Israel's spiritual life from state control. Faithful Jews under these conditions exercised two main options. Daniel and his friends resisted government commands to engage in pagan worship during the time of the Babylonian and Persian empires. Later under Persian, Greek, and Roman rule an uneasy truce between the pagan state and Israel allowed the Jews their "peculiar observances."

It is into this world that the church was born. The principle given by the Lord (Give to Caesar what is Caesar's and to God what is God's) implied a distinction of spiritual and civil responsibilities. While the Roman empire may have looked on the young Christian church as a mere sect of Judaism (while the Judaistic establishment regarded it as a heretical cult), clearly Christ and the apostles viewed it as a radically new and different organism. It was the body of Christ, a new kingdom with a King who ruled from heaven. No earthly state could regulate the spiritual life of such a kingdom. Nor would the subjects of such a kingdom desire to establish it in place of the existing state while their citizenship and their true King were in heaven. The political implications of this new kingdom require no special civil law for the Christian nor does it call the church to be an autonomous government (like Israel); the New Testament assumes that the church will operate within the secular state. Or, to put it in the most succinct words of Calvin: ". . . [the apostles'] purpose is not to fashion a civil government, but to establish the spiritual kingdom of Christ."[26]

Two points are critical to the previous discussion: I am not advocating a secular/sacred dichotomy; nor do I suggest that government must always disregard religious disorder. Christians are to be committed to Jesus Christ as Lord over all of life. This includes the way Christians respond to government. When the state demands worship, or violation of the laws of God, it must be disobeyed (Acts

5:29). But when the state operates biblically in its proper sphere of authority, we must obey (Rom. 13:1–7). We serve but one Lord, and He has instituted human government as one of His ministers.

We must support government and encourage its success in promoting justice and freedom. Not to do so may result in a weak government with at least two possible negative reactions. Either it allow the lawless to set their own standards of conduct, bringing about anarchy, or conversely, the government reacts to societal chaos or crisis and erupts into full-blown totalitarianism, exercising complete control over a country's social life.

The Role of Satan in Government

Scripture is clear that Satan influences government and that he rules the sinful world system (John 12:31; Dan. 8:16). It is equally true that "the Most High is sovereign over the kingdoms of men and gives them to anyone he wishes" (Dan. 4:17). Proverbs 21:1 tells us that "the king's heart is in the hand of the LORD; he directs it like a watercourse wherever he pleases."

So then, though I do not question that Satan influences unregenerate political leaders and societies, I do deny that the Devil has authority apart from that specifically allowed to him by God. God allows Satan to exert authority only as far as it furthers His plans. Our God does not tremble on His heavenly throne, wringing His hands and worrying about what Satan will do next. It is the Lord Jesus Christ who controls the events and course of history.

Since Satan does influence ungodly men and nations, Christians should seek to become a leavening, countervailing influence in government and society.[27] For the Christian, there can be no dividing line between sacred and secular. Jesus Christ is Lord of all. Christians should proclaim this truth and live in light of it.

The Nature of Law

When considering whether Christians should be obedient to the government, we are really asking whether we should obey a particular law of the land. It is usually recognized that for society to maintain order and justice for the good of all, laws in general must be respected and obeyed. Christians have been called to obey the laws of men that do not cause them to disobey the laws of God. We are not to disobey laws because we do not like them or simply because they interfere with our attempts to do religious work in the way we desire. The government has legitimate interests that God has established, and it expresses these interests through law. In performing its God-appointed task, however, the jurisdiction of the state is not allowed to nullify the jurisdiction of the church, though the two may overlap to some degree.

Ultimate Transcendent Reality and the Law

When conflict with the government occurs, it is not really a conflict with law per se; our conflict, first, is with the state's view of final or ultimate reality. Francis Schaeffer said,

> The difference lies in what the final reality is. Either the infinite-personal God to whom not everything is the same, or merely material or energy which is impersonal, totally neutral to any value system or any interest in man as man. In this view, the final reality gives no value system, no basis for law, and no basis for man as unique and important.[28]

The end of the twentieth century probably will not be remembered for its depth of thought, its unceasing grappling with the questions that have occupied the great minds of the last two thousand years. Instead, some future historian may recall our generation as the age of clichés, the inventors of bumper sticker philosophy. We are guilty of what may be called "non-thought," the unwillingness to explore the big questions of life that concern ultimate truth outside ourselves. Christians also have been guilty in not moving beyond a bumper-sticker theology to a full-orbed view of God and ultimate meaning. Too often Christians have unconsciously accepted a value system formulated by the world rather than being reflective. This failure to ask the big questions leads one down a road that leads to uncertainty and an experience-oriented life. The big questions may be answered in the exploration for ultimate transcendent reality, one that provides truth and rightness beyond oneself. Finding this ultimate meaning is of utmost importance, not simply some ethereal undertaking (a Tillichian ultimate concern); it gives meaning to life. One may interpret life with the pessimism of a Jean-Paul Sartre or with the exuberance of a Corrie Ten-Boon—one's perspective really matters!

What then is ultimate transcendent reality? It is a final and non-transitory reality beyond one's own person. The parts (inductive observation) need to fit into the whole (deductive reasoning). One must go beyond the *what's* to the *why's*. In a Sunday-school class I was teaching on the subject of civil disobedience, the class often had trouble working through this distinction. There was the feeling also that one would simply make the right decision when the time came. This is so different from the kind of deliberation that we observe with Daniel and his friends in Daniel 1 and that of Peter and John in Acts 4.

Every person has a worldview, a *weltanschauang*, through which he or she interacts with the world. One looks at facts (what is), develops a theory (how it is), and attempts to fit them into a presupposed philosophical model (why it is). To the one who adopts a nonbiblical worldview, the world does not appear to be cohesive. There is fragmentation (Schaeffer) and thus non-meaning and absence of purpose. When one sees God as the starting point for all reality or truth, the Bible as the explanation of the reality, Jesus Christ as the embodiment of the reality, and the Holy Spirit as the applier of that reality in the Christian's life, then the world makes sense. Humanists say they are searching for reality (*Humanist Manifestos I* and *II*), but how would they know if they have found it since they have no reference outside themselves?

How does all of this apply to the Christian and the law? In our struggles to promote equity and truth we need to recognize that spiritual forces are at work. Prayer must be mixed with hard work. The way a Christian views the law and disobedience to that law should be different from a non-Christian. God is the great Legislator and Judge, and His higher law is the final word on law. A constant vigilance must be kept to integrate the principles of God's Word to our societal structure, even to impose rightly understood Christian morality for the glory of God and the betterment of man. Lastly, there must be recognition of the lordship of Christ over law and all of life if we are to move toward all the purposes God has for us.

Definition of Law

The word law is generally used to refer to a *standard of conduct to which individuals are held*. The Greek word "novmo," translated "law" in the New Testament, carries the idea of what is distributed, or a custom. A major sense in which it is developed in the New Testament is the reflection of the Hebrew תּוֹרָה or "instruction." Instruction which is distributed to people to be followed is the resultant meaning.

Law Is God-Given

But Christians are not called by God to simply follow any given law because it is a law. Many laws are unjust and blatantly contrary to God's will. When they are not, however, we are not to resist these laws, to be rebels.[29] The reason we are to obey is that, ideally, laws reflect the will of God for an orderly society in which humans deal with their God and each other in a righteous manner. Thus, the *source of law is God*; it is His will and instruction for us. That law should be of divine origin is not unusual. As Rushdoony aptly and correctly recognized, law in every culture is religious in origin; and the source of law in any culture is the god of that culture.[30] When law fundamentally changes in a society, in

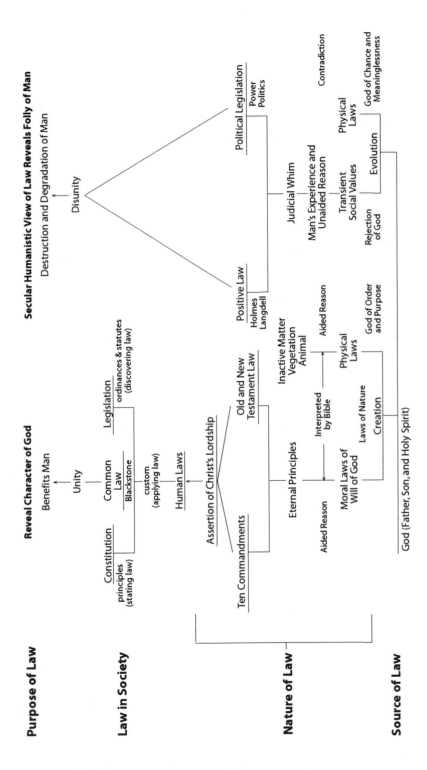

reality there is a change of religion; the separation of law and ethics is a myth. Though man may establish rules or laws to be obeyed, if they are not reflections of the divine character of God, they are, to use Jesus' words, "the traditions of men which pervert the law of God." Such laws have set up the will of man against the will of God.

God has revealed His will in three ways: Scripture (the Higher Law), nature, and the Holy Spirit. God has through creation revealed that He is a God of order and purpose. Not only in physical laws but in moral laws He has given us an understandable order for our lives. This law of nature, as Blackstone called it, is not understood by unaided reason; it is the will of God founded in justice and antecedent to positive law. Through the work of the Holy Spirit in interaction with Holy Scripture, Christians may see clearly principles by which society and individuals should govern their lives. Through the work of the Spirit in common grace, the unsaved imperfectly may know and follow God's law. But Christians may more fully realize the formation of Christ in them to imitate the Savior.

The nature of law may be confusing to some. One often hears that the laws of God are absolute. What is meant by that statement? Does one mean that the command not to steal is absolute so that the taking of shewbread by David and his friends was sin or a crime? Rather than seeing these commandments as eternal verities, it would be better to view them as expressing specific applications or eternal principles.

Note the following positive principles that flow naturally out of the apodictic law:

1st Commandment	Sanctity of the Special Claims of God on His people
2nd Commandment	Sanctity of the Incomparability of God
3rd Commandment	Sanctity of the Character of God
4th Commandment	Sanctity of the Worship of God
5th Commandment	Sanctity of the Parents as Reflection of God
6th Commandment	Sanctity of the Innocent Human Life
7th Commandment	Sanctity of Marriage as Reflection of God (Gen. 1:27)
8th & 10th Commandment	Sanctity of the Private Property or Sole Stewardship over God's Creation
9th Commandment	Sanctity of the Person's Character from Defamation

These are only suggestions as to how one may view the commands of God as having transcending principles behind them. That the Ten Commandments may be expressed in a given culture a number of ways is immediately illustrated in the casuistic law of the Book of the Covenant, Exodus 21–23. The desire to preserve sanctity of life may be applied in legal form from constitutional principles of rights, to statutory laws against murder, descending down to rules such as traffic ordinances that may vary. To understand how the will of God may be expressed in our legal system will require of the Christian "lawmaker" careful observation of natural law, Scripture, and wisdom from the Holy Spirit.

Why Has God Given Us Law?

The first reason God has given law *is because He is a God of order.* The Creation is to follow properly from its Creator. The intrusion of sin has "put a cog in the wheel," so that man is not as willing to obey the will of God. Second, since creation is to reflect the character of its Creator, *God has privileged us to magnify His character through obedience to His will.* Third, obeying the law of God will result in benefits to us. As the psalmist says, it is He who has made us, not ourselves. He knows the ways in which our lives will be more enriching to ourselves and others; He knows what will keep us from falling into the traps of sin or harm to ourselves.

With this understanding of the nature of law and the previously discussed function of the state as God's servant to preserve society through facilitating good and punishing evil, we may see why Christians, except in rare situations, should be obedient to law. The burden of this paper, however, is in what circumstances should the rule of law be violated by the faithful follower of our God.

THE NATURE OF CIVIL DISOBEDIENCE

A Definition of Civil Disobedience

It is important that we first know what we are describing. James F. Childress defines civil disobedience as a "public, non-violent, submissive violation of law as a form of protest."[31] This contains several key elements, and subsequent examination of the examples and teachings of Scripture will reveal whether these are accurate descriptions of civil disobedience for the Christian.

Acts of Civil Disobedience are Public

Concealment is not characteristic. Private disobedience does not directly confront the state and therefore, oftentimes does not greatly concern it. But external public actions that blatantly oppose civil authority do concern the state because they threaten its control, existence, and power. Even some clandestine disobedience—secret worship meetings, for example—while not public, still are considered "subversive" and are therefore judged illegal and criminal by some anti-theistic states.

Acts of Civil Disobedience Should Be Non-Violent

Revolution is not the goal. Practitioners of civil disobedience do not violently resist legitimate civil authority. They are simultaneously active but non-resistant.

Acts of Civil Disobedience Are Illegal

Christian Bay tells us, "The act of disobedience must be illegal, or at least deemed illegal by powerful adversaries, and the actor must know this if it is to be considered as an act of civil disobedience."[32]

Acts of Civil Disobedience Should Be Submissive

Those who disobey must accept the consequences for their actions out of respect for government authority. On the other hand, there are instances where Scripture accepts other responses (flight, for example).

Civil Disobedience Is an Act of Protest

Such an act is aimed at some sort of change in the existing code of law. A protester disobeying the law demonstrates he wants the statute altered. With this background to civil disobedience, let us now discuss its validity from a biblical perspective.

The Premise for Civil Disobedience

There is Something or Someone more important, or to what or whom we have greater allegiance, than the law.

We must sometimes disobey civil authority because, as Christians, we acknowledge only one Lord. No human institution can have greater authority than Jesus Christ. When government calls its citizens to violate a law of God, believers must submit to God and refuse to follow the dictates of human authority. The words of Peter are the motto of Christian civil disobedience: "We must obey God rather than men!" (Acts 5:29).

A similar principle teaches that Christians must submit to government as long as they do not violate a law of God in doing so. We are told in Romans 13 to obey governing authorities. This authority is not absolute—the government Paul describes is righteous and acts in accord with God's law.

Further, Paul does not suggest that a government demanding disobedience to the Word of God should be obeyed. When the government justly exercises its God-given authority (as Paul assumes), the believer is to submit. That includes areas where there is no clear biblical command—zoning laws (except in specialized cases), for example, or where government uses its authority correctly in taxation and the punishment of criminals.

Purpose of Christian Resistance

The glory of God is the point of faithful obedience. We have exchanged the yoke of sin for the cross of Christ. Let us count the cost, and in doing so recognize that eternal values far supersede any earthly benefit.

Principles for Civil Disobedience

We have seen that civil disobedience has a deep biblical tradition. How can a modern belief determine when and how to oppose the state?

One must disobey the laws of the state if

A. It commands a person to do what God prohibits (negative duty)
1. Hebrew midwives (Exodus 1)
   When Pharaoh ordered the Hebrew midwives to murder male infants, they disobeyed because they "feared God." The Lord was "kind to the midwives" because of their disobedience (Ex. 1:15–22).
2. Moses' parents (Exodus 1)
   Hebrew parents were commanded by Pharaoh to throw their children into the Nile. The mother of Moses instead placed her son in a basket and put him into the hands of Yahweh.
3. Rahab (Joshua 2)
   Rahab disobeyed and betrayed the government of Jericho in several ways because of her faith in the God of Israel. She first of all entertained the enemies of Jericho. Next she lied to the state authorities about the series of events and her knowledge of the situation. She hid the enemies of the state. She sent the spies on their way and led the authorities on a wild goose chase.
4. Daniel and his friends (Daniel 1)
   They purposed not to eat the king's food and drink that would be against the ceremonial requirements of Israel. If this "creative alternative" had not been accepted, there would have been a confrontation with the governmental authorities much sooner.
5. The three Hebrew children (Dan. 3:1–30)
   Daniel's three friends, Shadrach, Meshach, and Abednego,

refused to worship the idol that Nebuchadnezzer erected as god of his empire.

6. David fled from Saul (1 Sam. 19–26)
   David fled when Saul sought to kill him. Had David obeyed Saul, allowing the mad king to capture and murder him, the line of Jesus would have been substantially different.

7. Refusal of prophets to surrender to the king (1 Kings 18:3–4)
   The prophets of Yahweh did not turn themselves over to the king even though they were aware they were considered criminals who were wanted by the state.

8. The Magi (Matthew 2)
   Herod had told the wise men to come back and provide him information about the Messiah, but they sneaked out of the country after being warned by an angel.

9. Jesus evaded capture (Luke 13:31–33)
   Although Herod sought to kill Him, Jesus refused to submit to the king's authority and evaded capture. Our Lord obeyed God, not men.

10. Jesus' refusal to answer Herod or to perform a miracle for him (Luke 23:6–12)
    Our Lord refused to answer King Herod and would not perform miracles at the king's bidding. He continually rebelled against the ruling politico-religious community (the Pharisees, scribes, and teachers of the Law).

11. Jesus rises from the dead after angels remove the seal (Matt. 28:2–6)
    Jesus became involved in a conspiracy against the Roman state. Pilate had a seal put on the tomb. It was illegal to break this seal, as the angels did; and Jesus rose from the grave.

12. Refusal to worship antichrist (Rev. 13:14–15)
    Christians are persecuted for refusing to worship the antichrist or to receive his sign.

B. It prohibits a person to do what God commands (positive duty)

1. Daniel (Dan. 6:1–28)
   Daniel refused to stop his semipublic prayer even for thirty days. As a result, he was thrown to the lions.

2. Prophets spoke against the kings of Israel and Judah
   The prophets of Israel, despite their kings' wishes, spoke against the evil of their governments. Many were murdered for their trouble.

3. Esther (Esther 5)
   Esther knew the law against entering into the presence of the king unless being summoned. Because of the need to save the

Jewish people she deliberately violated the law for the sake of others.

4. John the Baptist (Mark 6)
   John the Baptist refused to stop preaching against Herod's sin and was therefore beheaded (Matt. 14:1–12). This was certainly outside his mission as the forerunner of Messiah, but it was very much in line with the prophetic call to righteousness on the part of peasant and royalty alike.

5. Peter and John (Acts 4)
   Peter and John placed the law of God before the law of man (Acts 4:13–22; 5:17–42, especially v. 29).

6. Peter's escape from prison (Acts 5:17–22; 12:5–19)
   When an angel took off his chains, Peter escaped from prison. This was not a legal act.

7. Paul in Philippi (Acts 16)
   When Paul was commanded by the city magistrates to leave the jail and the prison after they had violated his civil rights as a Roman, he refused to go and publicly pressured them to lead him out.

Why is there no evidence in the New Testament for civil disobedience in the case of issues like abortion or euthanasia? I believe this may be addressed in two ways:

Why no social action in the New Testament? Abortion and euthanasia in the ancient world was not public—no government action or sanction—but early Christians did rescue babies on the hills who were left to die. Remember this abandonment was legal and their parents' decision. Should Christians have intervened against the wishes of the parents?

Anti-civil disobedience dictum: The moral force of Scripture only applies when exact examples are found in Scripture. What about principles, wisdom, analogies, and type meaning for application?

HOW WE APPLY THE BIBLICAL EXAMPLES TO CONTEMPORARY PROBLEMS

Comparisons Between the Disobedience of Esther and the Actions of Those Involved in Operation Rescue: A Paradigm

A law was passed that was unjust against innocent lives but did not require believers to do anything contrary to the law of God, that is, a direct violation of His law.	A law was passed that is unjust against innocent lives but does not require believers to do anything contrary to the law of God, that is, a direct violation of His law.
Esther violated the law of the land.	Rescuers violate the law of the land.

Arrest is for violating a law that does not directly relate to reason for which Esther was disobedient, namely going before the king without permission.

Arrest is for violating a law that does not directly relate to reason for which rescuers are disobedient, namely trespassing.

The law disobeyed was a just law. It provided protection for the king.

The law being disobeyed is a just law. It provides for protection of persons and property.

The reason for breaking the law—coming into the presence of the king without permission—was not in order to obey a direct law of God that was contrary to the king's law or to disobey a law by the king that was directly forbidden by God.

The reason for breaking the law—trespassing—is not in order to obey a direct law of God that was contrary to the law of the state or to disobey a law by the government that was directly forbidden by God.

The motivation for breaking the just law (coming into the king's presence without permission) was to circumvent an unjust law (permitting non-Jews in Medo-Persia to take the lives of innocent persons, the Jewish people).

The motivation for breaking the just law (trespass) is to circumvent an unjust law (permitting abortionists and women to take the lives of innocent persons, unborn children).

Upon breaking the law the king could exempt Esther or exact the penalty of death.

Upon breaking the law the court can exempt rescuers due to common law defense to trespass, that is, necessity, or fine and/or put the trespasser in jail.

The king did not demand that the Jews be killed but only that citizens could kill them.

The government does not require that unborn babies be killed but only that abortionists may kill them.

Esther obeyed the higher law of coming to the aid of her people who were under the sentence of death.

Rescuers obey the higher law of coming to the aid of innocent babies who are under sentence of death.

The non-Jewish citizens generally chose not to do what the law allowed when the Jews were able to defend themselves.

Women often choose not to do what the law allows when rescuers stand in the way of babies being killed.

The Jews were able to defend themselves.

Unborn babies only have us to defend them.

Implications of Resistance

Faithful obedience sometimes resulted in deliverance (Daniel and his friends) and sometimes in death (Jesus, John the Baptist). Deliverance does not always come from civil disobedience. The issue is faithfulness, a faithfulness consistent with biblical revelation, which leaves the consequences up to God. Jesus said, "If anyone serves Me, the Father will honor him" (John 11:26 NASB). This honor sometimes has a temporal effect: God's deliverance from physical harm. At other times civil disobedience may end in martyrdom, as with the Lord Jesus.

We could do no better than to follow the example of Daniel's friends. When Nebuchadnezzar threatened to cast them into the intense, flaming heat of his furnace, they cried out: "The God we serve is able to save us from it [the furnace], and He will rescue us from your hand, O king. But even if he does not, we want you to know, O king, that we will not serve your gods or worship the image of gold you have set up" (Dan. 3:17–18).

GUIDELINES FOR DISOBEYING THE GOVERNMENT

Initial Considerations

The Dangers of Disobedience

Civil disobedience, biblically motivated or not, can be used by those who want to undermine the social order. It should be the last recourse, the final act. In the interim, and during legal protests, believers must remain faithful to God. Should the state forbid evangelism, for example, we must still testify to the saving work of Christ while legal means of changing the order are sought.

When Should We Disobey the State?

God has ordained government and delegated to it authority over people. Christians have freedom to disobey government only when it demands them to violate God's law. Freedom to disobey the state is not absolute, just as the state's authority is not absolute.

We may dislike our tax rates; but we must still pay taxes. Despite the enormous, unjust tax rate of New Testament times, Jesus paid taxes (Matt. 17:24–27). Paul commanded that taxes be paid to corrupt Rome (Rom. 13:6–7). Lack of agreement with every state decision is no justification for civil disobedience.

Discerning the Law of God

How do we know, then, when a law of God is at stake? There is only one way: We must know the Scriptures intimately! As James Montgomery Boice writes:

> The only way the right will be known . . . is by the teaching of God's Spirit through Scripture. Even then some areas remain ambiguous . . . But without the Bibl~there are no sure answers at all. This is the point. Consequently, no substitute exists (even for the busiest Christian) for studying the Bible and conscientiously striving to submit one's life and thoughts completely to it.[33]

Practical Value in Knowing Scripture

The effort to legally resolve conflict may be impossible in some cases. "Some persons are in situations of such urgency that their opportunities to explore alternatives to civil disobedience are quite restricted," writes Daniel B. Sterick. "They have only time enough to react—with little reflection—to a demand which they cannot but think it incumbent for them not to obey."[34] Knowing beforehand the teachings of God's Word is the only sure way to judge whether we must immediately disobey. Still, it is one thing to know when to disobey; it is quite another to know how.

How Should We Disobey the State?

Prayerfully

Paul commanded believers to pray for governing authorities (1 Tim. 2:1–2). We should also pray about how to obey them—and, when necessary, how to disobey. Every situation is different and should be bathed in prayer before, during, and after we take action. What kind of prayer? Prayer for wisdom to know what specific actions are appropriate; prayer for strength to carry them out; prayer for perseverance under persecution; and prayer for the hearts and minds of those in authority. That is the most powerful action a believer can take to effectively bear witness to the lordship of Christ and to change the objectionable law.

Peacefully

Avoid violence. Although non-violence has not always been a part of civil disobedience, for the faithful Christian it is the norm. "To be violent and to physically hurt someone is contrary to the teaching of the Word of God," writes George Sweeting. "The riots that shake our world are violent and evil."[35]

When refusing to obey state authority, believers must refrain from acts of violence designed to incite anarchy or that victimize other persons and society itself. When the disobedient Christian becomes violent, he scorns God's Word: "Love your neighbor as yourself." Harming others has no place in Christian civil disobedience.

Are there exceptions? Granting that nonviolent Christian resistance is the norm, do we allow for exceptions? Can a Christian participate in a civil war? These are important questions, but we will save discussion on them for the section entitled, "Christians and Revolution" (p. 164).

Respectfully

Disobedience to immoral laws is not disrespectful of law in general.

Civil disobedience "in its purest form . . . breaks laws that Law may prevail. Failure to comply with specific civil demands is not equivalent to general rebellion."[36] Legitimate civil disobedience is designed to force government to recognize the primacy of the laws of God, and to thereby properly exercise an authority that furthers social order. Respect for the idea of law as a God-given means of assuring social order is basic to biblical civil disobedience.

Respect for lawmakers must accompany this. Paul not only submitted to harsh treatment by the Romans (Titus 3:1), he also apologized for insulting the high priest when dragged before the Sanhedrin (Acts 23:1–5; cf. Ex. 22:28). The Lord Jesus was respectful to Pilate, acknowledging the governor's God-given authority to punish criminals (John 19:10–11). Although Pilate abused his authority to crucify our Lord in the most evil miscarriage of justice in history, the authority itself went unchallenged. Both Paul and Peter demand that honor be given to the king (Rom. 13:7; 1 Peter 2:13). The counsel of the Lutheran Church-Missouri Synod is helpful:

> The breaking of an unjust law, as civil disobedience is at times defined, need not necessarily reflect a spirit of anarchy, criminal intent, or general contempt for laws. It may, in fact, reflect an earnest desire to respect the rule of law and to test the validity of a specific law and so to provide a larger measure of justice.[37]

Civil disobedience respects law by opposing lawless demands.

When Christians are called upon to disobey government for their Lord's sake, they should pursue all legal avenues to avoid conflict with the government. Because God calls Christians to have profound respect for government authority and government leaders, followers of Christ should work within their legal systems to keep from breaking civil law.

Submissively

Flight for safety or legal resistance is fully acceptable. It is foolish to invite harm to either yourself or your companions when it is clear that danger is near. In a democracy where courts protect even common criminals, it is both logical and expedient to use the legal system for self-defense. But should the arrest come, non-resistance is the biblical pattern.

None of the apostles (all of whom were either murdered or exiled by the government) called on their followers to break them out of prison or help them resist arrest. Daniel and his friends willingly and bravely faced punishment for their disobedience. Resisting the consequences of civil disobedience shows contempt for law. "If you are insulted because of the name of Christ, you are blessed, for the Spirit of glory and of God rests on you . . . if you suffer as a Christian, do not be ashamed, but praise God that you bear that name" (1 Peter 4:14, 16). Boldly bearing witness for the cross of Christ may cost dearly. We must be willing to surrender everything—even, if necessary, our lives.

Should Disobedience be Public or Private?

Private Disobedience

Disobedience may be public or private. Private disobedience is a form of personal protest (and a matter of faithfulness) just as public disobedience is. But private civil disobedience has no direct impact on those laws found repugnant to the law of God. Still, it may affect non-believers who are impressed and convicted by the faithfulness, despite persecution of God's people.

Public Disobedience

Disobedience should bear witness to the lordship of Jesus. Public disobedience bears witness to the lordship of Christ, calls attention to His sovereignty and the validity of His Word, and seeks to change immoral laws. When disobedience is concealed or clandestine, it has an indirect effect; public disobedience is an open challenge to immoral civil law.

We need to disobey publicly when the state demands that we act immorally. The case of Daniel's three friends is a case in point. Christians disobey privately when the government tells them to stop reading their Bibles or meeting with other believers, and they refuse. Both forms of disobedience are biblical.

Wrong Reasons to Disobey Government

The Problem of "Standard"

Although civil disobedience is a biblical concept, when it is motivated by wrong reasons it becomes just as invalid as compliance with an evil law. The critical issue is deciding what standard should determine when it is right to disobey government.

The Viewpoint of Thoreau on Civil Disobedience

Henry David Thoreau, in his classic "Civil Disobedience," wrote: "The only obligation which I have a right to assume, is to do at any time what I think right."[38] Thoreau believed that one's own conscience provided the basis for civil disobedience. That implies one is a law to oneself and has the right to select one's own code of morality.

There is no way to enforce civil law under this view, since each person has the right to obey or disobey at will. The obvious consequence is anarchy and social chaos. Thoreau acknowledged as much when he endorsed the slogan, "That government is best which governs not at all." He doubted, though, that men could survive without government; and if he properly understood human depravity, he might have realized they never would. While Thoreau taught correctly that one should not "resign his conscience to the legislator," he erred in believing that a conscience indifferent to Scripture provides a basis for rebellion. The values of unregenerate humans often fall short of biblical standards. Rationalization, selfish interest, and personal arrogance color the value systems of everyone, Christians included. These render conscience a slippery guide for conduct. Only the Bible offers a trustworthy standard. As humans, we are always the subject of God's moral law, not the creator of our own moral code.

To follow Thoreau's view is to damage the entire idea of ordered society and do harm to the good that government does do. When looking at unjust laws, we must not see that each one demands that we disobey, even those that seem to impinge on our desire to fulfill our work as Christians. John Rawls rightly says, "Whether noncompliance is justified depends on the extent to which laws and institutions are unjust. Unjust laws do not all stand on a par, and the same is true of policies and institutions."[39]

The Argument of Infringement of Personal Rights

The infringement of personal rights is another reason often cited for civil disobedience. Although justice is clearly served when Christians lawfully seek to protect their rights, nowhere does Scripture permit us to actively rebel against government when it curtails personal freedoms or selfish interests. Paul told Titus after extensive Roman abuse, "Remind them to be subject to rulers, to authorities, to be obedient, to be ready for every good deed" (Titus 3:1 NASB). Charles Ryrie writes:

> Maltreatment at the hands of Rome had evidently not provided Paul with sufficient existential grounds for changing his teaching ... Wherever a believer feels obliged to disobey his government, he must be sure it is not because the government has denied him his rights but because it has denied him God's right.[40]

Additional Invalid Arguments for Civil Disobedience

There are several invalid reasons for civil disobedience. The Lutheran Church-Missouri Synod in 1967 listed several:

1. an exaggerated individualism that breeds contempt for law and due process of law;
2. an anarchic spirit, which pits one segment of the population against another;
3. the asserting of individual rights at the expense of others.

As we seek to know when the state has overstepped its bounds, let us make sure our disobedience is based on the will of God as revealed in Scripture, not on the whim of personal preference or the arrogance of self-righteousness.

CHRISTIANS AND REVOLUTION

Samuel Rutherford's Perspective

Samuel Rutherford in 1643 published his classic work on political science, *Lex Rex*. Profoundly influential in the history of political theory, apparently Rutherford's book was both secularized and popularized by the more well-known John Locke. Rutherford proposed several points about Christian participation in revolution:

> A ruler and his citizens have an implied, if not explicit, contract of mutual obligation. When the ruler reneges on his role or abuses his authority, he illegitimizes that rule and forfeits his authority. The ruler's power is only conditional.

> A power ethical, political, or moral, to oppress, is not from God, and is not a power, but a licentious deviation of a power; and is not more from God, but from sinful nature and the old serpent, than a license to sin.

> If officials in the government choose to resist the abusive and illegitimate tyranny of the ruler, Christians can join with them and fight the ruler.

> All tyranny is Satanic. Tyranny defies the laws of God; therefore, failure to oppose tyranny is allegiance with Satan.

> Three types of resistance are appropriate: Protest (legal action); Flight; and Self-defense when the other two fail.

Commenting on Rutherford, John Whitehead writes,

> Only when the magistrate acts in such a way that the governing structure of the country is being destroyed (when he is attacking the fundamental constitution or covenant of society) is he to be relieved of power and authority. This is an application of God's grace and mercy to man through man.[41]

Interaction With Rutherford

Remember that Rutherford was reacting to a grave social evil. In seventeenth-century Scotland and in the whole of that period in Western civilization, the king (as divinely appointed ruler) ruled above and outside the law. Rutherford sought to call the king to moral and political responsibility. Several questions surface when Rutherford's view is analyzed.

Is It Up to the People to Overthrow Government?

Rutherford's view is logical, but is it biblical? We certainly want rulers who are both responsible and accountable to their citizens; but in a totalitarian state—or in a state where political rule becomes despotic—are Christians *really* called to topple their rulers?

David refused to harm Saul because the king was "the Lord's anointed" (1 Sam. 24:6). Saul had become despotic and evil, yet David refused to oppose him. Certainly the latter part of Nero's regime was one of the most corrupt in Roman history, yet Paul demanded submission to it (Titus 3:1).

Non-violent resistance is appropriate toward a law or government that opposes God; but is an armed rebellion valid?

No, according to George Sweeting, because both good and bad rulers fall within God's permissive and directive will.[42]

No Scripture appears to permit the active overthrow of government (which, by the way, is not what happened in the so-called Revolutionary War). The state may be despotic, but *only* when it calls for flouting the laws of God is it to be disobeyed.

Should we not, then, indict rulers for injustice and evil (as the prophets of the Old Testament did)?

Yes, but such protest should be directed against sin, not the legitimacy of the ruler.

What Happens When a Government Ceases to Be Legitimate?

When elected representatives disregard their constitutional function, they cease being true representatives and therefore deserve to be resisted. For the sake and in the name of legitimate government, Rutherford believed Christians in that case are called to actively revolt.

It is unlikely that will soon occur in America, however. The people themselves are the government in our system, and the true law of the land is not found in the courts or in the legislatures but in the Constitution of the federal government and in the constitutions of the several states. Christians here do not have to use force to resolve problems; they may seek to change policies and laws through political means.

What if Political Means Do Not Work?

Then comes another option: non-violent resistance. Are we to resist non-violently? Peter urged us to accept suffering with joy (1 Peter 4), and the early Christians were glad they were worthy to suffer for the Name. Legal protest and flight are biblically acceptable, but for the circumstances given below, violent resistance is not. Non-violent resistance agrees with the commands of Jesus and demonstrates submission to authority. Armed revolt does not.

Is Submission to a Tyrannical Ruler Sinful?

Yes, when this submission is absolute. No, when it is conditioned by higher allegiance to the laws of God. When a government sins, Christians should bear witness to its sins in the pattern of biblical prophets and the apostles (Isa. 3:14–15; Acts 4:10–12). When the state demands we obey a statute that violates a law of God, we must refuse.

Early Christians showed both submission to God and to the state by their nonviolent refusal to worship the emperor. Caesar did not exercise his rule legitimately, and on a moral level was not worthy to govern. But the church let God remove him and did not seek to do so itself.

Where Do We Draw the Line Against Government?

Francis Schaeffer writes, "Only when the magistrate acts in such a way that the governing structure of the country is being destroyed— that is, when he is attacking the fundamental structure of society—is he to be relieved of his power and authority."[43]

When Is This Point Reached?

The Bible does not tell Christians how to deal with armed resistance to government. I believe, however, that under certain circumstances it *may* be biblically acceptable for Christians to take up arms in defense of legitimate government.

Rutherford deserves credit for trying to develop a Christian theory of protest. His emphasis on seeking legal ways of eliminating wrongs is commendable, and his advocacy of flight instead of defense also has biblical support. Furthermore, he called for governing authorities to submit to the laws of God. By proclaiming that rulers were appointed by God to fulfill His laws—in the case of government, to do justice, promote good and maintain social order—he struck a powerful blow at philosophies that would make rulers a law to themselves.

Rutherford's *Lex Rex* contains another implication about the Bible's teaching on the use of force. Anyone choosing to violate a civil law must be willing to accept the consequences of that act. Resistance to arrest may involve flight but not violence.

When citizens not involved in civil disobedience suffer because they are somehow related to those who disobey, another principle comes into play—the strong defending the weak. A family may suffer for the act of one of its members, but the person who disobeys should do all he can to safeguard his family from brutality. That may mean the use of force in defense. Accepting persecution for one's own actions is the biblical pattern. Failing to help and (if necessary) defend one's family from persecution and attack is loveless. To stand idly by and allow the innocent to suffer amounts to assisting the aggressor.

Rutherford taught that Christians should support the efforts of one group of state officials seeking to overthrow other members of government who unjustly use their power. Now, if a local water bureau employee should try to overthrow an American president in the name of justice, it would be both immoral and impractical (and silly!) to join him. On the other hand, if a plurality of elected leadership (local, state, and most importantly, national) seriously challenged officials in the national government—based on the government's lack of biblical responsibility to do justice, promote good, and maintain social order—Christians would have to seriously consider, in light of Scripture, whom they should follow. If the insurgent group harmonized with biblical revelation, Christians would have to weigh carefully their political loyalty. Because government has the right to demand military service (Rom. 13:3–5) and if the insurgent group truly represented legitimate government, it may even be that military service in the revolt is valid.

Francis Wayland in 1847 published a series of lectures given in the Brown University chapel on "The Duty of Obedience to the Civil Magistrate." His words are a fitting conclusion:

> A virtuous man is bound to carry his principles into practice
> in all the relations of life. He can no more do wrong in

company alone, and be guiltless. If he be a true man, he must love right and justice and mercy, better than political party or personal popularity. If he fears God, he must obey God rather than man, and this fear must govern his conduct universally. In this matter every man must begin not with his neighbor, but himself, and if he wish our country to be reformed, let him begin the work immediately. Let us all then lay these things solemnly to heart and may God grant us grace to carry them into practice.[44]

To leave these ideals unfulfilled may be obedience to the state; but it is a rebellious slap in the face of God.

NOTES

1. This account is taken from the Appellants' Opening Brief, *Robert E. McCurry, et al. v Fred Tesch, et al.*

2. During the writing of this paper, a former student of mine sent me a letter from Florida, where he is involved in new church planting. He has been told by the city in which he works that he is not permitted to have Bible studies with couples in his home because it is a violation of a city zoning ordinance.

3. Randall A. Terry, *Operation Rescue* (Springdale, Pa.: Whitaker House, 1988), 126.

4. In an earlier draft of this paper I gave considerable attention to the historic development of the civil disobedience perspective both in Christian and non-Christian circles. For the purposes of the consultation I will offer only a cursory evaluation and concentrate on the biblical and theological questions.

5. I am not making any distinction between resistance to the state and civil disobedience as was done by Ghandi.

6. F. F. Bruce, *New Testament History* (Garden City: Doubleday & Co., 1980), 253.

7. G. M. Carter, *The Government of the Soviet Union* (New York: Harcourt, Brace, Jovanovich, 1972), 6.

8. Alfred Meyer, *Communism* (New York: Random House, 1967), 22.

9. Cf. the words on the tomb of Thomas Jefferson: "The God who gave us life, gave us liberty at the same time. . . . Can the liberties of a nation be secure when we have removed their only firm basis, a conviction in the minds of the people that those liberties are the gift of God." As cited by John Eidsmoe, *Christianity and the Constitution* (Grand Rapids: Baker Book House, 1987), 245.

10. John Murray, *The Epistle to the Romans* (Grand Rapids: Wm. B. Eerdmans, 1965), 151.

11. Donald Guthrie, *New Testament Theology* (Downers Grove: InterVarsity Press, 1983), 948.
12. See G. E. Ladd, "The Christian and the State," *Command* (March, 1982): 13.
13. Ibid.
14. Helmut Thielicke, *Ethics: Politics,* vol. 2 (Philadelphia: Fortress Press, 1969), 252.
15. Alan Johnson, *Romans: The Freedom Letter,* vol. 2 (Chicago: Moody Press, 1977), 86.
16. Murray, 151.
17. Ibid.
18. Ladd, 13.
19. E. F. Harrison, "Romans," in *The Expositor's Bible Commentary,* vol. 10, ed. F. E. Gaebelein (Grand Rapids: Zondervan, 1976), 137.
20. Ibid., 138.
21. Barclay M. Newman & Eugene A. Nida, *A Translator's Handbook on Paul's Letter to the Romans* (London, New York, & Stuttgart: United Bible Societies, 1973), 248.
22. John Calvin, *Institutes of the Christian Religion,* transl. Ford Lewis Battles (Philadelphia: The Westminster Press, 1960), 1497.
23. Peter Gilchrist has argued that "It is . . . inconsistent with the Scripture to consider that human government derives its legitimate authority ultimately from a 'social compact,' or from 'the consent of the governed,' or even 'the will of the majority'" (Peter R. Gilchrist, "Government," *The International Standard Bible Encyclopedia,* ed. C. W. Bromiley [Grand Rapids: Eerdmans, 1982], 545). Gilchrist is correct if one is speaking of specific scriptural declarations. However, we may ascertain the validity of representative government by examining the difference between the governmental structures of a republic, democracy, or autocracy and determine how they fare in adhering to biblical teaching, principles, and examples of governmental functions found in the Old and New Testaments. The value of a constitutional government to ordered society and the provision for maximum freedom within moral government may be seen through this process of investigation. Remember that behind the Constitution stands the Declaration of Independence, a document that recognizes the hand of God in establishing this nation's rights.
24. Wayne Boulton, "The Riddle of Romans 13," *The Christian Century* 93, no. 28 (Sept. 15, 1976): 760.
25. Ladd, 14.
26. John Calvin, *Institutes,* 1500.
27. R. D. Culver, *Toward a Biblical View of Civil Government* (Chicago: Moody Press, 1974), 57.

28. Francis A. Schaeffer, "The Secular Humanistic World View versus The Christian World View and The Biblical Perspectives on Military Preparedness," a speech given at the Mayflower Hotel, Washington, D.C., June 22, 1982.

29. Rebellion to law itself occupies a status like witchcraft we are told in the Hebrew scripture (1 Sam. 15:23).

30. Rousas J. Rushdoony, *Institutes of Biblical Law* (Philadelphia: Presbyterian and Reformed Publishing Company, 1973), 4.

31. James F. Childress, *Civil Disobedience and Political Obligation: A Study in Christian Social Ethics* (New Haven and London: Yale University Press, 1971), 11.

32. Christian Bay, "Civil Disobedience," *International Encyclopedia of the Social Sciences*, vol. 2, p. 473, quoted in Childress, 5.

33. James Montgomery Boice, *God and History: Foundations of the Christian Faith*, vol. 4 (Downers Grove: InterVarsity Press, 1981), 241.

34. Daniel B. Sterick, *Civil Disobedience and the Christian* (New York: The Seabury Press, 1969), 106–107.

35. George Sweeting, "Civil Disobedience: Right or Wrong?" *Moody Monthly* 81, no. 7 (March 1981): 42.

36. Richard Bardolph, "Some Reflections on Civil Disobedience," *Concordia Theological Monthly* 38, no. 6 (June 1967): 381.

37. The Commission on Theology and Church Relations of the Lutheran Church-Missouri Synod, 379. ("Civil Obedience & Disobedience").

38. Henry David Thoreau, *The Variorum Civil Disobedience* (New York: Twayne Publishers, Inc., 1967), 33.

39. John Rawls, *A Theory of Justice* (Cambridge, Mass.: Harvard University Press, 1971), 352.

40. Charles C. Ryrie, "The Christian and Civil Disobedience," *Bibliotheca Sacra* 127, no. 506 (April–June 1970): 157, 160.

41. John Whitehead, *The Second American Revolution* (Elgin, Ill.: David C. Cook, 1982), 154–55.

42. Sweeting, 42.

43. Francis Schaeffer, *A Christian Manifesto* (Westchester, Ill.: Crossway Books, 1981), 101.

44. Francis Wayland, *The Duty of Obedience to the Civil Magistrate* (Boston: Little, Brown, 1847), quoted in David R. Weber, ed., *Civil Disobedience in America: A Documentary History* (Ithaca and London: Cornell University Press, 1978), 84.

PART THREE

How Christians May Influence the Future Direction of American Law

SEVEN

The Religious Roots of Western Liberty: Cut Them or Renew Them?

D. F. Kelly

THE NINETEENTH-CENTURY Virginia theologian and political philosopher, Robert L. Dabney, must have been wearing the mantle of a prophet when he wrote these sobering words in 1897:

> The history of human rights is, that their intelligent assertors usually learn the true grounds of them "in the furnace of affliction"; that the posterity who inherit these rights hold them for awhile, in pride and ignorant prescription; that after a while, when the true logic of the rights has been forgotten, and when some plausible temptation presses them to do so, the next generation discards the precious rights bodily, and goes back to the practice of the old tyranny. . . .
>
> You may deem it a strange prophecy, but I predict that the time will come in this once free America when the battle for religious liberty will have to be fought over again, and will probably be lost, because the people are already ignorant of its true basis and conditions.[1]

THE WESTERN LEGAL CRISIS

Much more recently, Harold J. Berman Professor Emeritus of Harvard (now working at Emory University) stated in an important volume in 1983:

> That the Western legal tradition, like Western civilization as a whole, is undergoing in the twentieth century a crisis greater than it has ever known before . . . we are in the midst of an unprecedented crisis of legal values and of legal thought, in which our entire legal tradition is being challenged—not only the so-called liberal concepts of the past few hundred

years, but the very structure of Western legality, which dates from the eleventh and twelfth centuries.[2]

If Dabney is right, this profound crisis of Western civilization is directly related to our forgetting what made the blessings of our culture, with its healthy if imperfect balance between liberty and order, possible. And even more to the point, if Berman is right, this crisis of law and liberty is on us because in his words

> . . . the legal systems of all the nations that are heirs to the Western legal tradition have been rooted in certain beliefs or postulates: that is, the legal systems themselves have presupposed the validity of those beliefs. Today those beliefs or postulates—such as the structural integrity of law, its ongoingness, its religious roots, its transcendent qualities— are rapidly disappearing, not only from the minds of philosophers, not only from the minds of lawmakers, judges, lawyers, law teachers, and other members of the legal profession; but from the consciousness of the vast majority of citizens; the people as a whole; and more than that, they are disappearing from the law itself.[3]

The massive public forgetfulness of the past and the epidemic unbelief of truth that are causing our society to break down have flooded in on us at a strange time; a time when as American evangelicals we might have least expected it. After all, has America not experienced a powerful evangelical resurgence for more than forty years? There is not the slightest doubt in my mind that in the years after World War II, God, in His mercy and grace, has raised up and mightily used such people and institutions as Billy Graham, Harold John Ockenga, Carl F. H. Henry, *Christianity Today*, Fuller, Gordon-Conwell, Trinity, Dallas, and Reformed Seminary; and many other institutions and associations, not least, the National Association of Evangelicals. Many called the 1970s "the decade of the evangelical." In much of the United States (except the South), evangelical Christianity had tended to be on the fringes of society between the two Wars. After the Second World War, it entered the mainstream in a way no one could miss.

WHY OUR CRISIS?

So, with more than forty years of unmistakable evangelical witness at the very heart of the culture, how could things be as bad as they are right now in our crumbling society? Let me suggest two possible factors here, one inside evangelicalism, and one outside it.

An Internal Problem

First, our internal problem. The late Francis Schaeffer may have been simplistic and may have overstated the case in his last two books, A Christian Manifesto and The Great Evangelical Disaster; but I suspect he had a valid point to make, painful as it may be for us to accept it. Namely, with greater popularity, we evangelicals have too readily yielded to the temptation to water down the pure wine of our theological values with the bacteria-laden liquid of the dominant secularist culture. David F. Wells, in his book No Place for Truth, updates the kind of compromise I am talking about from the time of Schaeffer's death in the early 1980s to 1993.[4] This is a theme requiring the urgent attention of all evangelicals but I must bypass it for the sake of getting on with the central concern of this chapter, the second factor in the crisis of our civilization, a factor external to evangelicalism.

An External Problem

Whereas our internal problems are caused by our own weakness and wrongness, most (though not all) of our external problems are being caused by our strength and rightness (that—insofar as we possess them—are gifts of undeserved grace). If the first element in the crisis of our culture has come about because evangelicals are weak and inconsistent, this second element has occurred for the opposite reason; it is a deep reaction to our strength and sincerity in the cause of truth, frail and fallible though we know our grasp of the situation to be. (What I am proposing may seem paradoxical at first, but a little thought will show how natural a reaction it is in a fallen world.)

We do not understand the severity of the problems confronting us at the end of the twentieth century until we realize that evangelicalism is not the only religious faith that has been on the move for the past forty or fifty years in the Western world. I refer to what is generally called secular humanism (as expressed in the two humanist manifestos of the 1930s and 1970s). The more violent Eastern variety of secularism in its Euro-Communist form does seem to have peaked and to have entered rapid decline. But the Western varieties of secularism, whether the traditional Democratic Socialism of Europe or the individualistic materialist debt capitalism of America, although sick and ailing, are still strong enough to dominate the political and economic scene.

Would it be fair to compare these varieties of secularism to a wounded animal who is all the more dangerous when he perceives a threat to his turf that is now harder to keep than when he was well? Or to change the figure, could we compare the reaction of many secularist thinkers to some prominent person who suddenly realizes he is losing the dominance he once had in almost every area he touched?

No serious scholar can doubt that what we are speaking of as secular humanism, whether in its seventeenth-century English Deist form, its eighteenth-century French Enlightenment form, its nineteenth-century German Idealist form, or its twentieth-century pragmatic, modernist American form was and is a substitute religion and total life response in place of historic Christianity. And who could seriously deny that for more than a century secularism has held dominant sway in most of the significant institutions of our culture?

Obviously, dominant secularists have not been pleased to see the evangelical resurgence of the last forty-five years. Our increased influence in the mainstream of society has constituted a challenge to those who are deeply committed to an alternative—indeed, a contradictory—set of values from those of traditional biblical theism.

A Worsening Conflict

Thus our very strength has brought us into a kind of conflict that has not been seen in this country since the forces of Deism and evangelical revival did battle from the 1780s to the 1830s during the Second Great Awakening. I wish I could believe that the conflict we are presently passing through could come to such a happy conclusion! But back to the 1990s.

During the nineteenth century and especially during the earlier years of this century, the inevitable conflict between influential forces committed to secularism and influential forces committed to Christian values was held in check for several reasons. First, at least as far as this century is concerned, the secularists do not appear to have perceived evangelical Christians to have constituted a serious challenge to their cultural hegemony before mid-century. After all, as Harold O. J. Brown pointed out a few years ago, "normal people do not mobilize against a nonexistent danger. By far the largest and most self-aware group of Americans with vision and purpose today consists of Christians." Then, he rightly concluded, "From the perspective of a contemporary Christian dynamism, it seems almost inevitable . . . [that] the A.C.L.U., People for the American Way and others are frightened."[5]

Breakdown of an Old Coalition

Second, I think Professor Carl H. Esbeck of the faculty of law, University of Missouri-Columbia is right in pointing to the significant breakdown of an old coalition between what he calls rationalists on the one hand and religious enthusiasts on the other. He writes:

In the eighteenth century, American rationalists—students of the Enlightenment in its milder form—and religious enthusiasts, whose numbers were greatly increased by the revivals of the First Great Awakening (1730s–1750s), combined forces on the practical outworkings of religious liberty against the older established churches. This alliance between rationalists and religious enthusiasts (principally Baptists, "new side" Presbyterians, "new light" Congregationalists, Dutch Reformed, and Anglicans later identified with Methodism) was possible because both sought the same end, namely independent churches in a nonsectarian state. Their reasons for seeking this arrangement, however, were quite different. The religionists sought religious liberty. To them this meant deposing the established churches that, in their linkage to the state, had become cold and formalistic. The rationalists acted on a different purpose. Some were anti-clerical, but nearly all were pro-religion. To rationalists, religion served the utilitarian function of infusing society with the necessary morality to make self-government possible. Nevertheless, disestablishment was sought by these rationalists to avoid sectarian strife and promote domestic peace.[6]

Then Professor Esbeck poses this important question:

So why is this old coalition that held for years and stood against those who threatened religious liberty now breaking up? Their common cause held so long as the debate in the courts focused on keeping ecclesiastical interests from capturing the instruments and power of state. Now that the intensity of First Amendment litigation has shifted to include issues of keeping the state from interfering with religious affairs, secularists and institutional-separationists find themselves on opposite sides of the courtroom.

Institutional-separationists have always held to the reciprocal nature of church-state separation: the church did not capture the state and concomitantly the state did not entangle itself in the affairs of the church. It is the secularists who have changed. Unlike the rationalists in the eighteenth century, secularists of modern bent devalue the utility of traditional religion for instilling the moral base and common vision necessary to hold a free society together. Indeed, some secularists view religion as a reactionary force retarding the moral evolution that they deem desirable.[7]

ILLUSTRATIONS OF THE CONFLICT

An illustration of the breakdown of this old coalition and the open conflict following in its wake is seen in the unprecedented way the courts have changed their interpretation of the First Amendment of the Constitution so as to abridge religious freedom, rather than protect it—as had been the case until mid-century. In this same article, Professor Esbeck discusses "the misconception that the Establishment and Free Exercise Clauses are in constant tension," and shows how this false construction of the First Amendment has been "a setback for religious Liberty."[8]

Similarly, Robert L. Cord in his significant study of the First Amendment stated that 1947 was a pivotal year in bringing about a more hostile relationship of state to church in America through the *Everson v. Board of Education* case rendered by the Supreme Court of the United States.[9] The results of this increasing hostility to religious expression in the public marketplace has been carefully traced by Steven A. Samson in a 1984 doctoral dissertation written for the University of Oregon, with particular reference to the secularists' usage of the state against traditional Christianity:

> The role of the judiciary as an arbiter between the social regulatory policies of the state and the free exercise of church doctrine is not a new one. What is new is the growth of affirmative as well as prohibitive rules directly affecting churches. To their credit, many courts have resisted this trend and have frequently dismissed suits brought against churches by public agencies simply for what William Ball has called "hasty overbreadth in regulating." But demands for church files, special permits, and employment statistics frequently lead to a hardening of battle lines. Typically, confrontations may be the result of mistakes, ignorance, suspicion, or alarm on either side. But many disagreements appear to arise from the sometimes different logic by which church and state pursue their professed goals.[10]

Concrete examples of this kind of conflict were listed by the Conference on Government Intervention in Religious Affairs, held in 1982 in Washington, D.C.:

- efforts by state and local governments to regulate fundraising by religious bodies
- efforts to require religious bodies to register with and report to government officials if they engage in efforts to influence legislation (so-called lobbying disclosure laws)

- efforts by the National Labor Relations Board to supervise elections for labor representation by lay teachers in Roman Catholic parochial schools (which have been halted by the United States Supreme Court)
- Internal Revenue Service's (I.R.S.'s) definition of "integrated auxiliaries" of churches that tends to separate church-related colleges and hospitals from the churches that sponsor them and to link them instead to their "secular counterparts"
- attempts by state departments of education to regulate the curriculum content and teachers' qualifications in Christian schools (which have been halted by state courts in Ohio, Vermont, and Kentucky, but upheld in Nebraska, Wisconsin, and Maine)
- attempts by federal and state departments of labor to collect unemployment compensation taxes from church-related agencies that hitherto were exempt, as churches are
- imposition by the (then) Department of Health, Education and Welfare of requirements of coeducational sports, hygiene instruction, dormitory and off-campus residence policies on church-related colleges (such as Brigham Young University) that have religious objections to such ways
- efforts by several federal agencies (Civil Rights Commission, Equal Employment Opportunities Commission, Department of Health and Human Service, Department of Education) to require church-related agencies and institutions, including theological seminaries, to report their employment and admissions statistics by race, sex, and religion, even though they receive no government funds. This is done with threats to cut off grants or loans to students unless they hire faculty, for instance, from other religious adherences.
- sample surveys of churches and church agencies by the Bureau of the Census, requiring them to submit voluminous reports under penalty of law, even though the Bureau admitted to a church attorney that it had no authority to do so, but refused to advise churches that they were not required to comply
- grand jury interrogation of church workers about internal affairs of churches
- use by intelligence agencies of clergy and missionaries as informants
- subpoenas of ecclesiastical records by plaintiffs and defendants in civil and criminal suits
- the placement of a church in receivership because of allegations of mismanagement of church funds made by dissident members

- conservatorship orders, granted by courts, allowing parents to obtain physical custody of (adult) offspring out of unpopular religious movements for purposes of forcing them to abandon their adherence thereto
- the I.R.S. determination of what is "religious ministry," often in contradiction to the religious body's own definition of "ministry" when qualifying clergy for exclusion of housing allowance from taxable income
- redefinition by the civil courts of ecclesiastical polity, so that hierarchical bodies are often in effect rendered congregational with respect to their ability to control local church property, and dispersed "connectional" bodies are deemed to be hierarchical with respect to their ostensible liability for torts committed by local entities, contrary to their own self-definition in both cases[11]

Allan C. Carlson sees the crux of the problem as follows:

> Religious organizations are seeing their activities and autonomy compromised indirectly by governmental definitions that confine unrestricted "church activity" to an ever smaller circle. . . . Joining most other private institutions, the churches are facing for the first time the discomfiting adjustments demanded by a bureaucratic state pursuing a set of abstract policy goals. Social regulations have spread far beyond its once limited domain. The government's commitment to an "affirmative" vision of individual and group equality and to augmented collective security, together with state protection of a new set of "rights" unknown several decades ago, is altering the religious community.[12]

The continuing secularist-Christian conflict has been clearly summed up by Steven Samson:

> Americans today are forgetting their cultural traditions and losing their moral consensus. The problem is both religious and political, not simply one or the other. . . .
> The American constitutional system is founded on the Reformation ideal of individual self-government. It is expressed in the cherished rights of free speech, religious liberty, and private property. But the center of American life has been shifting so dramatically that many of the old customs of local self-government, like the town meeting, are becoming

cultural artifacts fit only for display. . . . Any standard of value other than an ultimately hedonistic utilitarianism is apt to be rejected as an intolerable imposition.[13]

THE NEED FOR A UNIFIED CHRISTIAN RESPONSE

We are experiencing unprecedented conflict between secularists and believers, which is part of the general breakdown of social cohesion and of the structures of law itself in our Western culture. As threats to civil and religious liberties loom and moral and legal structures of the society crumble, one longs for the various branches of Christ's church to stand shoulder to shoulder to address the crisis of the century and thus to speak with a united voice and act with united hearts on the absolutely crucial issues concerning our inalienable rights to propagate and live out the truths we believe.

This will not be easy to do, granted the many historical, theological, and cultural differences among various denominations of American Christians. But as Christians begin perceiving the seriousness of the threat to religious freedom, they are going to become far more willing than ever to work together in a cause far transcending even important traditional, denominational concerns.

Not that we should water down our theological convictions in order to merge them into a thin, lukewarm ecumenical soup! On the contrary, Christians in many different quarters are realizing that the only way in which we can go into the twenty-first century with full rights to proclaim publicly the theological distinctives we hold most dear may well depend on our building a broad and strong coalition now with groups of believers whose biblical exegesis and theological stance are very different from our own. We can no longer afford the luxury of not working together in such a time of massive cultural as well as legal crises. And the good news is that on most of the crucial issues that are now pressing in on us as Christians in a hostile secularist environment, we really can march forward together in the common cause of truth and right without having to deny our own historic theological heritage.

WE MUST SEEK TO UNDERSTAND ONE ANOTHER

In order to understand one another, it is essential that we have at least an elemental understanding of some of the major ways in which our own theological traditions differ on matters of church-state relations, law and liberty, as well as ways in which they agree. The time and trouble we take to do this will later be richly repaid in mutual respect, clear conscience, and general harmony of coparticipants in what may be the most demanding struggle of our lives.

Work of C. L. S. Jurisprudence Panel

The Christian Legal Society was farseeing when more than ten years ago it convened a jurisprudence panel to seek understanding. It was composed of Christian scholars, both lawyers and theologians, from the five major Christian traditions that have historically had the most influence in America. That is, Roman Catholic, Lutheran, Calvinist, Anglican, and Mennonite (or Anabaptist). It was believed at that time that other important denominations in this country would probably fit into one of these five traditions insofar as law and liberty, church and state are concerned.

Professor Harold J. Berman, then of Harvard University, and his assistant, Dr. John Witte, professor of law at Emory University, helped raise the basic questions regarding the approach we should take to understand one another's tradition in order to seek some kind of consensus that could guide Christians involved in contemporary legal problems. As John Witte wrote in 1984:

> In order to deepen the Christian's understanding of Biblical teachings on law, to encourage discussion among Christians about perspectives on law and authority, to isolate differences, to highlight commonalities, and to foster cooperative Christian witness, we have begun to explore first-order philosophical questions about the origin, nature, and function of law and legal authority . . . Within the history of Christianity lie buried roots of differences among Christian traditions today, including differences in concepts of law and authority. Informed and responsible dialogue among contemporary Christians about concerted biblically-based witness in law requires awareness of these historical differences and commonalities of perspective. Scripture, together with the past, must guide our future, direct our jurisprudence, ground our institutional theories. . . .[14]

Principal Themes in Five Different Traditions

This jurisprudence panel during the five or six years of its existence generally tried to follow the advice of Harold Berman, who said: "We should continue, as we have started, to focus *on the various perspectives on law that have been presented by the principal branches of the Christian community in the history of the West.*"[15] Professor Berman went on to suggest two principal themes to be taken up in the five different traditions and then thought through together: first, the relationship of the church to the state—negatively, considering the doctrines of civil disobedience and right of resistance to tyrannical laws, and positively, the responsibility of the church to influence the state and secure reform of the law. Second, the theme of the responsibility of individual Christians to participate in the state was considered.[16]

Throughout these studies, it was advised to keep such things in mind as the relation of Biblical hermeneutics to legal hermeneutics and places and not to forget "what all branches of the Church have always had in common," such as the conviction "that law derives its legitimacy not from itself (this would be idolatry) but from something beyond itself."[17]

Curran Tiffany skillfully guided the deliberations and kept the studies on track. Originally it was hoped that volumes dealing with such questions in all five traditions would be published, but it was not possible to secure the funds to carry this out completely. Nevertheless a great deal of material was forthcoming on these topics in each of the traditions, comparing and contrasting their perspectives and finding withal some crucial commonalties for the guidance of God's people in the moral and legal crisis at the end of the twentieth century. A good bit of this material has been published, and other parts of it are still available in unpublished form from the Christian Legal Society.

Roman Catholic Tradition and Western Law

Protestant historiography, undoubtedly under the influence of the antimedieval European Enlightenment, has been very slow to recognize the obvious: other than the inspired biblical tradition itself, no institution has been so significant in making liberty and order a reality in the Western world as the early and medieval Catholic Church. What is well known is the way the Christian Church stood as a sort of alternative government, legal system, and refuge when the Roman Empire was falling and all Europe became radically decentralized in the early Middle Ages or so-called Dark Ages.[18] But what is much less known is what Harold Berman has pointed out—that in the very middle of the so-called static Middle Ages, a dynamic movement occurred from about 1050 to 1150 that would lead to the legal transformation of European life and make both the modern state and modern civil and religious liberty possible because of the new relation worked out in the Gregorian revolution between church and state.

Though one should refer to Harold Berman's *Law and Revolution* for the details of this perspective—and other important Western legal revolutions—for our purposes it will be sufficient to quote from an article by Berman and Witte as a way of looking at this looming mountain peak. They refer to the Roman Catholic "two-swords" theory as it had developed since the eleventh and twelfth centuries. The Papal Revolution [i.e. of Hildebrand through Gregory VII] had established a duality of spiritual and secular authority. The Church became a visible corporate hierarchical polity governed by canon law with jurisdiction not only over its own priesthood but also over the laity in a very wide range of matters. This was the "spiritual sword." The "temporal sword"—whose function was primarily to keep the peace and to protect rights of property— was wielded by emperors and kings, now deprived of their earlier ecclesiastical supremacy, as well as by feudal lords, urban authorities, and others. Papalists sometimes claimed the ultimate supremacy of the spiritual sword over the temporal, but the reality was generally one of competition and cooperation between them.[19]

The beneficial results of the legal revolution are summarized later in the article:

The basic structure of Western legal philosophy was first established during and after the revolutionary upheaval of the late eleventh and early twelfth centuries. Then for the first time, great scholars of the newly revived and resystematized Roman law and the new system of canon law undertook to formulate a coherent set of principles concerning the nature and purposes of law, the sources of law, the various kinds of law, and the relationship of law to justice and order. They drew, to be sure, on the works of Plato, Aristotle, and the Greek and Roman Stoics as well as on the writings of the Church Fathers and later moralists and theologians. Nevertheless, none of their predecessors had treated legal philosophy as a separate comprehensive body of knowledge, distinct from, though related to, both moral philosophy and theology.

Not only the basic structure but also the basic postulates of Western legal philosophy were first articulated in the twelfth and thirteenth centuries. The early scholastic jurists taught that human law, including both customary and statutory law, derives its legitimacy from natural law, which is in turn a reflection of divine law. Natural law was thought to be immediately accessible to human reason. Divine law was revealed to human reason in sacred texts and in the traditions of the Church. At the same time, the scholastic

jurists recognized that human selfishness, pride, and the drive
for power are sources of unjust laws, which are contrary both
to natural law and to divine law. Thus, human law, though a
response to divine will, was seen to be also a product of a
defective human will, which could be and needed to be
corrected by human reason. Human reason, it was said,
coincided with natural law and divine law in postulating that
crimes should be punished, that contracts should be enforced,
that relationships of trust and confidence should be protected,
that accused persons should be heard in their defense, and in
sum, that legal rules and procedures should conform to
standards of justice.[20]

Rosenstock-Huessy many years ago in his *Out of Revolution* had
perceived the relationship between medieval canon law and the
supposedly unique liberties of English common law. While
appreciating the liberties of the English common-law tradition, he
pointed out that it was not unique; it was part of the all-European
heritage of Catholic canon law.[21] Certainly there were periods when
the Roman hierarchy abused its power both in relationship to civil
states and to its own people. Out of these abuses arose another
movement within the Catholic Church that would be pregnant with
possibilities for moral and legal renewal—the conciliar movement.
Contemporary scholars, such as Francois Wendel, Thomas F. Torrance,
Heiko Oberman, Quentin Skinner, and others, have rightly pointed
to the thought and practice of the late medieval conciliar movement
as the immediate context in which such magisterial Protestant
Reformers as Luther, Calvin, Zwingli, Bucer, and Bullinger were
nurtured and from which they drew.

Joan O'Donovan has discussed the advances for law and liberty
gained in this movement in her writings on "The Theological
Precursors of the English Reformation."[22] She particularly emphasizes
the way in which William of Ockham separated "epistemological or
cognitive authority from political (in this case, prelatical) authority,
and elevated the former over the latter."[23]

Lutheran Tradition and Western Law

Lutheran theology is like the rest of the sixteenth-century
Protestant Reformation in that it bodily takes over crucial elements
of traditional Catholic theological, moral, and legal doctrine, and at
the same time, "introduces revolutionary changes in that tradition."[24]
Berman expresses this change:

By their theology, and especially by their twin doctrines of justification by faith alone and the priesthood of all believers, the Lutheran reformers undermined the canon law and the sacramental system, and therewith, the entire jurisdiction of the Roman Catholic Church. This gave to civil rulers the sole prerogative of legislation, administration, and adjudication within their respective territories. By the same token, however, laws enacted by civil rulers now lacked the sanctity that they had formerly had by virtue of ecclesiastical endorsement under the two-swords theory, with its division of powers between the universal church organized under the papacy and the plurality of secular kingdoms, feudal lordships, and urban polities.[25]

The Lutherans attacked "the synthesis of reason and revelation that underlie the Roman Catholic doctrine of natural law" on the basis of the corruption of human will and human reason.[26] But then the Lutheran authorities were faced with a massive problem for an organized civil society. "Lacking the endorsement of an independent ecclesiastical hierarchy, and lacking a foundation in objective and disinterested human reason, what was to justify civil laws other than mere expediency? The theological answer to these fundamental jurisprudential questions was rooted in the Lutheran two kingdoms theory."[27]

There was certainly a tendency to dualism in the two-kingdoms theory of the Lutherans and also a tendency—which could be healthy or unhealthy—to desacralize public life, decreasing the influence of Christianity on the state. Berman and Witte point out that:

Indeed, the Lutheran Reformation created the modern secular state by allocating to the holders of state offices ultimate responsibility for the exercise of functions that had previously been in the jurisdiction of holders of ecclesiastical offices. . . . The elimination of the checks on secular authority traditionally exercised by the Roman Catholic hierarchy substantially increased the danger that the prince would assert absolute power, that is, a power above the law.[28]

While leaving the door open for the development of a certain kind of dualism and secularism, Lutheran theology, especially under such successors of Luther as Melancthon and Olderdorf, made great contributions to the growth of such foundational moral-legal concepts as the guidance of the Christian conscience in statecraft and the role of equity in the fair application of law.[29]

Calvinist Tradition and Western Law

Since John Calvin is in the generation following Luther, one might have thought that he would have distanced himself even more from the traditional Catholic church-state approach. But in fact, Calvin's mature thought, as well as the British and American Puritanism that it engendered, is in some central respects closer to the Roman two-swords theory than it is to the Lutheran dualism between church and state. As I have written elsewhere:

> John Calvin was lastingly influenced by the ancient Constantinian settlement and by late-medieval Roman Catholic conciliarism, as well as by a close study of Old Testament Hebrew polity and Roman civil law. He believed in a relatively independent church supported and reinforced by a Christian civil magistrate. In other words, Calvin held the ancient "two powers" view that both church and state are directly ordained by God with neither subordinate to the other and neither entitled to control the other. Both have coordinate authority under God's ultimate authority, which is expressed through his infallible Word. Calvin held a much more positive view of the guidance of God's law for Christian life and polity than did Martin Luther, the elder statesman of the Reformation.
>
> While Calvin emphasized a positive value of law, his strongly theocentric vision clearly limited the power of all human authorities and institutions of the law. They are all equally under the higher authority of God's transcendent law, including natural law engraved on the consciences of all men, and most importantly, the revealed law of Scripture. This meant, that under extreme circumstances, the people have a right to resist civil tyranny in the name of that higher covenant law, insofar as they are led by duly constituted "lesser magistrates."
>
> The French Huguenot tractarians who followed Calvin, with their need to placate moderate Catholics in France, took Calvin's thought on the covenant basis of civil government much further in the direction of a constitutionalist view of the state by developing the concepts of natural liberty and popular sovereignty. In many respects they were ahead of their time in seeing the chief end of civil government as the protection of the liberty and safety of the people. They developed a more political (and less theological) theory of revolution on the basis of a legal, bilateral contract between ruler and people while retaining the understanding of accountability to God for fidelity in contracts.

In Scotland, John Knox was like Calvin in holding to an essentially medieval and Catholic concept of a Christian civil magistrate's protecting and reinforcing a largely independent church. But he differed from Calvin in holding to a more radical view of civil resistance. Knox, unlike Calvin, actually taught the right and duty of the common people to undertake revolution against the ruling authorities, even without the leadership of lesser magistrates if the secular authorities refused to stamp out idolatry and establish the Reformed religion. Knox developed more thoroughly than Calvin the appeal to scriptural precedents, especially of the Old Testament Hebrew theocracy, as a basis for shaping—and overturning—contemporary legal institutions.

Knox's successor, Andrew Melville, in his development of a Presbyterian ecclesiastical system at the time of growing absolutist monarchical designs on the part of James VI (I of England) emphasized the headship of Jesus Christ over his church. This carried implications for the balance of power between church and state and for the resultant liberty of the people to take whatever political action may be necessary to maintain the rights "of Christ's crown and covenant." Years of costly struggle in Scotland and England resulted in a vast increase of personal civil and ecclesiastical liberties, especially after the Glorious Revolution of 1688, not only for Scotland and England, but for much of the Western world.

The Puritan struggle during the various phases of the seventeenth-century English Revolution saw an unprecedented debate and experiments in applying in practice Calvinist-inspired, covenantally based constitutional theory. During the Commonwealth phase of the revolution, it first appeared that the Presbyterian (and Catholic) view of two independent and coordinate powers of church and state (with strong limits of state authority over individual religious and civil liberties) would prevail. But this was not to be.

The 1660 restoration of King Charles II restored also the older English one-power theory of the state. (The power of the church is held to flow through the power of the state, and in certain respects to be subordinated to it.) While the final phase of the English Revolution clearly limited the power of the monarchy in 1688, it left intact the one power of "the crown in Parliament" over all things, including the church. This led to problems both in Scotland and in the American colonies, problems from which we have never fully escaped.

The American colonies were heavily influenced by large numbers of Calvinist immigrants, of both Congregational and Presbyterian persuasion. New England Congregationalists and middle- and southern-colony Presbyterians were united in their desire to limit the tyrannical propensities of fallen human nature by asserting covenant limits on governmental power. God reigns and His law gives His people the right to governments "instituted among men which derive their just power from the consent of the governed." This implies the right to resist civil tyranny in terms of transcendentally based, covenant obligations binding on both ruler and ruled.

As this approach was worked out in the North American colonial and then revolutionary events, a system was developed in several states and the nation that provided historically unprecedented civil and religious liberties. This American system drew from many sources, including secular Enlightenment thought, but the Calvinist outworking of the two-powers view of church and state was prominent in the process. This view, to the Presbyterian mind, upheld the headship of Jesus Christ directly over his church without civil intermediaries. The two-powers view contributed much to the American establishment of consent of the governed's— covenant or constitutional limitations of all civil power and all institutions—being seen in terms of God's transcendent law—checks and balances of power in the political and legal structure, liberty of conscience, and the inalienable right to resist tyranny, no matter how powerful or legal its pretensions.[30]

Anglican Tradition and Western Law

As we have noted, a central emphasis of Calvinist thought in Great Britain is the two-powers view of church and state, a development and modification of the older Catholic two-swords theory. Very different from both Catholic and Calvinist on this point, and indeed, a crucial contention in the English Civil Wars and a matter for strife in Scotland and America for over a century after 1688, was the Anglican one-power theory of church/state unity.

In her chapter, "Hooker's Theological Consolidation of the English Church," Joan O'Donovan notes that the greatest exponent of the Anglican "via media," Richard Hooker, follows his fourteenth-century predecessor, John Wyclif, in "a continuous thread: namely, the point of complete identity of church and realm." And she also notes the Erastianism of both Wyclif and Hooker: "Wyclif and Hooker alike propound the supreme authority of the secular sovereign over the church."[31]

Hooker believed and taught in his influential *Ecclesiastical Polity* that, "in respect of its territorial scope and personal membership, the church or ecclesiastical society is identical with the commonwealth or civil society."[32] He held that "the English Parliament, as embodying the 'general consent' of the English political community, has the preeminent right to legislate for the church" (*Ecclesiastical Polity* VIII, p. 410).[33]

Hooker worked to establish a middle way or via media position between the Calvinist-Puritan appeal to the sole authority of Scripture as the "regulative principle" for establishing the proper form of government on the one hand and the Roman Catholic synthesis of reason and revelation in its ancient authoritative church tradition on the other hand. Both accord the church strong rights apart from the state. He did so by circumventing the authority structure that both used to uphold church rights apart from the state by making "the law of reason," which is essentially the law of nature, more basic to the organizing and administration of society than appeals to Scripture or church tradition.

In the words of O'Donovan:

> It is not incidental that Hooker expounds the relationship between Reason's law and Divine law within the context of circumscribing Scripture's authority, for the burden of his exposition is to demonstrate the pervasive dependence of the latter on the former. . . . God's supernatural law is bound to reason's autonomous operation in manifold and diverse ways. . . . He formulated the dependence of divinely revealed law on the law of Reason as a refutation of the Puritan axiom "that Scripture is the only rule of all things which in this life may be done by men" (*Ecclesiastical Polity* II, p. 286). His arguments were designed to prove that unassisted reason authorizes many human actions that are approved by God even though not explicitly commanded by His Word of Scripture. . . . In breaking down the Puritans' opposition of God's eternally valid decrees to the blind and transient dictates of man's depraved rationality, Hooker retained a separation of reason and revelation that works to the advantage of reason's autonomy and jurisdiction.[34]

Of course there is much more to the long and powerful Anglican tradition in church-state relations than the justly famous Hooker. Philip Edgeumbe Hughes dealt with the contributions of this rich tradition to modern form and freedom in "The Law, the State, and the Christian: Conceptions of the Relationship between Civil and Ecclesiastical Authority in England in the Sixteenth and Seventeenth Centuries."[35] He laid particular emphasis on the importance of Christ-like character, or "a godly meritocracy," in leadership positions.[36]

Anabaptist Tradition and Western Law

If the Roman Catholics and Calvinists theoretically would have stood together against the Anglicans on two-swords or two-powers of church and state over against the one-power view, nonetheless, all three of them would have stood together against what scholars such as William Balke called "the Anabaptist Radicals" on the state establishment of churches.[37] Political and religious history would show that "the radicals" were actually the wave of the future, and would prevail against all odds. The idea that prevailed throughout the entire Western world after 1776 of "a free church in a free state" owed more to these people at the fringe of the Reformation than to any other influence.

The Anabaptists or Mennonites generally came to have a rather negative moral assessment of the civil state and thus tended to separate themselves from it. A typical illustration of this viewpoint is provided in a sermon preached around 1575 by Hans Schnell:

In this prohibition [i.e., Mark 10:42 and Matt. 20:25] the church of God and of Christ has been obedient to the Teacher's word and has never had the power of government within it; nor has it called on this power to place the hangman beside them, but always suffered persecution until the reign of Constantine. He was baptized by Pope Sylvester, the antichrist, the son of perdition, whose coming took place through the work of the terrible devil. Therefore he received the name Christian falsely. For the Christian church was thereby transformed into the antichristian church."[38]

The Anabaptists made an even more radical split between church and state than the Lutherans and tended to withdraw from life in the state to life in the religious community. Unlike the Calvinists, they did not look to the Old Testament for specific guidance in civil-religious relations but, rather, concentrated on the New Testament. Hans Schnell's words are representative: "It has been sufficiently shown that in the New Testament, Christ has annulled the vengeance in the law of Moses and made it powerless and transformed all into love and mercy."[39]

The writings of such Anabaptist leaders as Hans Denck, Balthasar

Hubmaier, Menno Simons, and Conrad Grebel as well as the widely received Schleitheim Confession of 1526 and Waterland Confession of 1580 demonstrate the hesitancy of these Christians to participate in the polluted civil order, and also their belief that their greatest contribution is to set an example for all by living in a community that operates in terms of the New Testament ethic of love.

The major Reformers such as Luther, Zwingli, and Calvin were so offended by the Anabaptists' negative assessment of the civil order and their withdrawal from it as hopelessly compromised that they could not hear the latter part of their testimony—the contribution of a community based on practical living of the radical love of Christ in every relationship. John Howard Yoder, perhaps the leading contemporary Mennonite theologian, has specified the Anabaptist New Testament political ethic as involving a rejection of violence, a confrontation of evil, and an acceptance of the action of God in overcoming evil through suffering. He emphasizes that "the Kingdom is the cross" and that "the alternative to how the kings of the earth rule is not spirituality but servanthood (Luke 22:25)."[40]

Two factors helped spread the Anabaptist view. Given this powerful disjunction between church and state, it is no surprise that the Anabaptists and their heirs would have been utterly opposed to an established state church. They would have seen it as inherently polluted by the civil state and also would have experienced persecution at its hands. Even so, it is doubtful that this strand of the Reformation could have exercised such massive influence in disestablishing churches across the Western world by the late eighteenth century had it not been for two contributing factors that strengthened their position.

First, and probably of most importance, is the influence of the Mennonites on the Baptist movement in England, Holland, and the American colonies. This connection is difficult to trace because English Puritan Calvinism seems to be the true parent of American Baptists. Yet Professor W. R. Estep of Southwestern Baptist Seminary has shown a definite influence of Anabaptists on Baptists, especially in matters touching religious liberty.[41] Estep quotes Roger Williams, the famous colonial Rhode Island Baptist, who argued for "the absolute necessity of an uncoerced faith for an authentic Christianity."[42]

Separate Baptist ministers such as Isaac Backus in the Congregational establishment of Massachusetts and John Leland in the Anglican establishment of Virginia preached widely, suffered bravely, and agitated constantly for disestablishment of the formal churches in order to follow an uncoerced conscience in worshipping God freely in a free state.

The second contributing factor to the success of the Anabaptist belief in uncoerced religious freedom in the young American republic was the assistance of the milder wing of the European Enlightenment thinking in such figures as Jefferson, Madison, and Mason to whom these courageous Baptist preachers appealed (with tens of thousand of names on petitions in some cases).

Dr. Estep quotes the distinguished American church historian, William Warren Sweet, who comments on the Baptist influence on the defeat of the General Assessment Bill in Virginia in 17ᵛ (which in effect disestablished the Anglican Church there):

> Religious freedom had triumphed in Virginia and was soon to spread throughout the nation, and in a few years later in the form of the first amendment to the Federal Constitution was to become a part of the fundamental law of the land. Justice compels the admission that Jefferson's part in this accomplishment was not so great as was that of James Madison, nor were the contributions of either or both as important as was that of the humble people called Baptists.[43]

This was the basic beginning of the old coalition between religionists and rationalists, which, as Carl Esbeck has shown us, has been breaking up since the middle of the twentieth century. The consequences of this breakup are obvious today.

Having finished a whirlwind tour of the mountain peaks of the five major Christian traditions of America, we must briefly summarize their differences and then their commonalties. This should help us see what, if any, united direction they may give us in these times of confusion and loss.

DIFFERENCES AMONG THE FIVE TRADITIONS

We can usefully summarize the most crucial continuing differences among the millions of descendants of these five traditions in terms of a polarity, with the Roman Catholics and Calvinists together at one end of the pole and the Mennonites and many of their Baptist offspring at the other end. On the Catholic and Calvinist end of the pole is a view of civil government as God-ordained and as a worthy vocation for Christians. These traditions are eager to influence government directly as institutions, not just individually, while at the same time remaining suspicious of the magistrate's propensity to overstep his bounds and thus are protective of the church's freedom and standing as a coordinate institution along with the state.

History shows that they have taken their institutional involvement with civil government much too far at times. In the past, they were willing to use the state to enforce their views on others, but the vast majority of American Presbyterians, Congregationalists, or Roman Catholics would be as loathe to do this today as would the Baptists or Methodists. Thus, the Calvinist and Roman Catholic traditions seem to have engaged in genuine repentance and rethinking at the point of their excesses.

It is difficult to discern whether or not they have presently reached a viable balance concerning the practical influence of the Christian polity on the civil order. The contemporary secularist hostility to the Christian voice in the public marketplace makes the finding of such a balance urgent, though more difficult than ever, for this very reason.

At the other end of the spectrum are the classical Mennonites and a large number of the Baptists. The Mennonites tend to have a more negative view of the civil order and the inherent sinful tendencies of organized power and force than do most Baptists. And the Baptists *as individuals* are much more involved in the running of government than are the Mennonites. The two traditions, however, are generally agreed in drawing a strong dichotomy between the institutional church and the state, often spoken of in terms of (in Jefferson's letter to the Danbury Baptists) as "a wall of separation." This separation or dichotomy can be so strongly held that the state is functionally insulated from the influence of Christianity, leaving a vacuum that is then filled by secularist values.

In a paper summarizing discussions of the Christian Legal Society Jurisprudence Panel on 8 and 9 April 1984, Curran Tiffany made this significant observation: "the Anabaptist and Baptist focus on the primacy and purity of the gospel and its freedom from taint of governmental coercion appears to leave unaddressed the question of the covenant character of civil government, and human governmental responsibility in the light of possible divine vindication of covenantal obligations."[44]

As the Calvinists and Catholics had to do some rethinking of important aspects of their traditional positions and practices many years ago (without denying their central convictions on two swords and two powers), it appears that the Baptists and other "institutional separationists" (to borrow Carl Esbeck's term) may now be in a position of rethinking some aspects of their traditional stance on church and civil government (without denying their core commitment to an uncoerced conscience guaranteed by a free church in a free state). Specifically, when they speak of "a wall of separation between church and state," have they said enough to give sufficient guidance for their people to use their talents and vast influence in their current struggle between contradictory value systems? Outsiders (though even appreciative and sympathetic ones) can raise this question but not answer it.

Could it be that the experience of the Black Baptist Church in America since the 1950s has something to teach the broader Baptist tradition concerning the direct impact of the church's faith on the state?[45] Does the whole Christian tradition have something to learn here that could help us face the future?

The other two classical Christian traditions may summarily be fitted onto the theoretical pole as follows. For all practical purposes, modern Anglicans or Episcopalians would probably be very close in position to the Catholics and Calvinists in terms of interaction between church and state. Lutherans appear to be divided in approach. Those Lutherans more clearly in the Pietist tradition tend to be closer to Mennonites and Baptists, whereas the mainstream Lutherans would be somewhat closer on the pole to Catholics and Calvinists (practically, if not theoretically), although still holding more of a dichotomy between state and church than is allowed by the latter two groups.

SIMILARITIES AMONG THE FIVE TRADITIONS

For all their significant, continuing differences, the five traditions hold enough in common to make it possible to address the current moral, political, and legal crisis of their common culture. All of these traditions believe that only the infinite, personal triune God of Scripture is absolute. Every other person, every other institution is less than absolute, and therefore limited in legitimate power claims.

Because the one true God has created all things and has spoken His Word to guide His creation, all human formulations of law and all humanly organized civil and ecclesiastical structures stand under the judgment of His transcendent Word and must be held accountable in terms of its objective standards. This means that the source of human dignity and rights is transcendent. Humans did not give dignity and rights nor can they take them away. Attempts by humans to do so, no matter how apparently legal their pretensions, must always be resisted. (Calvinists and Catholics have tended to resist with arguments and then arms, and Mennonites have tended to resist by withdrawal and suffering; but all resist tyranny in God's name.)

Thus, when true to their own convictions, the Christian traditions do not allow an idolatry of the state nor an idolatry of human-law formulations nor of political orders. All of the traditions in one way or another believe in a variety of institutions as a sort of divinely ordained checks and balances to the fallen human lust for absolute power. And all of them believe in their deepest souls that the summary of all law and all obligation for time and eternity is the law of love: to love the Lord our God with all our hearts and our neighbors as ourselves.

WHERE DO WE GO FROM HERE?

What do we do with all this, and where do we go from here? Two problems of which evangelicals must be aware as they think of the causes for the moral and legal crisis of our society are (1) an internal problem within the evangelical community and (2) a problem largely external to it. The internal problem involves weaknesses and inconsistencies among evangelical Christians themselves and must be addressed at another time. My concern has been the external problem that the five major Christian traditions face together in an increasingly hostile secularist society. And my concluding remarks on "where do we go from here" must also focus on what I have called our second or external problem.

I fear something important might be lost regarding our united thought and action as we face our external problem if we do not make some short, action-oriented observations concerning our internal problem. Let me make three remarks; all of them concerning repentance by one who needs repentance himself.

Before the church goes forward in a secular, God-denying world, it must first go on its knees before God for its own lack of devotion to Him and lack of conviction about His truth. For all our talk, if we keep denying God where it matters, the secularists can do nothing but disdain us. The statement of James Hitchcock is to the point here: "In practice an orthodoxy which loses its authority has trouble even retaining the right of toleration."[46]

We must also repent of our indifference to one another across traditional, denominational lines, of our hesitancy to cooperate where we can without compromise of convictions, and of our historic readiness to believe the worst about one another without taking the trouble to get to know where the other Christian stands and who he or she is.

Finally, we have some repentance to do before our secular culture. If we appear to be more concerned with our rights than with the temporal and eternal well-being of the very people with whom we do not agree, then we will have little to say to them.

Many centuries ago, the early Christian church was in a cultural situation facing widespread and fierce secularist hostility, a situation far worse than ours. With clearest conscience, Christian leaders such as the apologist Justin Martyr could say to the second century pagan culture (paraphrased): "Look at our lives; look at our Gospel; such a look will melt your hostility."[47] And Tertullian, the second- and third-century converted lawyer of North Africa, could say to the hostile establishment of his day that the lives and worship of Christians were among the greatest assets the Roman Empire could possess. He invited them to consider how the Christians prayed for the emperors, helped the needy of all groups, and loved one another.[48] The triumph of the early Christians was ultimately the triumph of the love of Christ within them for all men, including their enemies. The church today can triumph on no other basis.

The external problem that all of us Christians face together is the moral breakdown and legal crisis of our Western society. This has been brought on, in no small part, by the secularist attempt to cut the religious roots of our liberty and order. Having taken you on what I sincerely hope is a fair survey of the differences and similarities of our five leading traditions, I would like to conclude by suggesting that our commonalties allow us—and indeed encourage us—to begin taking united action in the following way.

Simply stated, our united goal must be this. First, we must understand afresh the principles on which our American government is founded and its civil powers organized. Second, we must require all civil officials to acknowledge and honor these concepts. In so doing, we will discover that the things we agree on most, specifically, the transcendent nature of human freedom or "inalienable rights" and also the nonestablishment of any specific denomination or religious tradition by the civil powers are hereby fully upheld and safeguarded.

AN ANALYSIS THAT CALLS FOR URGENT DISCUSSION

The reader should consult two important works to find further guidance, works that could prove to be of highest importance in the survival of liberty and order in this confused nation. They have been written by distinguished, longtime attorney Robert C. Cannada of Jackson, Mississippi, a widely known Christian statesman and former Director of the Christian Legal Society. They are being extensively circulated and discussed throughout the country at present. The first one is "Inalienable Rights and the Declaration of Independence" (1992), and the second one, "Creator-God/Religion: There is a Solution to the Dilemma Facing America" (1993).[49] More recently he has authored a series of three articles: "America's Choice: Securing Our Unalienable Rights (The Process to be Followed by Office Holders)." They were published in the National Lawyers Association (*NLA*) *Review* in 1997. This series suggests practical steps that could be taken immediately to hasten the restoration of liberty in America.

America's True Form of Government

Robert Cannada provides a helpful summarization to the theses stated in his essay "Inalienable Rights and the Declaration of Independence:"

> The Organic Law for America was to consist of principles, serving as the support or base to the government, and a document "organizing" the government's civil powers.
>
> The document setting forth the principles on which the government is based is the Declaration of Independence. The document organizing the government's civil powers is the Constitution. To ignore or overlook either of these documents constitutes a departure from and a rejection of the structure of this government—a rejection of the Form of Government of this Nation. The principles set forth in the Declaration of Independence and the Constitution are inseparable as a matter of law and principle and each must be acknowledged and honored if our form of government is to survive.[50]

He shows that

> ·the principles identified in the Declaration of Independence and set forth as the base for the government of the new nation involved, among other points: the existence of God (as the first "principle"); the existence of certain "self-evident" truths; the principle that governments are instituted "to secure these rights," and the principle that the government derives its just powers from the consent of the governed.[51]

Unchangeable Principles and Changeable Documents

He demonstrates that these principles that are rooted in a transcendent source, the laws of nature and of nature's God are not amenable to change. "No provision was made in the Declaration for any change or amendment. . . . It was on this base that the government was to operate as long as the government existed."[52] But the instruments and procedures by which the principles were to be carried out could be changed.

> Documents . . . such as the Articles of Confederation and the Constitution . . . could be changed, altered or eliminated—they simply organized the powers of the government and should be changed as the society progressed. On the other hand, *all* such documents were to be subordinate

and subject to the principles constituting the base on which the government rested. Any failure to acknowledge and honor those principles by the government would have the effect of removing the support or base from under the government. This was not to happen.[53]

Mr. Cannada clearly shows that the Declaration created the nation more than ten years before the Constitution was written, and that this is recognized by the United States Constitution and by all the state constitutions. Specifically,

> the signers of the Constitution . . . recognized that the Declaration established the United States as a nation. They also recognized that the Declaration had set forth principles which were to serve as the support or base for the government and they were to write a document that would "organize" the powers of the civil government. They dealt with the civil powers and not with the "principles."[54]

The results of this recognition are of central importance to the solution of our religious liberty problems today. He states:

> Thus each state, with the exception of Oregon, not only adopted a Constitution that was not repugnant to the Constitution and to the Declaration but went further and affirmatively adopted the concept of the belief in a Creator-God—the cornerstone of the "principles" set forth in the Declaration.
>
> It would appear, therefore, that the only proper basis for interpretation of any statute or any question presented to the court is to interpret the statute subject to and in accordance with the Constitution and to interpret the Constitution subject to and in accordance with the principles set forth in the Declaration. To do otherwise violates the structure of our government and ignores one part of the Organic Law of our nation.[55]

CURRENT JUDICIAL CONFUSION COULD BE CLEARED UP

These papers by Robert Cannada show that much of the judicial problem facing religious organizations today comes from a failure to understand what constitutes the organic law of the United States of America. For instance, courts seem to conclude that the First

Amendment to the Constitution is the only source of religious rights for Americans, ignoring the very first principle of the Declaration that the existence of the Creator God guarantees our inalienable rights. This has led to what he rightly calls "some strange conclusions," such as, "the prohibiting of a prayer to the Creator-God in public schools."[56]

Such conclusions represent "(a) failure to acknowledge that the principles set forth in the Declaration constitute a part of the structure of the government."[57] For us to continue to allow this shrinkage of the structure of our government down to a written document—the Constitution—in effect means we give up the transcendent source of inalienable liberties for a very different sort of system. "It is the difference between a nation that acknowledges the existence of certain 'truths' and a nation that denies the existence of anything such as a 'truth.' It represents an entirely different 'Form of Government' from the 'Form of Government' established by the Declaration."[58]

Only a Transcendent Source Secures Human Rights

Once this is understood, all five of the Christian traditions will be thoroughly agreed that the original form of government must be returned to, because it alone limits governmental powers and secures inalienable rights. "The concept of a government with limited powers is premised on the acknowledgment of a 'Higher Authority' than the government or the people, . . ." otherwise, "there would be no limit on the power of the government and there would be no such thing as inalienable rights possessed by the people."[59] In other words, if a human government can give rights, it can also take them away. But if the Creator gives them, no mere creature—not even a civil government—can take them away. This insight is surely essential to a return to judicial and legal sanity in our land.

Creator-God, but No Established Religion

Another crucially important point is Cannada's sensible explanation of how the American founding fathers solved the problem of rooting inalienable rights in the Creator God without at the same time "forcing on its citizens the belief of any particular religion."[60] His second paper, "Creator God/Religion" especially shows how an understanding of this—and an insistence that our officeholders function in terms of it—is essential if our individual freedoms are to be preserved. He also shows how the cornerstone of our government is the recognition of a Higher Power, but the recognition of a "religion" is one that should be supported both by religious as well as nonreligious people.[61]

SUMMARY AND CALL TO ACTION

These two essays agree as far as it concerns united action by Christians of the five classical traditions this way. First, the traditions agree that law and rights have a transcendent basis in the Creator God, and second—at least since the late eighteenth or early nineteenth century—all agree that no one denomination or particular religious belief-system should be imposed by the civil order on the citizenry. And both of these crucial concerns will be safeguarded insofar as we understand our original form of government and cause our officeholders to return to it.

This will be extremely difficult to achieve; and if and when it is achieved, it will not solve all of our problems. But it will solve many of them and will particularly limit the serious erosion of our religious liberty. Beyond that, we will undoubtedly have different ideas of what kinds of further reforms, if any, are proper. But we must get to first base together before we can go any further, whether separately or in concert.

NOTES

1. Robert L. Dabney, *The Practical Philosophy* (1897; reprint. Harrisonburg, Va.: Sprinkle Publications, 1984), 394.
2. Harold J. Berman, *Law and Revolution: The Formation of the Western Legal Tradition* (Cambridge: Harvard University Press, 1983), 33.
3. Ibid., 39.
4. David F. Wells, *No Place for Truth or Whatever Happened to Evangelical Theology* (Grand Rapids: Eerdmans, 1993).
5. Harold O. J. Brown. "The Case for a Christian America" (an unpublished paper in the mid 1980s), 12.
6. Carl H. Esbeck, "Toward a General Theory of Church-State Relations and the First Amendment," *Public Law Forum* 4 (1985): 327.
7. Ibid., 327–28.
8. Ibid.
9. Robert L. Cord, *Separation of Church and State: Historic Fact and Current Fiction* (New York: Lambeth Press, 1982), 15.
10. Steven A. Samson, *Crossed Swords: Entanglements between Church and State in America* (Ph.D. diss., University of Oregon,1984; Ann Arbor, Mich.: University Microfilms International), 540.
11. Dean M. Kelley, "Religious Freedom: The Developing Pattern of Restriction," in *Freedom and Faith: The Impact of Law on Religious Liberty*, ed. Lynn R. Buzzard (Westchester, Ill.: Crossway Books, 1982), 82–83.
12. Allan C. Carlson, "Regulators and Religion: Caesar's Revenge," *Regulation* (May/June 1979): 27.
13. Samson, *Crossed Swords*, 536.

14. John Witte, "Law and Legal Authority in the History of Christian Jurisprudence" (paper prepared for the Christian Legal Society, 1984), iv, v.
15. Harold J. Berman, "Christian Perspectives on Law: An Agenda" (paper prepared for the Christian Legal Society, 1984), 2.
16. Ibid., 3.
17. Ibid., 4.
18. Charles N. Cochrane, William C. Bark, Lynn S. White, and other scholars have shown the period not nearly so dark as the anticlerical Petrarch denominated it.
19. Harold J. Berman and John Witte Jr., "The Transformation of Western Legal Philosophy in Lutheran Germany," *Southern California Law Review* 62, no. 6 (September 1989): 1589.
20. Ibid., 1652
21. Eugen Rosenstock-Huessy, Out of Revolution (reprint, Norwich, Vt.: Argo Books, 1969), 270, 278.
22. Joan O'Donovan, "Theological Precursors of the English Reformation," (paper prepared for the Christian Legal Society, 1988).
23. Ibid., 5
24. Berman and Witte, "The Transformation of Western Legal Philosophy," 1653.
25. Ibid.
26. Ibid.
27. Ibid., 1653–54.
28. Ibid., 1656.
29. Ibid., 1611–50.
30. Kelly, 139–41.
31. Joan O'Donovan, "Hooker's Theological Consolidation of the English Church," (paper prepared for the Christian Legal Society, 1988), 136–37.
32. Ibid., 157.
33. Ibid., 164.
34. Ibid., 153–54, 156–57.
35. Phillip E. Hughes, "The Law, the State, and the Christian: Conceptions of the Relationship between Civil and Ecclesiastical Authority in the Sixteenth and Seventeenth Centuries," (paper prepared for the Christian Legal Society, 1986).
36. Ibid., 96.
37. William Balke, *Calvin and the Anabaptist Radicals* (Grand Rapids: Eerdmans, 1981).
38. Hans Schnell, "Thorough Account from God's Word, How to Distinguish Between the Temporal and Spiritual Regimes, Each with its Order, and Concerning the Power of the Temporal Sword:

Whether the Government Official May in Accord with the Demand of His Office Wield the Sword Over Evildoers, Take Vengeance with it, Fight Against His Enemies, Preserve Shelter and Protection with Force; and Whether He May at the Same Time Be and Remain a Christian in the Peaceful Kingdom of Christ," © 1575, (trans. Elizabeth Bender and Leonard Gross; ed. Leonard Gross, for the Christian Legal Society).

39. Ibid., 17.
40. John Howard Yoder, "The Hermeneutics of Peoplehood: A Protestant Perspective on Practical Moral Reasoning," *Journal of Religious Ethics* 10 (1982): 46 (quoted in Thomas L. Shaffer, "Jurisprudence in the Light of Hebraic Faith," [paper prepared for the Christian Legal Society, 1984]).
41. William R. Estep, "Baptists: Exponents of Religious Liberty" (paper prepared for the Christian Legal Society, 1984).
42. Ibid., 11.
43. Ibid., 17.
44. Curran Tiffany, "Jurisprudence Study Report of Meetings, April 8–9, 1984" (paper prepared for the Christian Legal Society), 4.
45. See chapters 2 and 8 of C. Eric Lincoln and Lawrence H. Mamiya, *The Black Church in the Asian American Experience* (Durham, N.C. and London: Duke University Press, 1990).
46. James Hitchcock. "Competing Ethical Systems," *Imprimis* (April 1981): 2.
47. E.g., Justin Martyr, *Second Apology,* chapter 12.
48. See Tertullian, *Anpologeticum,* chapters 29 and 30.
49. These papers are available from Robert C. Cannada, P.O. Box 22567, Jackson, MS 39225-2567.
50. Robert C. Cannada, "Inallienable Rights and the Declaration of Independence," 1.
51. Ibid., 2.
52. Ibid., 3.
53. Ibid.
54. Ibid., 7.
55. Ibid., 7–8.
56. Ibid., 8.
57. Ibid., 9.
58. Ibid.
59. Ibid., 12.
60. Ibid.
61. Robert C. Cannada, "Creator-God/Religion: There Is a Solution to the Dilemma Facing America," 3.

EIGHT

The Abiding Value of Biblical Law

Larry Walker

INTRODUCTORY ISSUES

Jesus warned, "Do not think that I have come to abolish the Law. . . ." (Matt. 5:17–19).[1] We must remember the abiding value and continuity of biblical moral law. All of life is ethical and, therefore, requires a moral standard of right and wrong. For the Christian, this standard is found in the teaching of Scripture, including its laws. This codified law of God is by its very nature perpetual in its principles and is of obvious abiding value for all of humanity. A statement such as, "Be holy for I am holy" (Lev. 20:7–8 NKJV) would be meaningless if God's laws were not timeless.

God's eternal law did not originate with Moses.[2] Earlier, Abraham had laws to observe (Gen. 18:19; 26:5), and the New Testament commends Abraham's *obedient* faith (James 2:21; Heb. 11:8–19). God judged Sodom (Gen. 19) for violating the law against homosexuality (cf. Lev. 18:23) and for the lawlessness of the Sodomites (2 Pet. 2:6–8). Notice also that Romans 1:32 (in the context of homosexuality) says "they know God's righteous decree."

External changing conditions do not invalidate God's laws that address and apply to internal attitude as well as to external behavior. We are commanded to love with the heart (Deut. 4:29) and to circumcise the heart (Deut. 10:16). God's love commands should be part of our worldview and apply to all areas of life; we are to love with everything in us (Deut. 6:4–6), throughout the day (v. 7), at home, and away (v. 9).

The publisher's introduction to the Banner of Truth reprint of Samuel Bolton's work, *The True Bounds of Christian Freedom*, mentions the abiding importance of God's law:

> Grievous and alarming is the present-day deterioration in the moral condition of society. For this decay the Church is partly blameworthy because, as the preserving salt of the

community, she has largely lost her savor. Modern theology has defected. It has cut itself adrift from the ancient landmarks, and present-day society reaps "the evil thing and bitter" which is the inevitable consequence. The present prevailing theology has not been able to elevate society and halt its moral decline, and unquestionably, one explanation of this is its misunderstanding of the place of the law and its usefulness in the service of the covenant of grace.[3]

These words are even more appropriate now than when first written. Ignorance of both the content and the relevance of biblical law has resulted in an immoral society without a compass and individual believers without a standard.

ORIGIN OF BIBLICAL LAW

At Mount Sinai, God delivered to his people, through Moses, the famous Ten Commandments. But this was merely a republication of the eternal will of God already stamped on human nature. Much of this law, stamped on human nature, has been found explicitly and implicitly in the ancient pagan law codes discovered in the lands of the Old Testament.[4] Many remarkable parallels have been noted between these and the biblical laws.

Use by Prophets

The Hebrew prophets[5] repeatedly called the people back to the truth and to the divine standard revealed in God's written laws.

The Law (Torah) was the "Bible" of the Hebrew prophets; it provided the standard by which they measured the conduct of the people.[6] This law was viewed as a supreme gift from their God to be appreciated and obeyed. Without it the people were left without a reference for the difference between right and wrong. It was the basis for the prophets' charges of obedience versus disobedience. Without it the people were left in a spiritual vacuum in which they lacked a written standard by which to judge behavior.

Amos (2:6–8) uses the term rebellions or crimes when he itemizes violations of God's law that here includes the oppression of the poor and the perversion of justice. Oppression of the poor is forbidden in Exodus 22:20–21 and Leviticus 19:13a; perversion of justice is condemned in Exodus 23:1–3 and Deuteronomy 16:19. In Amos 5:12 we find use of the law in the prophet's continuing message against "offenses" (rebellions) that include the oppression of the righteous and the acceptance of bribes—in violation of such law passages as Exodus 23:1–3 and Deuteronomy 16:19.

Jeremiah's famous "temple sermon" reminds the people of their violations of the Ten Commandments and other laws when he declares, "Will you steal and murder, commit adultery and perjury [swearing falsely], burn incense to Baal and follow other gods you have not known." It is the people's transgression of several of the Ten Commandments that forms the basis for Jeremiah's accusation of their disobedience and the consequent disaster about to fall on them. Not only the Ten Commandments, but other passages from the laws are utilized in the prophetic proclamation: Jeremiah's accusation of king Jehoiakim's conduct (Jer. 22:13) is based on the principles of the law that is encoded in such passages as Leviticus 19:13 and Deuteronomy 24:14–15.

Use by Other Old Testament Spiritual Leaders

Not only the Hebrew prophets but other spiritual leaders such as priests and civic leaders taught the abiding value of biblical law as a standard for the people.

During the postexilic period, leaders such as Ezra and Nehemiah (along with the postexilic prophets) summoned the people to the law and the God of that law. Ezra brought "the book of the law" from Babylonia and made it the very foundation of the life of the new community.

Use in the New Testament

Because the Old Testament law does not appear to be an explicit part of the evangelistic message found in the gospel as proclaimed in the New Testament, some have assumed a negative attitude toward it. This is based in part on the fact that the New Testament does express negative observations about those who would attempt to use the law to earn or attain individual and personal salvation, which is only in Christ. This idea of earning salvation was often present in the early church and led to forms of legalism contrary to individual salvation by faith alone. The New Testament message was alert to this threat and emphasized personal salvation by grace alone through faith.

The apostles, especially Paul, very strongly denounced the error of this legalistic perspective; but they never denounced the abiding value of biblical law itself. On the contrary, Paul made it quite clear that our faith does not abrogate the law: "Do we, then, nullify the law by this faith? Not at all! Rather we uphold the law" (Rom. 3:31). The great apostle of salvation by faith alone points out the abiding value of biblical law in exposing sin: "Is the law sin? Certainly not! Indeed I would not have known what sin was except through the law" (Rom. 7:7). He continued in the same passage, "So then, the law is holy, and the commandment is holy, righteous and good" (Rom. 7:12). He even says the "law is spiritual" (Rom. 7:14) in contrast to his sinful condition, which he described as "unspiritual."

The problem is not with biblical law, which is described in the New Testament with such terms as good, holy, and even spiritual. The problem is with fallen and sinful humans and their inability to keep to perfection the perfect law of God. To the extent that God's law is obeyed, it is to the benefit and advantage of both individuals and society; to the extent that it is rejected and disobeyed, it is to the detriment and disadvantage of individuals and society.

In the book of James we find a focus on the fact that true biblical faith is one that reflects obedience to God's good laws. This gives a balance to Paul's strong focus on faith alone as the basis for individual salvation. This biblical use of faith must be defined for clarification; Paul certainly never had in mind a passive and inactive faith that some have attributed to his teachings. The book of James provides a helpful antidote to antinomianism and to this misunderstanding of Paul and the Christian faith.

Use in Church History

The Reformation[7]

The Reformers clearly recognized the abiding validity and value of Old Testament law and did not consider it abolished by the New Testament.[8] They did not hesitate to accept a valid role for biblical law in their social systems; it would have been unthinkable to reject or ignore God's good gift of the law. But they also recognized that the law had been abused by the Roman Catholic Church and that important issues of interpretation were involved in the application of God's gracious gift of the law.

Obviously, the Reformers were aware of the pedagogic use of biblical law—exposing sin, bringing conviction to the sinner, and creating a sense of spiritual need. The law was indeed a tutor to bring sinners to the Savior.

> The right use and end, therefore, of the law is to accuse and condemn as guilty such as live in security, that they may see themselves to be in danger of sin, wrath, and death eternal. . . .The law with this office helpeth by occasion to justification, in that it driveth a man to the promise of grace.[9]

In addition, the Reformers were aware of the obvious principle that when the teachings of God's law are spurned by a culture, it experiences the wrath of God revealed against it in the progressive breakdown of social order and moral decency (Romans 1). Therefore, the Reformers did not hesitate to use God's law as a means of defining and restraining the evil and lawless deeds of the ungodly. Such a Reformed perspective was reflected during the time of the Westminster Assembly when Samuel Bolton wrote:

> First of all, then, my work is to show the chief and principal ends for which the law was promulgated or given. There are two main ends to be observed, one was political, the other theological or divine. The political use is hinted at by the apostle in 1 Tim. 1:8–9 . . . ; that is, it [biblical law] was made for them in such fashion that, if it were not their rule, it should be their punishment. Such is the political use of the law.[10]

In brief summary, at least three uses of the law were recognized in traditional Reformed thought: (1) political use—the civil magistrate was to enforce God's good law as a restraining of ungodly behavior by ungodly men; (2) pedagogic use—the law was a tutor to bring sinners to the Savior[11] by exposing sin, bringing conviction to the sinner, and thereby creating a sense of spiritual need; (3) didactic use—the law was a standard of life for believers.[12]

The Calvinist branch of the Reformation stressed biblical law as a good gift of God's grace, and the Lutheran branch focused more on it as a constraint; they both agreed that the law was to be used to guide the life of the regenerate believer.

Most debate has arisen over the legal or political use of the biblical law in restraining the ungodly behavior of the unregenerate in our society. Paul warns that there are both lawful and unlawful uses of the law of God. First Timothy 1:8 goes on immediately to illustrate a correct use of the law as that of curbing the outward civil behavior of unruly men (vv. 9–10). The law by its very nature aims to restrain the misconduct of lawless men: murderers, kidnappers, homosexuals, perjurers, and the like.

Luther and Calvin (and other Reformers) agreed that God's law was an instrument of civil government, functioning to restrain crime and to promote civil order. Luther taught that

> the first use of the law is to bridle the wicked. This civil restraint is very necessary, and appointed of God, as well for public peace, as for the preservation of all things, but especially lest the cause of the Gospel should be hindered by

the tumult and sedition of wicked, outrageous and proud men.[13]

Calvin agreed:

> The first use of the law is, by means of its fearful denunciations and the consequent dread of punishment, to curb those who, unless forced, have no regard for rectitude and justice. Such persons are curbed, not because their mind is inwardly moved and affected, but because, as if a bridle were laid on them, they refrain their hands from external acts, and internally check the depravity which would otherwise petulantly burst forth.[14]

Calvin

Because of Calvin's profound influence on Western Christian societies, his understanding of biblical law is of great significance.[15] John Calvin followed Thomas Aquinas in dividing the Mosaic legislation into moral, ceremonial, and judicial laws.[16] He described the moral law as the division containing permanent abiding validity.

> It is the true and eternal rule of righteousness, prescribed for men of all nations and times, who wish to conform their lives to God's will. For it is his eternal and unchangeable will that he himself be indeed worshipped by us all, and that we love one another.[17]

He believed that this moral law is summarized in the Ten Commandments and in the law of love, and that the moral law is "that inward law ... engraved on the hearts of all" and that it affirms "the very same things that are to be learned from the two Tables."[18] He adds that because of our dullness and arrogance, "The Lord has provided us with a written law to give us a clearer witness of what is too obscure in the unwritten natural law."[19] Calvin certainly believed that ceremonial laws were fulfilled in the person and work of Christ.[20] His view on judicial law[21] is not as clear.[22] At times he seemed to indicate that judicial law is not authoritative on all the nations since the general principle of equity underlying it has to be adapted to differing situations and differing times.

Later, many Calvinists applied the implications of covenant theology to civil government. The practical implications of covenant theory were developed by Samuel Rutherford (1600–61) in his *Lex Rex*, or *The Law and the Prince*. He said rulers derive their authority from God, as declared in Romans 13:1–4; but God gives this authority to rulers through the people. The people establish a form of government and choose a particular man to be their ruler. The ruler then acts under the direction of God.

The covenant view of government also found secular expression in John Locke's social-contract theory—the belief that men in a state of nature formed a government by mutual consent and gave it certain limited authority to act in order to protect their basic rights of life, liberty, and property. Locke, a Puritan by background, based his political theories on Rutherford's *Lex Rex*.

Locke, who strongly influenced the thinking of our nation's founders, relied on Scripture—supernatural revelation—for his political principles (especially in his first and second treatises). He constantly appealed to Scripture for authority[23] and used examples from Scripture of how God intervened in history. He wrote that everything in the text of the Old and New Testaments is "infallibly true" since it is the "will of God . . . clothed in words."[24] He also said that the "Christian religion" was not devised by the minds of men but received "from revelation"[25] and "when God declares any truth to us, this is a revelation to us by the voice of his Spirit."[26] Locke said that God's moral law, decreed in creation, is carried forward in the specific decrees of Scripture and obliges Christians and all men everywhere, and is to all men the standing law of works.[27] Men are to obey the moral law revealed in Scripture, and that according to the "law of nature man ought to obey every positive law of God."[28]

Use of Biblical Law in Early America

Calvinism was of great influence in the law and order established in the early New England settlements. This perspective believed that God's law, as revealed in his word contains absolute and unchanging principles that are (for the most part) relevant to modern society. Calvin stressed that both moral and judicial laws of Scripture needed to be applied as principles, not as hard-and-fast rules. These laws reflected the eternal and unchanging character and will of God and could not be ignored. Biblical law revealed the character of God and proclaimed Him as the ultimate and benevolent Lawgiver (Ruler of the Universe). But law was also to keep the sinful proclivities of depraved men in check.

The Colonies

The words of the Mayflower Compact of 1620, without hesitation or reservation, proclaimed for "the glorie of God and advancemente of ye Christian faith." Later in 1636, the General Court of Massachusetts resolved to make a code of laws "agreeable to the word of God"; and at about the same time, John Cotton drafted a code of laws that made reference to "the Law of Nature, delivered by God" that closed with a reference to Isaiah 33:22.[29]

The application and enforcement of biblical law had its basis in the Puritan belief that the Scriptures contained the general principles of government. God left it up to men to work out the details of applying those principles to concrete situations. This application of God's revealed law to civil government was especially prominent in Puritan New England.

The Founding Fathers

The source of authority most often cited by the founding fathers was the Bible, which accounted for thirty-four percent of all their citations. The fifth book of the Bible, Deuteronomy, because of its heavy emphasis on law, was referred to frequently.[30] The most cited thinker was Charles Louis Joseph de Secondat, the Baron Montesquieu of France (1689–1755), whose best-known work was *The Spirit of Laws.*[31] He believed that all law has its source in God and that laws made by humans should conform to the eternal laws of God. He believed that humanity was basically evil and self-centered and understandably does not choose to follow God's laws.[32]

The second-most-cited source was Blackstone (1723–1780), whose *Commentaries on the Laws of England* are rated as the most famous treatise on common law. His God-centered view of law is out of fashion in today's legal community, but throughout the latter half of the 1700s and the first half of the 1800s Blackstone's popularity in America was uneclipsed. The founders of the nation were quite familiar with his views and at least one delegate to the Constitutional Convention, Charles Cotesworth Pinckney of South Carolina, had been Blackstone's student at Oxford. The founding fathers drew several points from Blackstone, the foremost being that all law has its source in God.[33]

When Jefferson penned the Declaration of Independence, he wanted the world to know that Americans were not lawless rebels; rather, England was the lawbreaker. Americans had a right to be free, a right flowing from the laws of nature and nature's God. In fact, the words he penned for the Declaration of Independence are " the Laws of Nature and of Nature's God." Jefferson carefully chose this terminology, which was then a legal phrase for God's law revealed through nature and his moral law revealed in the Bible.[34] It may well be one of the most misunderstood phrases in American legal history and must be understood in the context of that time and its previous history of usage.[35]

Nineteenth Century

Lawyer and evangelist Charles G. Finney spoke for many when he affirmed that the American Constitution and laws were borrowed from the Bible, not from Greece or Rome.[36] During the first part of this century, the Bible and its laws remained a norm of exceeding importance. Politicians were aware of when they followed it or when they strayed from it. At that time, to quote the Bible for many issues in life would have been to repeat the obvious. Over the remaining decades of the nineteenth century, however, biblical standards became less important, except in the national struggle regarding slavery and freedom for black people. As churches accommodated the secularization of culture, they became more marginal in exposing public issues to the standards of biblical law.

During the latter half of the last century, the negative influences from such things as the "higher criticism" of Scripture and evolutionism had the effect of undermining the traditional high view of the Bible. The result was that the authority of biblical law was undercut.[37] Increasingly, the abiding value of biblical law was neglected or rejected along with any abiding value of other parts of Scripture.

Twentieth Century

The twentieth century has witnessed biblical law being less understood and increasingly abandoned on both a personal and collective level in society. With the loss of biblical authority came the loss of biblical law as an authority. Humanity became autonomous and made its own laws. Truth was determined by "science," or a poll, rather than by a biblical revelation from God. The practical end of such thinking results in the acceptance of what the Bible condemns, for example homosexuality.

The value of biblical law is that the God who created us has not left us in the dark on what is right and proper (righteous and just).[38] To reject God's special revelation in biblical law and its abiding value leads to moral chaos.

A view of higher law is necessary to produce "the rule of law rather than the rule of man." Evolutionary or populist approaches to law are inherently dangerous. God's law, if obeyed, produces justice (from God's perspective); humanity's law produces justice (from humans' perspective).

Contemporary Evangelical Views of Biblical Law

It should be noted, however, that among modern evangelical Christians a wide spectrum of opinion exists on this important but controversial subject of the relevance of biblical law for us today. Several basic questions and problems emerge.

First, among some Christians may be found negative views of biblical law; they emphasize instead the good news of the gospel of Jesus Christ who changes individuals and then changes society through changed lives. In fact, those who hold this view have no interest in using biblical law to define or mold even Christian character; and they certainly have no interest in imposing Old Testament law on a pluralistic society. Such Christians do not believe in any kingdom or form of divine dominion in this present church age. Some of these believe that not only has the King been rejected; but also His kingdom has been rejected; and we should not expect or promote any divine rule now.

Second, most evangelicals would disagree with the view that biblical law is invalid and irrelevant today. Most earnest Christians would be pragmatically against the separation of God's laws and the nation's laws. They are aware that antinomianism and lawlessness do not lead to a law-abiding and God-fearing society. Furthermore, since it is obvious that laws must be in place for the safety and welfare of a healthy society, the issue is simply which or whose laws. Most evangelicals support the idea that biblical laws are relevant and beneficial even for our modern pluralistic American society.

Third, some Christians would attempt by biblical law to make or declare our country a Christian nation and place it under the standards of Christianity, including biblical law.[39] They see the abiding validity and authority of biblical law as fundamental for setting the standard and changing the course of our pluralistic nation. They have no reservations about bringing all non-Christian religions in our society under the authority of God's Word and Christ's kingdom rule. This would constitute a return to the days of the earliest Christian settlements in this new land when non-Christians, such as Jews, were rejected and literally put back on their boats and sent back to their ports of origin. This hardly seems an option today.

Finally, some modern evangelicals find it totally inappropriate to attempt the imposition of the laws of the Bible, especially as understood by Christians, on a pluralistic society. This would lead not only to anti-Semitism but anti every other religion. Many Christians believe that this country with its unprecedented religious freedom and liberty would suffer much if one religion or worldview is given favored legal status over others. They believe that it is wrong to impose a Christian worldview over the many non-Christian worldviews represented in our pluralistic nation. And obviously the non-Christian religions and worldviews that abound in our great American democracy certainly have no interest in allowing partisan Christians to use the Bible to decide legally what is best for the country.

Resulting Confusion

Largely as a result of such confusion over the value of God's law, today there is absolutely no moral consensus in the 1990s. Each one makes up his own moral code (Christian and non-Christian alike). The authors of *The Day America Told the Truth* describe "the real commandments, the rules that many people actually live by."[40] Three examples from their list of ten are: (1) I will steal from those who won't really miss it (75 per cent); (2) I will lie when it suits me, so long as it doesn't cause any real damage (64 per cent); (3) I will cheat on my spouse—after all, given the chance, he or she would do the same (53 per cent). Such statistics reflect the moral chaos resulting when biblical law is abandoned. Evangelical theologian J. I. Packer says that the Ten Commandments

> are in fact foundational to Christian morals [and] appeals to the ethic of Christ and the apostles that fail to find their roots in the Commandments (roots that are made very plain in the New Testament, be it said) slip and slide into all sorts of misconceptions. The unity of biblical ethics, starting with the Decalogue, needs rediscovery today.[41]

Michael Horton summons modern believers to the abiding value of biblical law when he writes,

> The Bible, particularly the Ten Commandments, calls us to discover our obligations to God and to our neighbor and society. It calls the people of God to their posts in society . . . as called-out men and women who have a heavy sense of moral duty - not to save their own souls, for that is by grace apart from works, but to bring glory and honor to that gracious King.[42]

David A. Noebel wrote in criticism of the contemporary philosophy of law,

> What is needed to restore man's proper sense of ethical and legal obedience? An absolute basis for law. Clearly, the

weakest aspect of the entire theory of legal positivism is its founding of law on an ever-changing basis: governmental authority. Legal positivists believe a "flexible" system of law is desirable, since man and his laws are caught up in the process of evolution.[43]

Similarly, A. E. Wilder-Smith observed,

Why have law and order deteriorated so rapidly in the United States? Simply because for many years it has been commonly taught that life is a random, accidental phenomenon with no meaning except the purely materialistic one. Laws are merely a matter of human expediency. Since humans are allegedly accidents, so are their laws.[44]

Some Continuing Uses of Biblical Law

For Unbelievers: A Restraining Use

When people fail to see that God's law is meant to operate as an external safeguard[45] for society, and when they doubt and oppose the "civil use" of the law (not to mention the moral use), their societies inevitably suffer the consequences.

To a remarkable degree, conservative and liberal professing Christians alike quote the Bible for standards of justice and for a basis for establishing laws in society that restrain the actions of criminals and evil people. Biblical standards have been regularly applied to issues of slavery, racism, hunger, abortion, poverty, and other social issues throughout Christian history; the law and the prophets (who used biblical law as a standard) have been repeatedly quoted and held up as a standard. A great variety of professing Christian people, Martin Luther King, Jerry Falwell, Billy Graham, Mother Theresa, Jesse Jackson, Bill Clinton, and so forth, have appealed and continue to appeal to the authority of biblical precepts. An endless array of individuals appeal to biblical standards for distinguishing right from wrong. Throughout Christian history the abiding value of biblical standards of justice was mostly assumed by nations in the West. Modern leaders still, perhaps unconsciously, find themselves in that tradition.

Carl Henry described the restraining use of the law in this way:

Even where there is no saving faith, the Law serves to restrain sin and to preserve the order of creation by proclaiming the will of God. . . . .By its judgments and its threats of condemnation and punishment, the written law along with the law of conscience hinders sin among the unregenerate. It has the role of a magistrate who is a terror to evildoers. . . . It fulfills a political function, therefore, by its constraining influence in the unregenerate world.[46]

For Unbelievers: A Pedagogic Use

Unbelievers need to be made aware that they are lawbreakers and, therefore, guilty before the Ruler of the universe.[47] The Gospel is not only for "the needy" but also for "the guilty." Sinners are guilty of breaking God's law and failing to keep His standards of justice and righteousness. Without biblical law, sinners fail to see how they are guilty before the holy God who gave such laws. A whole generation is growing up in our country totally unaware of God's standards and, therefore, totally unaware of their guilt before Him. In the past, even public schools posted and advertised at least the Ten Commandments. Now this has been made illegal in some places; or public officials fail to see any significance in such activity.

In an attempt to stem this growing tide of ignorance about the abiding value of God's law, many churches and at least one national organization are printing beautiful copies of the Ten Commandments for display purposes.

For Believers: A Pedagogic Use

Not only does the law serve as a tutor for unbelievers, it also is of pedagogic value for believers.[48] The law illuminates sanctification; it is a guide for the believer of what is pleasing, right, and good in God's sight. It provides the pattern and offers positive moral direction by divine revelation.

The Reformers clearly recognized this abiding didactic use—a standard for believers. Calvin wrote, "The law is the best instrument for enabling believers daily to learn what that will of God is which they are to follow."[49]

God's law identifies, defines, and illustrates sin so that the believer can understand and recognize the meaning of sin and salvation. Although God's law does not justify the believer, obedience to it is harmonious with grace and saving faith. Paul taught that although we are not saved by good works, we are saved for good works (Eph. 2:10). We are only able to identify good works and distinguish them from evil works by biblical law, the standards of a holy God revealed in Scripture.

Biblical law is of immense abiding value for God's people, and believers should not hesitate to delight in God's law (Ps. 112:1; cf. Rom. 7:22) and to love and appreciate it (Pss. 1:2; 119:16).

SUMMARY

The abiding value of biblical law must be taught, remembered, and appreciated today. Unless society has a fixed divine standard for truth, it flounders on vacillating human theories. God's standards are not determined by a poll or by scientific theories, but by revelation. He has revealed in biblical law the standards that reflect His holy nature and are beneficial for individuals and society.

NOTES

1. All the Scripture in this chapter, unless otherwise marked, is from the New International Version of the Bible.
2. For an insightful study of God's appearance and giving of the law at Sinai against its Ancient Near Eastern background, see Jeffrey J. Niehaus's *God at Sinai* (Grand Rapids: Zondervan, 1995).
3. Samuel Bolton, *The True Bounds of Christian Freedom* (London: Banner of Truth, 1964).
4. A useful survey and summary is available in R. Westbrook's "Biblical and Cuneiform Law Codes," *Revue Biblique* 92 (1985): 247–64.
5. For a helpful overview of this subject, see Richard V. Bergren's, *The Prophets and the Law* (Cincinnati: Hebrew Union College, 1974).
6. The closest analogy to the Hebrew prophets that has been found outside the Old Testament is the case of the Mari prophets from the eighteenth-century B.C. kingdom of Mari on the Euphrates. They were sent as messengers from a deity to a king or other person, but they did not have a "Bible" or Torah that they proclaimed as a basis for human conduct.
7. Because of the necessary brevity of this short survey, I will begin this simple survey of church history with the Reformers. They exercised the greatest influence on the thinking of the founders of this country.
8. For more details on Luther and Calvin, see David Wright, "The Ethical Use of the Old Testament in Luther and Calvin: A Comparison," *Scottish Journal of Theology* 36 (1983): 463–85.
9. Luther's *Commentary on Galatians* at Gal. 2:17 and 3:19.
10. Bolton, *The True Bounds of Christian Freedom*, 78.
11. "The right use and end, therefore, of the law is to accuse and condemn as guilty such as live in security, that they may see themselves to be in danger of sin, wrath, and death eternal. . . . The law with this office helpeth by occasion to justification, in that it driveth a man to the promise of grace" (Luther's *Commentary on Galatians*, 2:17 and 3:19).

12. Calvin wrote, "The law is the best instrument for enabling believers daily to learn what that will of God is which they are to follow" (*Institutes of the Christian Religion*, ed. John T. McNeill, trans. Ford Lewis Battles [Philadelphia: Westminster, 1960], 2.7.12).

13. Luther, *Commentary*, at Gal. 3:19.

14. Calvin, *Institutes*, 2.7.10.

15. For much of the following summary, I am indebted to Douglas F. Kelly, *The Emergence of Liberty in the Modern World* (Phillipsburg, N.J.: Presbyterian & Reformed, 1992), 19–22.

16. Calvin, *Institutes*, 4.20.14.

17. Ibid., 4.20.15.

18. Ibid., 2.8.1.

19. Ibid.

20. Ibid., 4.20.15 and 2.7.16.

21. Judicial law is usually termed civil law in contemporary debate.

22. Calvin's view of the use of judicial law has been debated. In a recent study of the teaching on God's law in Calvin's thought, Jean Carbonnier argued that Calvin's thinking on the subject of law developed toward a more positive view of the continuing validity of Old Testament judical law. Jean Carbonnier, "Droit et Theologie chez Calvin," in *Coligny ou les sermons imaginaires: Lectures pour le Protestantisme Francais d'aujourd'hui* (Paris: Presses Universitaires de France, 1970), 39–51, mentioned in Douglas Kelly's, *The Emergence of Liberty in the Modern World*, 22.

23. Gary Amos, *Defending the Declaration* (Brentwood, Tenn.: Wolgemuth & Hyatt, 1989), 53.

24. John Locke, *An Essay Concerning Human Understanding*, 2 vols., ed. Alexander Campbell Fraser (New York: Dover Publications, 1959), 2:120.

25. Ibid., 2:279

26. Ibid.

27. John Locke, "The Reasonableness of Christianity" with "A Discourse on Miracles" and part of a "Third Letter Concerning Toleration," ed. I.T. Ramsey (Standford, Calif.: Standford University Press, 1958), 31, sec. 23.

28. Ibid.

29. John Eidsmoe, *Christianity and the Constitution: The Faith of Our Founding Fathers* (Grand Rapids: Baker, 1987), 32.

30. This information is taken from the work of two professors, Donald S. Lutz and Charles S. Hyneman, who reviewed an estimated 15,000 items and closely read 2,200 books, pamphlets, newspaper articles, and monographs with explicitly political content printed between 1760 and 1805 (Cf. Donald S. Lutz, "The Relative Influence of

European Writers on Late Eighteenth-Century American Political Thought," *American Political Science Review* 189 [1984]: 189–97).

31. Montesquieu, *The Spirit of Laws* (1949; reprint, New York: Hafner, 1962).

32. Ibid., 1:2–3. These references are given in John Eidsmore, *Christianity and the Constitution*, 34.

33. Eidsmoe, *Christianity and the Constitution*, 57.

34. Amos, *Defending the Constitution* (Brentwood, Tenn.: Wolgemuth & Wyatt, 1989), 35n.3.

35. A good summary of this material may be found in Amos, *Defending the Declaration*, 35–37.

36. Charles C. Cole, *The Social Ideas of the Northern Evangelists, 1820–1860* (New York: Columbia University Press, 1954), 145.

37. A very clear example of the undercutting of biblical authority and therefore it's irrelevance for modern-law study is found in Edward McGlynn Gaffney's "Biblical Law and the First Year Curriculum of American Legal Education," *Journal of Law and Religion* 4 (1986): 63–95. The author (not a biblical scholar) accepts the critical conclusions of the "biblical scholars" who reject the integrity of Scripture and from that deduces that biblical data should not be brought into issues of law education. For a contrary view that biblical law should be studied as a subject in the humanities see Dale Patrick's "Studying Biblical Law as a Humanities," *Semeia: An Experimental Journal for Biblical Criticism* 45 (1989): 27–47.

38. The Hebrew concepts behind these terms (*justice* and *righteousness*) are fundamental, rich, and significant. These concepts are at the very heart of Old Testament morality and ethics. The related Greek terms used in the New Testament continue the Hebrew usage and concepts.

39. Most notable of these would be the Theonomists or Christian Reconstructionists who have helpfully reminded us of the value of biblical law.

40. James Patterson and Peter Kim, *The Day America Told the Truth* (New York: Plume, 1992), 2.

41. J. I. Packer, foreword to *The Law of Perfect Freedom*, by Michael S. Horton (Chicago: Moody Press, 1993), 10.

42. Michael S. Horton, *The Law of Perfect Freedom* (Chicago: Moody Press, 1993), 15.

43. David A. Noebel, *Understanding the Times* (Manitou Springs, Colo.: Summit Press, 1992), 545.

44. A. E. Wilder-Smith, *The Creation of Life* (Costa Mesa, Calif.: TWFT Publishers, 1970), ix.

45. Sometimes labeled the civil use. When our sinful nature wants to

break the bonds of the law, the only thing that stops some of us is the threat that violation of the law imposes. This use of the law is that of a deterrent in the civil sphere, with the police and prisons to back up the threat.

46. Carl F. H. Henry, *Christian Personal Ethics* (Grand Rapids: Eerdmans, 1957), 355.

47. This is called the pedagogical use because of Paul's reference to the law as God's tutor, that leads sinners to faith in Christ (Gal. 3:24). The law reveals how we fall short of the righteousness that God requires and therefore teaches us, hopefully, our need of His grace. It serves as an exposé of the unbeliever.

48. This is sometimes called the moral use. Biblical law is an expression of God's eternal character that does not change. Believers appreciate and obey this good law not in order to meet perfectly God's requirements (which can only be attained in Christ) but to profit personally and collectively from living in obedience to this gracious and good instruction from a loving God.

49. Calvin, *Institutes of the Christian Religion*, 2.7.12.

NINE

Sin, Rights, and Equality

William J. Stuntz[1]

OUR LEGAL SYSTEM IS less Christian than it used to be. That is, the system's orientation, its vision of what law is and what separates good law from bad, is more at odds with a Christian view of the world than once was the case. This is not to say that our legal system once was thoroughly Christian, or that in some happy days gone by it was free from evil. Neither of those things is true. Nor is it to say that the law today is wholly inconsistent with Christian thinking. On the contrary, the influence of Christian culture remains strong in many areas of the law.

Still, that influence is less strong than it once was. The reason, at one level, is simple: fewer Christian judges and legislators. At another level, it is much more complicated. We are in the midst of some very large changes in the reigning legal philosophy, the view of law that judges and legislators alike take for granted. Those changes are subtle and often go unnoticed even among Christians, but they are important, for they shape the way courts and legislatures and ordinary people think about our law.

What follows is a rough attempt to grapple with those changes at a very general level. Two concepts—rights and equality—are key. Much of the law that governs the relations between the government and its citizens rests on these two concepts. Their meaning thus has a great deal to do with what worldview our legal system fosters. Each also has two quite distinct meanings, one structural and systemic, the other more individualistic. Over the course of the past two generations, there has been a gradual shift in the way in which legal theory approaches both rights and equality, a shift toward greater individualism. This presents a curious contrast: In a time when the size of government has grown dramatically, the dominant legal ideology has moved farther away from communitarian thinking toward a greater focus on individual entitlements. But though curious, the shift is real. It is also, in my view, hostile to Christian principles.

RIGHTS

It is best to start with what rights are, and why they might be a problem for Christians. For my purposes, rights may be defined as entitlements to choose a course of action free from government interference. This is not the only sense in which the word is used. People often speak of having a right to recover damages for some wrong done to them by others. For example, my neighbor has a right to some of my money if, when mowing my lawn, I carelessly run the lawn mower over his prize roses. Rights in this sense—entitlements to relief from harm done wrongfully—seem unproblematic, and for a fairly simple reason: The right is necessarily coupled with an obligation. My neighbor's right to recover damages is based on my wrongful behavior; that is, I must pay for the harm done to him because I breached my obligation to take reasonable care—to take account of his interest in preserving his rose bushes.[2] Not only are rights in this sense always coupled with obligations, but the same people both hold the rights and owe the obligations. I am obliged to take care not to harm my neighbor's rose bushes, but so too is he obliged to take care not to injure my tulips. He has a right to recover damages if I breach my obligation, and I have the same right if he breaches his obligation.

The picture is quite different when one turns to rights that arise in disputes between the government and individual citizens. Here, there are no reciprocal obligations directly tied to the entitlement. It is my right to say what I wish to say about our political leaders, and they may in no way punish me for criticizing them. I have no legal duty to temper my criticisms with mercy or even good sense, and our leaders have no obligation to respond in any way to my complaints. Every citizen has the right to be free from intrusions by the police into his home, absent probable cause to believe evidence of a crime will be found there. But citizens have no legal duty to report crimes to the police or otherwise assist the work of law enforcement, nor does the government have any enforceable obligation to give us good police protection or to search vigorously when they do have probable cause. Rights against the government are generally freestanding entitlements to be left alone—to take some action (or not) without fear of official punishment. They are not coupled with duties, either for the government or for the right-holders.

To put it differently, rights protect choice. Those who defend legal abortion have been criticized for calling themselves "pro-choice," but their terminology is both correct and revealing. The right to abortion is indeed a right to choose—pregnant women are not compelled to abort any more than they are compelled to give birth. It is up to them to decide, and the government cannot dictate their selection. As

Lawrence Friedman notes in his book titled *The Republic of Choice*, this is the nature of almost all rights against the government. The right of free speech is a right to choose what to say, or whether to speak at all. The right to the free exercise of religion entitles rightholders to believe or not, to worship or not, and to decide what or whom to believe in and bow down to.

Rights are thus essentially procedural in nature. The point is not which choice ought to be made, but which decision maker—the individual or the government—ought to make it. Where rights against the government exist, individuals are given a sphere of autonomous decision making within which the government may not disturb them, at least not without a very good reason.[3]

Rights and Christians

This sort of protection seems, on the surface, quite problematic for Christians. The idea of a sphere of autonomous decision making is in serious tension with the idea that there are right decisions and wrong ones. From a Christian perspective, what to say, whom to worship, and whether to abort are not simply matters of individual taste or preference about which the rest of us should have no concern. They are matters of grave spiritual import; questions that have right and wrong answers. Either it is right to assail the character of the local school-board chairman or it is not; worshipping Allah is either a good choice or an evil one. Yet rights forbid society to look to the substance of the choice, focusing instead on the process by which it is reached. A right to choose permits the chooser to opt for sin, and to legitimize the choice simply by announcing that he made it. This would not be a problem if sin were nobody else's business. But Christians cannot easily take that posture. The apostle Paul states that the government exists to punish evildoers, not to protect our spheres of autonomous choice.

Yet if sin is in serious tension with rights, sin is also the best argument for having them. The point of legal regulation, for a Christian, is to limit the ability of sinful men and women to do wrong. But our laws are not divinely administered; the regulators are themselves men and women who live in the shadow of the Fall. Thus, something is needed to regulate the regulators, to limit their ability to do wrong. That is the role that rights play. Sinful people in a position of great power may be tempted to abuse their power. Rights limit the potential for abuse. (Naturally, such limits are necessary even for Christian rulers; Christians, of all people, ought to be aware of the extent of their own sin.)

It is thus possible to see rights not as something to which individual citizens are entitled (and whose exercise is thus out of the bounds of proper public debate) but as limits on the potential abuses of sinful governors. On this view, people have rights not because they deserve them nor because their choices should not be subject to any outside evaluation or censure but solely because without rights the government might do grave harm. Granting a right, or upholding the claim of a right-holder, in no way validates the choice in question. Rather, the idea is that some evils are tolerated for the sake of preventing still greater evils.

Of course, this view of rights as limits has an important corollary: The existence and scope of any particular right ought to be determined by the potential for harm from wrongful government action balanced against the likely gain from proper government regulation. The possibility of government error is not enough to invalidate all government; the point of rights must be to protect against the worst kinds of harms.

A great deal follows from this shift in perspective from protecting right-holders to limiting government. Consider two modern free-speech issues: the question whether to forbid the production and sale of pornography, and the question whether to bar so-called hate speech, speech that is insulting to members of particular groups. The pornography issue becomes relatively easy. The usual attack on censorship is that it interferes with the individual's entitlement to read and watch what he wishes. In the context of pornography, this is obviously problematic for the Christian who recognizes that books and movies, like the rest of life, have their share of evil (and perhaps more dangerous evil at that). But in a world of rights as entitlements, the Christian response is illegitimate: One cannot respond to an assertion of a right to choose by saying that the choice in question is wrong; the whole point is that the chooser gets to decide what is right and what is wrong. This problem disappears, however, if the right of free speech derives from a need to police official oppression rather than from a desire to protect people's choices. The question becomes whether the harm from bad government censorship outweighs the gain from good censorship.

We should not underestimate the harm in this balance. There is no doubt that some paintings or books that we might regard as uplifting and valuable contributions to the culture would have been condemned as pornographic by Christians of some times and places; indeed, such disagreements exist among Christians in our own society today. These disagreements prove that the possibility of error is substantial even among decision makers with a common moral baseline. Books like Joyce's *Ulysses* or Whitman's *Leaves of Grass* may indeed be banned under a regime that allows censorship of sexually explicit material (as they were). But we should not overstate the harm either. Whether one looks to highbrow literature or the popular culture, a comparison of late twentieth-century America with, say, midnineteenth- century Britain—a society with a great deal of censorship—hardly makes the case for the proposition that censorship causes grave social injury. And suppression of some kinds of artistic expression does not seriously risk suppression of political dissent; a number of societies (including our own not so long ago) have had the former without the latter.[4] On the other side of the scale, even the secular media are beginning to acknowledge the possibility that a culture that touts sex at every turn and in every setting may promote seriously destructive conduct by its youth (not to mention the effects on adults). Of course, one might weigh the harms and gains differently, and the lines are not easy to draw. But if one begins from essentially Christian premises about morals, it is hard to imagine not permitting a good deal more censorship than our society presently allows.

The hate-speech issue is harder. There, the question is whether the government (or, as the issue typically arises today, state universities) can punish people for saying rude and insulting things about blacks, or Jews, or homosexuals, or perhaps other groups. On the one hand, the argument for regulation is strong. Racial slurs and the like are wrong and stopping them prevents real injury. There is much to be said for insisting on a degree of civility in public communication. But the harm from error is also great, perhaps much greater. A government that may punish speech hurtful to protected groups may find speech hurtful when it is no more than appropriately critical of the established wisdom. Statements that homosexuality is sin have triggered accusations under university hate-speech codes, and speakers may hesitate with good reason before making strident attacks on race-based affirmative action. If such speech is deterred by hate-speech laws or campus codes, the democratic process cannot function effectively, because communication of opposing viewpoints on important issues is suppressed. And it would be naive to trust government officials to draw the necessary lines, since they have a strong self-interest in punishing any speech that is critical of them.

Hate-speech laws thus create the opportunity for serious error, even oppression, by government officials; and that is a fair reason for granting to individuals a right to engage in even rude speech on topics of political concern. Once again, different people may weigh the balance differently, and once again the lines will be hard to draw. (For example, even a society that protects rude speech about politics might draw the line at some forms of profanity in public.) But note what the claim of right is not based on: The argument for protecting the speaker in no way implies that the speaker's conduct is good or right. The argument for protection is structural and consequential in nature; it is focused on the protection of the community, not on any notion of individual entitlement.

Rights and History

The preceding discussion suggests an approach to rights that makes a good deal of sense for Christians. Interestingly enough, it is roughly the same approach that our legal system took for most of our history. The best recent work on the origin of the Bill of Rights, an article by Akhil Amar,[5] argues quite persuasively that the rights contained in the first ten amendments to our Constitution were designed not as a series of individual entitlements, but as structural limitations on a potentially distant and oppressive federal government. This point emerges most clearly from the First Amendment's protection of free speech and press. For at least the past generation, historians and legal scholars have understood that the men who wrote and ratified the First Amendment were prepared to tolerate a good deal of government regulation of speech, even of political speech.[6] The one practice they most clearly wanted to prevent, however, was the use of prior restraints on speech—meaning orders issued by judges or executive officials shutting down newspapers or silencing speakers in advance. Jury trials for sedition might be permissible. Civil and even criminal punishment for libel and slander certainly were permissible; but orders not to print the supposedly seditious or libelous material were not. This line seems odd to us today: One might think that after-the-fact punishment is as big a threat to free speech as before-the-fact injunctions. But after-the-fact punishment could only be meted out with the cooperation of a jury, an institution composed of ordinary people drawn from the community. Prior restraints could be issued solely on the say-so of government officials. Thus, preventing prior restraints, but allowing many other limitations on speech, made sense as a way of ensuring some sort of democratic check (in the form of the jury) on government regulation of speech and of the press.

The same idea—rights as a check on government oppression rather than as protectors of individual choice—may also explain the many procedural rights that the common law and our Constitution gave to criminal defendants. The right to indictment by a grand jury, for example, ensured that the Crown could not bring ordinary citizens to trial on serious charges without the assent of representatives of the broader community. The same is true of the right to be tried by a jury of one's peers, together with the right not to be tried twice for the same offense (meaning that a jury's decision to acquit was absolutely final). These protections were vital in a system, like the one that prevailed in England and the colonies at the time of the Revolution, where treason and sedition were defined broadly to include a great deal of ordinary criticism of those in power. Because of juries and grand juries, the government was unable to convict political or religious dissidents without the cooperation of the citizenry as a whole. The theme holds for other provisions of the Bill of Rights as well. When English judges announced that a man could not be made to answer potentially incriminating questions, they did so in cases where the questions went straight to the defendant's religious or political beliefs.[7] So too, the right to be free of unreasonable searches and seizures of one's home and one's personal papers entered the law in a case where the Crown was seeking to hold a pamphleteer liable for sedition.[8] Of course, one cannot know the judges' motives in these cases; but it seems plausible to suppose that common-law judges of the seventeenth and eighteenth centuries created or expanded rights as a means of throwing obstacles in the path of government officials who sought to punish their religious or political opponents. The rights did not serve to protect individual choice but to protect the community as a whole against sinful officials. Hence the important role of juries and grand juries in the system of common-law rights (a system we inherited through our Bill of Rights): Juries represented not the interests of the defendant, but the interests of the society.

Throughout the first century-and-a-half of our nation's existence, rights continued to play this role. That is one reason why the Bill of Rights lay largely dormant until well into this century. After the furor over the Alien and Sedition Acts,[9] neither the Federal government nor (for the most part) the states tried to criminalize ordinary criticism of political leaders.[10] And by the midnineteenth century, no state sought either to establish an official church or to compel worship. (Because of the First Amendment, the Federal government was disabled from these paths as well.) Later, beginning in the 1930s, some of the provisions of the Bill of Rights were adapted to the purpose of protecting against the conviction of innocent defendants in ordinary criminal cases—again, a basically structural role. But the idea of rights as guardians of individuals' interests in maximizing choice remained essentially absent from the law. That is why, until the 1950s, censorship of artistic speech—books and movies—raised no First Amendment issue. It was generally assumed that the First Amendment protected the community against government officials who might be tempted to perpetuate their power by jailing their opponents. That might sometimes mean protecting unpopular speakers like Socialists or Jehovah's Witnesses, but it did not translate into anything like a general entitlement to choose what to say or write or read.

Rights and Modern Legal Theory

Today the picture is quite different, as the following pair of examples should show. Artistic speech is now thoroughly protected by the First Amendment. As a practical matter, government censorship of written material is completely forbidden, while censorship of pictures and films is limited to the most hard-core sexual content (and typically absent even there). The second example is equally familiar. The most talked-about right of late twentieth-century America is one that focuses not on limiting government but on protecting individual choice. By its very terms, the notion of a right of privacy elevates individual choice over the claims of the community to prevent wrongful conduct. Why has such a dramatic change occurred? A major part of the answer has to do with a change in the underlying concept of rights, a change that has taken place only since the middle of this century.

Consider the two most popular justifications for rights of free speech and religious expression. The first is the notion that such rights are necessary to the proper functioning of the "marketplace of ideas." The market metaphor captures this justification well. The theory is that ideas (and religions) must be allowed to compete freely for public favor, and that good ideas or religions will over time win more "buyers" than bad ones, just as companies that make good cars will rack up bigger sales figures than companies that make lemons. To carry the metaphor further, one might say that command economies do not work any better for speech and religion than they do for food or automobiles. Just as bureaucrats cannot do a good job of deciding what a good car design is (compare the former East Germany's Trabant with a Volkswagen or BMW) or anticipate consumer wants, they cannot tell worthwhile ideas from bad ones or anticipate which ideas or religious expressions will sell well among the general public. Indeed, the theory goes, that is even more true of speech than of products such as automobiles, because there is no such thing as a false idea— ideas have an irreducible element of subjectivity to them, so that certain ones are better for some people than for others.

The second conventional theory of speech and religious rights is that they exist in order to allow people to "express" or "fulfill" themselves. This argument breaks down into three propositions: (1) Man's highest end is self-fulfillment or self-expression; (2) speech, whether it is political or artistic or religious, is the most important means by which people achieve that end; (3) thus, government must avoid regulating speech at all costs, since regulation would have the effect of stifling this process of self-fulfillment, leaving people less fully human than they otherwise might be. Under this theory, speech is protected because it is inherently more valuable than other activities.

These theories have a common thread: the idea that across a wide spectrum of expression, one cannot reliably distinguish truth from error. That is plainly the premise of the marketplace theory—one must leave discipline to the market, since the government will not know which speech to encourage and which speech to punish. It is also the premise of the self-fulfillment theory: That theory assumes that individuals alone can judge what political or religious expression will best fulfill them. It follows that no one can properly say that another's choice of art or religion is wrong or evil; such choices are necessarily subjective. Indeed, such choices become primarily a matter of personal taste that is beyond criticism, much like one's choice of ties or hairstyles.

The justification for the modern right of privacy is similar— consensual transactions between adults that cause no tangible harm to third parties (or at least third parties whose interests count)[11] are nobody else's business. The community's desire to prevent wrong conduct is not a sufficient reason to override the individual's interest in making his or her own choices.

The idea takes its most extreme form in Justice Blackmun's dissent in *Bowers v. Hardwick*, the Supreme Court case that upheld a state's power to punish homosexual sodomy.[12] In *Bowers*, the state argued that it had an interest in regulating private sexual conduct when that conduct was wrong. Blackmun treated the argument as ridiculous; he went so far as to say that moral interests of this sort are illegitimate— that they represent an improper attempt by religious groups to impose their beliefs on the population as a whole.[13] Indeed, Blackmun associated moral arguments with "religious intolerance" and equated the state's argument with arguments based on racial bigotry.[14] Blackmun's position lost in *Bowers*, but the notion that moral claims do not count is a necessary premise for the right to abortion.

Bowers reveals how fully our concept of rights has shifted. Both sides took the issue to be whether individual adults have an absolute entitlement to choose when to have sex and with whom, as long as they do so in their homes. Yet there was a very different, more structural argument available to the claimant in *Bowers*, one that was not pressed. Though Georgia nominally criminalized consensual homosexual relations, at the time *Bowers* arose there had apparently been no prosecutions for such conduct for some time. This raises a serious concern that has nothing to do with privacy. Thousands of Georgia's citizens violated its sodomy statute regularly, and the state had given them no reason to believe that it had any interest in their conduct. Yet, by leaving the sodomy statute on the books, Georgia could *threaten* any of those violators with prosecution, not because of any concern with homosexual sodomy but for other reasons. Rather than standing up for a particular view of sexual morality, Georgia might prefer to keep sodomy a crime in order to extort information or confessions from homosexual suspects or in order to permit local officials to harass political opponents who are homosexual. The point can be generalized. If the state can criminalize conduct it does not really care about, everyone can be made a criminal; and the state can punish whomever it wishes.

This is a real and substantial problem; it suggests that not only sodomy statutes but any statutes that criminalize commonplace conduct should perhaps be invalidated. But the argument has nothing to do with privacy or individual choice. It is rather concerned with protecting the community against sinful leaders. That no one thought to raise this argument in *Bowers* says much about the legal culture's vision of rights.

EQUALITY

If the concept of rights underlies much of the law governing the relationship between rulers and citizens, the concept of equality underlies all law. This poses no difficulty for Christians; one version of an equality principle is necessary if one starts from Christian premises.

But the nature of equality arguments has taken an important shift in recent years. As with rights arguments, the shift has been away from Christian principles.

To see the point, one must first see what is meant by the equality principle, why (like rights) it seems initially problematic for Christians, and why (also like rights) the problem disappears when one considers the pervasiveness of sin. Consider these two simple progressions, using as examples my eight-year-old daughter and my five-year-old son:

Sarah threw a ball in the living room, broke a lamp, and was sent to her room.

Sam threw a ball in the living room and broke a lamp. Sam *should be* sent to his room.

Sarah threw a ball in the living room, broke a lamp, and was sent to her room.

Sam tripped on a box that someone else left sitting on the living room floor. As he fell, he hit a lamp and knocked it over, breaking it. Sam *should not* be sent to his room.

The first example is an instance of the familiar principle, "like cases should be treated alike." Sarah and Sam committed the same wrong in roughly the same circumstances, and their misbehavior caused the same injury. They should therefore receive the same punishment.

The second example is a necessary corollary to the first; relevant differences ought to be taken into account. Sarah again misbehaved (apparently my wife and I should work harder on the no throwing-balls-in-the-house rule) and caused harm, and Sam caused the same harm, but this time Sam's conduct was not wrong. He simply tripped, something that (in my house at any rate) five-year-olds do wholly innocently and with some regularity. He should perhaps have been a little more careful, but plainly should not be punished in the same way as his sister.

This pair of examples is the equality principle in a nutshell.[15] No one—or at least no one with any sense—believes that all lawsuits should be decided in favor of the plaintiff just because some plaintiffs win, or that all criminal defendants should be acquitted because a few are. That is, no one believes in equal legal outcomes for everyone. Results of criminal litigation should depend on what the defendant did, and on what the law defines as a crime. Yet, when two cases are alike, the results should be the same. That, after all, is what equal justice means.

The point goes even farther. The very nature of law requires equal treatment for similarly situated parties. If the results of criminal prosecution do not depend on rules evenly applied—that is, if the equality principle is absent from criminal justice—then they must depend on the whims of the decision maker. That is not law, but discretion, and it is the hallmark of dictatorships.

Equality and Christians

That much seems simple, indeed trite. Yet when one looks at the same idea through a Christian lens, the equality principle seems a good deal more complicated. Consider two stories from the gospel of Matthew. In chapter 20, Jesus tells the story of the laborers in the vineyard who all receive the same wage, though some worked only an hour while others worked the whole day. When the laborers who worked longest complained, the employer answered by saying that they had received what they were promised; the fact that others had been treated with great generosity was, in effect, none of their business (Matt. 20:1–15).

The point of this story is far removed from equality arguments in American law. Yet the story only works as a parable if it works on its own terms—that is, it works only if the employer's response to the workers' claim is fair. (And in Jesus' story, the employer says he is being fair.) Note what that response is: What the workers are entitled to does not depend on what anyone else gets; the measure of their proper payment is absolute, not comparative. In spite of what anyone else received, the worker who worked all day was entitled to one denarius—no more, no less. This entitlement could not be enlarged by payments to others.

The point is sealed, in a negative way, by an even more famous story from chapter 19. When Jesus spoke with the rich young ruler, He told him to sell all his possessions and give them to the poor (Matt. 19:16–22). This command is interesting in part for what is missing: Christ does not say that all His followers, or even all who have great wealth, must sell their goods and give the proceeds away. Elsewhere in the Gospels, Jesus encounters wealthy people (think of the Roman centurion in Matthew 8) and does not command them to dispose of their wealth. Nor is such a directive to be found elsewhere in Scripture. The conclusion seems inescapable: The rich young ruler was asked to bear a cost that at least some others are not asked to bear.

Was Jesus being unjust? Did the owner of the vineyard treat his workers unfairly? The answer is no, for (at least) two distinct reasons. The first, and simplest, is that justice requires that one be treated no worse than one deserves. That much seems clear from the parable of the laborers in the vineyard. Some may be (of those in grace, all are) treated better; and generosity to some does not invalidate the outcomes for others. It follows that comparative claims do not necessarily carry any weight; like-cases-should-be-treated-alike is not a norm that always must be followed. The story of the rich young ruler and the parable of the laborers in the vineyard suggest that if one guilty bank robber is mistakenly acquitted, his equally guilty accomplice cannot claim injustice when he is convicted.

There is, I believe, an even broader sense in which Christians must approach the equality principle with great caution. Divine justice is perfectly individualized. None of us is the same, and hence our treatment by the Father—our opportunities, temptations, roles in the body of Christ—is special and uniquely tailored to us. The metaphor of the body captures the idea well: We each have a place that is like none other's and that no one else can fill. A perfectly just Father knows that place. We do not. Hence, worrying about how my lot stacks up against my neighbor's (except in order to prompt generosity toward my neighbor) is not only wrong, it is silly. My neighbor is not meant to have a life like mine.

The same point holds true when one shifts to legal cases. Return to the simple picture of my daughter and son, both throwing balls in the living room, both breaking lamps. The end of the progression, which we are tempted to accept too quickly, is that both should receive the same treatment—punishment by isolation in their respective rooms for a brief time. But formally equal treatment may not be just at all. After all, my daughter is eight and my son only five; moreover, she is much less naturally impulsive than he. Finally, she does not mind going to her room very much; he cannot stand it. All these things point to quite "different" outcomes for the "same" offense. But different and same are the wrong words to use here, for the reality is that the people, the circumstances, indeed all the things that make up the offenses in question are unique. Perfect justice would treat them that way.

This leads us back to the equality principle. On the one hand, if that principle means that identical cases should be treated identically, it means nothing; no two cases are identical in all relevant respects. The range of relevant circumstances, the number of individual characteristics that bear on the defendant's fault and the victim's injury are limitless; each case, like each person, is different from every other. If, on the other hand, equality means that superficially like cases should be treated alike, it seems wrong, for it requires ignoring relevant circumstances. Should Christians then abandon equality? No, for much the same reason we should not abandon rights. The Divine Will is perfectly individualized and also perfectly just. But our laws are administered by fallen people. The treatment that judges give the defendants who come before them may be individualized if we tell judges to decide each defendant's fate according to all the circumstances. But it will not necessarily be just. If we vest too much discretion in the hands of judges and other officials, we might reasonably worry about what factors cause them to be lenient and what factors lead them to be strict. Rough equality—treating superficially like cases alike—may be the closest to justice that we can come.

Imagine, for example, a town that makes spitting on the sidewalk a misdemeanor punishable by up to a week in the local jail. Imagine further that in the past five years, there have been fifty prosecutions for this low-level offense and all fifty defendants were black. The town is three-fourths white. It may be that the white residents of this hypothetical town do not spit, but that seems unlikely. The more plausible explanation is that the government is nominally criminalizing spitting on the sidewalk but is actually punishing something else—something associated with being black. If officials really cared about spitting on the sidewalk, there would likely be at least an occasional white defendant in the mix.

But while comparisons to other cases may reveal hidden injustice, they may reveal nothing worse than the parable of the laborers in the vineyard. Take two rapists, one with the money to hire the best lawyer in town, the second forced to take a mediocre court-appointed attorney. The first rapist's lawyer recognizes that the police search that uncovered the critical evidence was conducted without a warrant. The lawyer moves to suppress the evidence, the motion wins, and the prosecution drops the charges because there is not enough evidence left to convict. The second rapist has a similar claim available, but his lawyer does not make it, perhaps because he is ignorant of the law of search and seizure. The case goes to trial, and the second rapist is convicted.[16] There is obvious inequality here. But the second rapist has no just claim entitling him to relief solely because his more fortunate counterpart received a windfall. The only reason for giving either defendant a claim to suppress evidence is to send the police a message—get a warrant when you search a home. It may not be necessary to suppress evidence in every case where the police violate the law in order to send that message. An occasional slap may do a reasonably good job of deterring police misbehavior. It follows that we should not be troubled just because a few guilty defendants are convicted when they could have been acquitted with better defense lawyers. The second rapist, after all, seems clearly to be getting no more than his just deserts.

Note the difference between these examples. With the second rapist, it is possible (indeed, easy) to know whether conviction is just without reference to how any other cases were decided. Rape is a serious wrong of the sort that any decent society would punish. But spitting on the sidewalk is not so easy a call; it is hard to say what the right outcome is in the abstract. So too, it is not obvious what the right sentence for a given narcotics offense is. Comparisons seem helpful, even essential, to determining what any given defendant deserves. And the comparison might reveal the possibility of real misconduct by the government. The unifying theme in these examples is that equality is not an end in itself, but a means to an end, a tool for avoiding excessive official discretion and for spotting government misbehavior. Seen in this way, equality arguments play the same structural role that right arguments traditionally have played. It is a role that Christians should find appealing.

Equality and History

Modern-style equality arguments were simply absent from the legal culture of two centuries ago. The equality principle was protected, to be sure. The common-law process itself ensured that judges would aim for consistency, i.e., equality, by forcing them to square their decisions in the cases before them with past decisions in similar cases. But this protection was only partial; it left two important gaps.

First, governments were free to create arbitrary legal distinctions among their citizens. The most obvious example was race—not only were blacks enslaved in much of the United States, they were denied many legal protections in the supposedly free states of the North. This kind of direct legal inequality was widespread. Second, even where laws were nominally equal, the government could simply refuse to enforce the law for some classes of citizens. After the Civil War, this was precisely the behavior that prompted the Ku Klux Klan Act that required state governments to protect the rights of black citizens in the same manner as it protected the rights of whites. Both phenomena blatantly violate the like-cases-should-be-treated-alike principle, for blacks and whites are not obviously different in ways relevant to their need for basic legal protection. For the same reason, both phenomena amount to government oppression of the sort that a structural equality-principle ought to condemn.

That is what the Fourteenth Amendment, with its guarantee of equal protection of the laws, aimed to do. The two sets of events that prompted the Fourteenth Amendment were the Black Codes passed by many Southern states and the tacit cooperation of southern governments with crimes committed against newly freed blacks. The Black Codes were directly discriminatory—they simply abolished ordinary legal protections for blacks—while the actions of local law-enforcement officials were more subtly discriminatory; the law remained nominally equal, but crimes against blacks went unpunished. The Fourteenth Amendment sought to eliminate both kinds of government misconduct.[17]

It is possible to see this guarantee of equality as a kind of individual entitlement—a right given to black citizens to be treated the same as whites. But it is equally possible to see it not as an individual-centered entitlement but as a structural limitation on government. The conduct that the Fourteenth Amendment aimed to confront was oppressive government; just as a structural-equality principle would prevent the government from criminalizing spitting on the sidewalk and then prosecuting only blacks, the same kind of principle could easily justify requiring the government to eliminate laws and customs that treated blacks and whites differently for no reason save prejudice.

Sadly, this protection against government misbehavior largely passed from the law beginning in the late nineteenth century. Both official and unofficial race discrimination were legally tolerated, and the Fourteenth Amendment was deemed consistent with a system that resembled South African apartheid. Entering the 1950s, our legal system guarded the equality principle in essentially the same manner as English common law: The rule of law led courts to strive for consistency, but little effort was made to prevent either unjust discriminatory laws or unjustly discriminatory enforcement of fair laws.

To put it another way, our law traditionally respected the equality principle by placing great importance on precedent and consistency in legal doctrine. But race was a blind spot. Throughout the legal system, blacks and whites were treated differently, either through formal law or informal custom. These differences were not the result of relevant factors; they did not stem from any effort to do individualized justice. Instead, they flowed largely from the premise, usually unspoken but sometimes horribly explicit, that some of those made in the Father's image are worth less than others.

Equality and Modern Legal Theory

This blind spot is the starting point for modern legal theory about equality. The one proposition that everyone in the legal system accepts today is that institutionalized race discrimination is wrong. The intellectual battle is about why.

One answer is the kind of structural equality argument discussed above. When a (white) majority gives its children the opportunity to go to good colleges, such opportunity is probably a good thing for all children. Denying black children the same opportunity is thus denying them something they ought to have—not just because white children have it, but because it is good. This does not suggest an individual entitlement to equal treatment but rather a social obligation to fair treatment for all citizens.

This is the view of equality that the law takes, for the most part. For example, current constitutional law holds that those who claim that the government has discriminated against them on account of race must show that the discrimination was intentional—not the accidental by-product of circumstances. Many government policies have different effects on blacks and whites (or on Asians and Latinos). Those different effects do not necessarily show that any injustice has been done; a host of circumstances can lead, quite innocently, to statistical disparities between different groups. On the other hand, in cases where, say, government officials intended to disadvantage blacks, the strong likelihood is that injustice was done. When the majority denies to some what it provides for itself, we ought always to be suspicious.

A quite different possibility is that race discrimination is wrong simply because all citizens are entitled to equal treatment—that whenever two like cases are not treated alike, the litigant who is treated worse has been done an injustice. This idea is common among legal academics and has made some inroads in the legal doctrine. Recall the example of the two rapists, one of whom is let off because his attorney made a prompt motion to suppress incriminating evidence while the other is convicted because his attorney neglected to make a similar motion. Current law holds that the second rapist wins— that a defendant is entitled to relief if his lawyer's incompetence affected the result of his criminal trial, even if there is no doubt about the defendant's guilt. The rationale for this rule is equality as entitlement: The wealthy defendant who hired a better lawyer won his case, so the poor defendant is "entitled" to the same treatment. Note the necessary premise: It does not matter what the just outcome in the poor defendant's case is; justice is measured comparatively by how the poor defendant's case stacks up against his counterparts. This is equality as an individual right, not as a tool for remedying injustice.

A more common example of equality as entitlement is the current rage of reverse-discrimination claims. In most places, in the hiring of police officers or fire fighters or in the admission of freshmen into state universities, blacks are given a substantial edge over whites. This means that black applicants may be hired or admitted with worse paper credentials or test scores than some white applicants, who are rejected. These schemes are often challenged in court by whites who claim that they have been subjected to unconstitutional race discrimination. The challenges are increasingly successful. This trend makes perfect sense if we are all entitled to equal treatment, if like-cases-should-be-treated-alike is a right. After all, white plaintiffs in reverse discrimination cases can point to others who were treated differently for a reason that seems irrelevant to their ability to do the job (or for college admissions, the academic work).

But the inequality in these cases does not necessarily amount to injustice. When a mostly white society treats black college applicants worse than white ones, the majority is giving opportunities to its children that it denies to others. A fair inference is that the opportunities are good and right; they ought to be given to everyone. So-called reverse discrimination is something quite different: The majority is denying opportunities to its own children in order to give them to children of a group that has long suffered at the majority's hands. This may not be unjust at all. Affirmative action as practiced in America today may have its problems. As one who has been actively involved in the law-school hiring process, I have my qualms about it. Still, it is not true that any fair-minded person would necessarily think it a bad thing. After all, there is something noble about a majority giving a minority good things the majority does not give itself. Seeing the issue in terms of entitlements only distorts the picture. It would be better to look at the effects on the community as a whole, to see whether affirmative action is in fact helping its intended beneficiaries at acceptable social cost. That is surely preferable to the casual presumption that I am entitled to whatever my (black) neighbor gets.

CONCLUSION

The progression with respect to these two foundational concepts, both intellectual and historical, is not quite the same. Most obviously, it is hard to argue that we ought to return to our former vision of equality when that vision so easily tolerated the oppression of blacks. A certain degree of nostalgia for an older vision of rights, however, might be appropriate. Then too, the change in our legal culture's approach to rights seems quite powerful, at least to one who inhabits the world of law schools. The change in approach to equality is much more subtle, indeed mostly unconscious, and has to date had much less effect on the law itself.

Yet, while there are important differences, there are some common threads. The fighting issue in many disparate areas of law, areas having to do with either legal rights or arguments about equality, is whether we ought to give broad scope to claims of individual entitlement, claims that a certain outcome or an ability to make a certain choice is my *right*—not subject to regulation by a society that might view that outcome or choice as wrong. This view, the notion that results are good if they promote choice or look fair compared to other results, necessarily undermines the ability of a society to define the good by defining those norms of behavior to which decent people should adhere. Entitlements are radically relativist, for they deny the relevance of any constant standard, and whether one looks at the legal culture's view of rights or its vision of equality, the trend is toward more and more entitlement-based thinking.

The second common thread is less obvious, perhaps especially to

Christians. Our inclination when it comes to public issues is to make a moral judgment and stick with it. If rude, hateful speech is wrong, then we ought to see to it that people do not engage in that sort of conduct. So too with homosexual conduct; if it is sin, it ought to be prohibited; and so we should seek to preserve the criminalization of such behavior. But when one looks at the twin problems of rights and equality through a Christian lens, one quickly discovers that crafting good law is not so simple. The reality of sin, both in the citizenry and in those who govern it, demands a more consequentialist approach. Adultery is indeed wrong, but it is such a pervasive wrong that no state makes any systematic effort to punish it any more. In these circumstances, keeping the crime on the books creates the potential for genuine evil on the part of police or prosecutors who want to punish not adultery but something else. The idea applies equally to hate speech, or homosexuality, or a range of other types of conduct that may be quite wrong, and yet might also be best left unregulated in order to prevent government misconduct.

Christians ought to be more willing to engage in this kind of structural thinking about law and government. The pervasiveness of sin makes some government enforcement of morals essential. But the pervasiveness of sin also makes it essential that we regulate the regulators—that we pay attention to the ways in which rulers can manipulate the rules. Our advantage in public discourse is precisely our understanding of sin and the hold it has on people's day-to-day conduct. That understanding should lead us to be skeptical of quick conclusions based on surface appearances; at the same time it should make us amenable to structural, consequentialist arguments that look to the ways in which rulers and ruled alike might try to take advantage of different kinds of legal doctrine. (And, most clearly, it should make us wary of undue optimism about the curative powers of the law.) In our effort to promote morals in the public square—a noble effort in a society where moral argument is increasingly frowned on—we may be too quick to abandon the hard business of advocating rules that seek to minimize the effects of sin in both the citizenry *and* the government.

This task is important precisely because of the magnitude of the problem to which it responds. Throughout this essay, I have been discussing arguments mostly in the context of constitutional law— the body of law that defines what the government cannot do. Yet the arguments themselves go much farther. Thinking about abortion in terms of the individual's right to choose removes the question of justice, of right and wrong, from the table. That leads naturally to a mind-set that calls into question any government policy that starts from the premise that some conduct is right and some wrong. Such policies are thought to be intolerant and oppressive, because they presume to decide a question that individuals are entitled to decide for themselves. This is not a view that any large segment of the population held fifty years ago. It is surely no coincidence that the change in our vision of rights has accompanied a similar change in our willingness to make collective moral judgments.

So too, thinking about race discrimination in terms of individual entitlements to equal treatment makes justice relative rather than absolute. Thus, if my neighbor is better off than I, something is wrong, and I am entitled to feel aggrieved. This way of looking at the world discourages responsibility (because it does not look to whether I deserve what I have gotten) and promotes envy (because it focuses on whether my lot is as good as others'). Of course, irresponsibility and envy have played a large role in law and life ever since the Fall. But one does not have to be mindlessly nostalgic to believe that our law and our politics are less oriented toward the broader interests of the community than they once were. Our changing view of equality may have something to do with that.

The source of the problem is the same in both instances. Rights as entitlements measures justice by whatever choices please me. Equality as entitlement measures it by comparison with what my neighbor gets. This gets it exactly backward. Our conduct ought to be measured by a standard external to ourselves, to combat our natural tendency to excuse whatever we wish to do. And the material opportunities and outcomes of our life ought to be measured primarily by an individual standard—by whether we have done at least as well as we deserve—to combat our tendency toward envy. Both points rest on the reality of sin. Entitlement-based thinking about law flows naturally out of a world view that sees people as essentially good, as corrupted only by corrupt institutions. An understanding of sin leads, equally naturally, to abandonment of entitlements, to a focus on justice and community rather than on rights and comparisons.

This is not a problem that is restricted to political liberals; consider the prevalence of reverse-discrimination claims, or the growing attention paid by judges and politicians to property rights. Nor is it a problem for non-Christians alone. We seek after our entitlements as well; consider the recent growth of groups whose prime goal is to enlarge the First Amendment rights of religious speech. All of us— Christians and non-Christians alike—need to think about law and politics in terms of justice for individuals and the welfare of the community. Such a change would have significant effects on some important areas of constitutional law. It would have even greater and more beneficial effects on our society's politics and its culture.

NOTES

1. I thank Barbara Armacost, John Hart Ely, and Michael Klarman for helpful comments on an earlier draft.

2. This form of right is thus consistent with—perhaps compelled by—the Golden Rule: People are required to treat the interests of others as of equal importance to their own interests. When they breach that obligation and cause tangible injury to persons or property, they must pay for the damage. That principle is the heart of the common law of tort, and it is quite thoroughly Christian in character.

3. This last qualifier is of some significance, and I want to return to it below. No rights are absolute, in the sense that the right-holder can make any choice he wishes, come what may, and the government cannot interfere. Rights of free speech are constrained by defamation law, for example, and the freedom of religion does not encompass human sacrifice. Still, for now it is enough to note that within broad bounds, a right gives the right-holder the ability to choose from a range of options without fear of official punishment or reprisal.

4. Any regime that permits censorship of artistic speech but not political speech must distinguish the two and that task is surely difficult in some cases. Still, given our own extensive experience with censorship of books and movies, it seems hard to imagine that, say, obscenity law could become a vehicle for across-the-board suppression of political dissent. Even on issues like the regulation of sexual conduct, it is easy to send a strong political message without being even arguably pornographic.

5. Akhil R. Amar, "The Bill of Rights as a Constitution," *Yale Law Journal* 100 (1991): 1131.

6. This has been understood, at least, since the publication of Leonard W. Levy, *Legacy of Suppression: Freedom of Speech and Press in Early American History* (1960). Levy updated and somewhat moderated his claims in   (1985). However, the essential point—that the framers of the Constitution accepted a degree of regulation of speech that we would today consider plainly excessive and impermissible—remains solid.

7. See Leonard W. Levy, *Origins of the Fifth Amendment* (1968).

8. The case is *Entick v Carrington*, 19 Howell's State Trials 1029 (1765).

9. The Alien and Sedition Acts were passed by a Federalist Congress during the administration of John Adams; they were then used to criminalize a good deal of straightforward political dissent. The Acts were repealed after Thomas Jefferson took office.

10. There are two important exceptions to the statement: Some Southern states effectively criminalized antislavery speech during the Civil War, and during that war, the Lincoln administration jailed a number of political opponents, particularly in the border states.

11. The interests of fetuses do not count, at least for most purposes.
12. 478 U.S. 186 (1986).
13. Ibid., 211–12 (J. Blackmun, dissenting).
14. Ibid., 212.
15. See Peter Westen, "The Empty Idea of Equality," *Harvard Law Review* 95 (1982): 537, for the best discussion. Obviously, equality can mean different things in different settings. In political discourse, it often refers to efforts to redress imbalances in the distribution of wealth or income. In law, the meaning I am using in the text—treat like cases alike, and exclude irrelevant factors (the chief example in our own law being race)—is more common.
16. The hypothetical is based on *Kimmelman v. Morrison*, 477 U.S. 365 (1986), in which the second rapist won his case.
17. That is not to say the Fourteenth Amendment did nothing else. There is a lively debate, far from resolved, about what its framers meant to accomplish by this most important of the post-Civil War amendments. But all sides agree that the core of the amendment was designed to ensure the constitutionality of recently passed civil-rights legislation, and that that legislation was in turn designed to confront both the Black Codes and the cooperation of southern officials with private violence against blacks.

TEN

Mission and Civil Law

Arthur F. Glasser

HOW DOES THE MISSION of the Church relate to civil law? Does it mean that a benevolent Caesar will welcome expatriates into his country and promise to protect "their rights" as they seek to persuade his people to change their religious allegiance?

In considering this question, one should reflect on what has been called the "Devil's Great Commission." The details are familiar. In the gospel of Matthew we learn that on the Sabbath following the crucifixion of Jesus, a delegation of chief priests and Pharisees went to Pilate with the request:

> Sir, we remember how that impostor said, while he was still alive, "After three days I will rise again!" Therefore order the sepulchre to be made secure until the third day, lest his disciples go and steal him away, and tell the people: "He has risen from the dead," and the last fraud will be worse than the first (Matt. 27:63–64).

Pilate readily agreed. He had no desire to have a religious riot on his hands. The record states that the authorities "went and made the sepulchre secure by sealing the stone and setting a guard" (v. 66).

But the resurrection of Jesus completely frustrated all plans. The great earthquake, the rolling back of the stone, the emptiness of the tomb, and the appearance of an angel of the Lord—all these overwhelmed the guards, and they "became like dead men" (Matt. 28:2–4). Upon recovering, they ran into the city and told the chief priests all that had taken place. An assembly was hastily convened and counsel was taken. The record then states that the Sanhedrin gave a sum of money to the soldiers and said, "Tell people, 'His disciples came by night and stole him away while we were asleep.' And if this comes to the Governor's ears, we will satisfy him and keep you out of trouble" (Matt. 28:13–14).

We all readily grasp the substance of the Devil's great commission: Proclaim that Jesus remains dead; his body was merely stolen. Behind this large lie was a "large sum of money" (money talks). Indeed, the "money itch" is such that "men can be bribed to hide the truth and spread an untruth, as modern propaganda well proves."[1] The political establishment could also be counted on to support this deliberate deception. In the end the soldiers proved obedient. The lie was widely propagated, and among the Jewish people this explanation of the empty tomb was widely accepted (vv. 14–15). It still is!

So much for civil law in the first century protecting the religious liberty of Rome's subjects. Actually, this pattern of Caesar as no friend of Jesus Christ has largely characterized the long history of the worldwide expansion of the Christian movement. In the Gospels, Jesus warned his disciples:

> They will deliver you up to tribulation, and put you to death; and you will be hated by all nations for my name's sake (Matt. 24:9).

> You will be delivered up to councils, beaten in synagogues, and you will stand before governors and kings . . . to bear testimony before them (Mark 13:9).

It is not without reason that the apostle Paul later affirmed that the ongoing of the Gospel to the nations would only become possible through individual Christians "completing what is lacking in Christ's afflictions for the sake of his body, that is the church" (Col. 1:24; Phil. 1:29–30). The China Inland Mission, in whose ranks my wife and I served (1946–1951), lost more than a hundred of its missionaries to mob violence during its eighty-six years of effort to plant the church in China.

Even so, there is considerable relevance to the subject before us: the worldwide mission of the church and its relation to civil law. To this we turn.

FOCUS: CHURCH AND SYNAGOGUE

This topic needs a focus so that its exploration will not end in a host of generalities of little practical benefit to the worldwide Christian movement. Hence, the attempt of the author is to develop this chapter from the perspective of the church in her missionary encounter with the synagogue. Through this procedure we can derive specific principles that can be related to the growing complexity of mission and civil law throughout the world today.

But this choice of focus demands a brief digression. The terms "church" and "synagogue" are notoriously difficult to define because of the broad areas covered by their current usage. The concern is not with cultural Judaism or cultural Christianity, with differences in ethnicity or tradition, with the accident of birth that largely determines in which building one worships. Rather the concern is theological and missiological. The focus must be on the essential issue that is present when the church faces the synagogue, or rather when the Christian Jew or Gentile who is *in* Christ faces the Jewish person who is *without* Christ. According to rabbinic Judaism, Jews save themselves. In sharpest contrast, the Bible witnesses to the reality of those Jews and Gentiles who have been to the cross, have become conscious of their need for forgiveness and cleansing, and have found this need met in the Savior. It was this contrast that particularly burdened the apostle Paul (Rom. 9:1–3; 10:1–3).

Jews and regenerated Christians differ fundamentally over the knowledge of God and of themselves before God. Because of this, "synagogue" represents human religious activity—whether Jewish or Christian, i.e., rabbinic Judaism or liberal Christianity.[2] In contrast, biblical Christianity seeks to represent Jesus Christ as God's response to human bankruptcy. Evangelicals contend that if rabbinic Judaism can manage without Jesus Christ, so can liberal churches, and so can ethnic faiths and world religions.

Nothing so tests the loyalty of evangelical Christians—to Jesus Christ and to His mission to the nations—as their commitment to Jewish evangelism. Hence, before we can explore the issue of mission and civil law, we must identify the mandate behind the missionary impulse. According to the Gospels this mandate is patently clear. The followers of Jesus Christ are to "make disciples of all nations" (Matt. 28:19). The Gospel is "to the Jew first and also to the Greek" (Rom. 1:16). Admittedly, this is a most difficult and demanding task. Most Christians who engage in mission shrink from the tension of hostile, personal encounters that evangelistic work often precipitates. Furthermore, many missionaries will candidly admit that they do not feel themselves particularly adept at pressing the claims of Christ on those to whom He is a total stranger. In the final analysis, those who seek to evangelize others will readily confess that they do so because Christ has commanded them to do so. They believe that it is the essence of the Church to seek the reconciliation of the human race to God (2 Cor. 5:16–21). Despite all the problems inherent in mission, one overarching reality must be affirmed: Mission is nothing less than obedience to God through involvement with him in his mission to the nations.

CASE STUDY

I first became aware of the complexities of mission and civil law through an encounter with a Jewish official on the streets of Manhattan in the fall of 1940. At the time I was both a seminary student and an informal agent (weekends and throughout the summer of 1941) of the New York Bible Society. A woman had given the society a generous donation with the expressed wish that it be devoted to the Jewish people. This resulted in the production of thousands of copies of a special issue of the gospel of Matthew. It was the venturesomeness of youth that pressed me to offer to distribute these gospels, and to do so in a responsible fashion. Fortunately, I had a mature Christian companion, and the two of us spent hours during those long weekends and summer months contacting Jewish people with a friendly greeting and then asking the question: "Have you ever read the life of Jesus by a Jew who knew him?" On this particular occasion a small crowd of Jewish people gathered around me, and we had what appeared to be the beginning of another one of those public wrangles that we occasionally, though unwittingly, precipitated.

It all began when a well dressed, older Jewish gentleman came forward and in a civil fashion challenged me: "Is it right for you to come into our midst and do what you are doing?" Before I could compose a responsible reply he added, as far as I can recall, the following:

> I am the leader of a Jewish social organization. One of my particular responsibilities is to contact Jewish homes in which their sons and daughters have come under the influence of people like you. They have broken with our Jewish heritage and our Jewish religion, and most painfully have brought anguish and a sense of shame to their parents and family. I ask then, is it right for you to do this and thereby bring all manner of trouble to our community? Hitler is destroying our bodies, but isn't what you are doing even more destructive? Is it right for you to seek to destroy our souls and the social cohesion of our people?

What could I say by way of reply? It so happened that the crowd took up this challenge, and soon I was hearing all sorts of voices pressing me for an answer: "Is it right that you do to us what you are doing?" Fortunately, my associate across the street saw the crowd close in upon me, heard their cries, and came to my rescue.

He came to the edge of the crowd and listened. Since he was considerably older than I, and rather impressive in appearance, the crowd opened to him, and he soon faced the Jewish leader. The crowd became silent. He graciously identified with me and then answered the leader's question in the following fashion:

> Friend, you have asked whether it is right for Christians deliberately to come among your people with the specific intent of sharing the Christian Scriptures with them, knowing full well the disruption this may provoke in Jewish families. Let me ask you a question: Was it right for God to call Father Abraham from Ur of the Chaldeans and disrupt his family in the process? You will recall that he said: "Go from your country and your kindred and your father's house to the land that I will show you" (Gen. 12:1). Was it right for him to demand this, knowing full well the anguish of social dislocation this would precipitate?

You can be sure that this identification of our work with the will of God provoked an uproar. Did we not know that the Abram whom God called out of Ur of the Chaldeans was an idolatrous Aramean? Were we unaware that the Jewish people today know all about God? On and on. My friend would not draw back. He pressed on and spoke of the desire of God to have personal relationship with his people, the descendants of Abraham, Isaac, and Jacob. Did they not know that this was why he sent them prophet after prophet to call them to personal faith and to vital contact with himself?

We shall return to this incident later. Suffice it to say, involvement in the Christian mission is nothing less than a way of expressing one's obedience to Jesus Christ. No opposition—human or demonic—has the right to oppose the mission of God's people. When confronted by such opposition from the Jewish authorities in their day, the apostles could only affirm: "Whether it is right in the sight of God to listen to you rather than to God, you must judge; for we cannot but speak of what we have seen and heard" (Acts 4:19).

So then, missionary obedience is an expression of one's obedience to Christ. And it is particularly tragic to find increasingly in Protestant churches a turning away from the God-given mandate to evangelize the Jewish people. A case in point would be the paper, "A Theological Understanding of the Relationship between Christians and Jews" (submitted to the 199th General Assembly [1987] of the Presbyterian Church [U.S.A.]). Its drift is to encourage dialogue with the Jewish people and discourage evangelism (denigrated as "proselytism"). The following sentence is representative: "Proselytism by Christians, seeking to persuade, even convert, Jews often implies a negative judgment on Jewish faith."[3] Commenting on this, Frederick Dale Bruner states: "To arrogate Jesus to ourselves seems to many of us to be an arrogation of arrogance and to be itself a form of anti-Semitism. Jesus belongs to the Jewish people first of all (Rom. 1:16); He deserves them; and in their depths, they (like all others) need him."[4]

There was a time when the World Council of Churches was unambiguously explicit in its endorsement of this obligation. In 1988 the WCC published *The Theology of the Churches and the Jewish People*, in which it recorded all statements made by member churches on Jewish issues from 1948 onward.[5] In 1948 when the WCC was formed, it was confidently affirmed: "All of our churches stand under the commission of our common Lord. . . . The fulfillment of this commission requires that we include the Jewish people in our evangelistic task."[6]

However, in 1988—forty years later—the leaders of the WCC spoke differently. The next to the last page of this volume contains the curious admission that although Christianity and Rabbinic Judaism are "distinctly different religions," God apparently approves of both. Then on the last page we read that the "next step may be to proscribe all proselytism of Jews on the theological ground that it is rejection of Israel's valid covenant with God."[7] Not only can evangelicals be counted on to challenge this flawed understanding of God's covenant with Israel on biblical grounds, they will also resist this threatened curtailment of their religious liberty. And they will be dismayed at this disregard for Christ's lordship.

MISSION AND BIBLICAL ETHICS

It is rather significant that Christ has not merely given us the Great Commission. If so, unprincipled Christians might feel free to utilize every means, every argument, and every type of persuasion to cause people to change their religious allegiance. This would be to violate the high regard God has for human beings—the people whom He has created and to whom He has imparted His own likeness. Furthermore, unethical conduct of any sort carried out in His name to further His redemptive purpose would violate what He is in essence. So then, as civil law has the function of protecting the legitimacy of a person's fundamental rights, so God's ethical guidelines revealed by precept and apostolic example, have the purpose of shaping the manner in which His people are to carry out their mission to the nations.

These guidelines are as imperative as the mission task itself. God is very jealous for His name. The Old Testament is replete with the record of God working mightily through His servants when their lives and service reflected His nature and submission to His will. They were enabled to further His purpose for Israel in ways that gained even the reluctant approbation of those who did not confess His name. Conversely, when His servants failed to conduct themselves in an ethical and law-abiding manner, He made war against them and thereby chastened them grievously.

Admittedly, mission of necessity involves encounter and persuasion; but for encounter to be effective, it demands grace. One can utilize the powers of persuasion in an offensive manner. People can be exploited through abusing the truth that should lead to repentance and faith. Truth can be distorted or deceptively used. Gospel proclamation can utilize symbols and nomenclature falsely and thereby manipulate the unwary. All told, the ethical guidelines God has laid down for His partners-in-mission are fashioned to maintain respect for the dignity of all persons and to protect their freedom of choice. These guidelines were wonderfully embodied in the life and witness of Jesus himself. Indeed, Christ is the great model for the church's missionary obedience. He identified Himself fully with the human race—we call this the Incarnation—and drew men and women, boys and girls into relationship with Himself through His outgoing love and persuasive proclamation of the "good news of the kingdom" (Matt. 24:14). This does not mean that He was not a controversialist. His mission involved almost continuous debate, and His loyalty to truth made Him unafraid of dissenting publicly, often using rather outspoken language—yet always in a fashion compatible with love.[8] And His missioners have no alternative but to express His loyalty to truth and follow His example as courageous and loving missionaries.

Space forbids our exploration of the ethical and social dimensions of this biblical instruction. Needless to say, the apostolic record of missionary service recorded in the Acts and alluded to in the Epistles is replete with the specific ethical guidelines that shaped their activity and paved the way for their "words in season" that drew people to Jesus Christ. The dynamic that empowered their lives and shaped their verbal witness was nothing less than the Holy Spirit. In 2 Corinthians 4:2–7 we learn that they were Christ-centered in their message and Christ-controlled in their lifestyle. They made themselves His bond-servants as they lovingly yet persistently proclaimed the truth of the Gospel to the consciences of those whom they addressed. In 1 Thessalonians 2:3–8 they speak of their experienced freedom from impurity, deception, flattery and greed. The love of God, triumphant in their hearts, enabled them to demonstrate that love in every way to those whom they sought to reach. Gentleness was their hallmark, and God was pleased to use them to fulfill the ministry that He had entrusted to them.

Suffice it to say that if we are to explore in depth the whole matter of mission and civil law, we must particularly take these ethical guidelines to heart. No dimension of the church's worldwide mission is so caricatured and denounced as her efforts to evangelize the Jewish people. We have already referred to the growing mood in most WCC member churches that increasingly regards all efforts to evangelize Jews as utterly unnecessary, if not altogether unwarranted. Furthermore, the Jewish community is relentless in its hostility to the least suggestion that their leaders in the first century were wrong in their response to Jesus Christ and His claims. In their eyes Christianity is nothing but a pious fraud, largely invented by the apostle Paul. Jesus was only a flawed Jew, and His resurrection never happened. The most recent example of this rather classical Jewish thesis is Hyam Maccoby's *The Mythmaker: Paul and the Invention of Christianity.*[9]

For these reasons, those who would obey Jesus Christ and seek to evangelize the Jewish people find themselves and their service the object of misrepresentation and scorn. The media tend to lump them with the activities of minority religious groups and utilize their penchant for prejudicial lingo to destroy any semblance of integrity. Jeremiah S. Gutman gives the party line:

> That which we would destroy, we first label pejoratively: A religion becomes a cult; proselytizing becomes brainwashing; persuasion becomes propaganda; missionaries become subversive agents; retreats, monasteries and convents become prisons; holy ritual becomes bizarre conduct; religious observance becomes aberrant behavior; devotion and meditation become psychopathic trances (1977:210).[10]

Evangelicals are concerned that the truth concerning Jesus Christ—who He is and what He has done—be the issue between themselves and the Jewish people. They want to discuss, for instance, the witness to Jesus in the gospel of John, because its author selected his material to bring people to the conviction "that Jesus is the Christ, the Son of God" (20:30–31). Rarely does this happen. There is almost a wistful longing for what happened among the Jewish people in Berea in apostolic times. Luke tells us that "they received the word with all eagerness, examining the Scriptures daily to see if these things were so" (Acts 17:11). Almost 2,000 years of "Christian anti-Semitism" have heightened Jewish resistance to this biblical witness concerning their Messiah. Because of the wariness with which the Jewish people regard religious dialogue with evangelicals in our day, we do well to heed the surprising advice of Francis of Assisi. It particularly applies to any mission to the Jewish people. He directed: "All the brothers should preach by their deeds." This has been expanded and is expressed widely today in a more contemporary fashion: "Go into all the world and preach the Gospel, and use words if you have to."[11] Of course we must use words, but what is to be stressed is the primacy of living evangelistically in response to our Lord's injunction to let our light so shine before the Jewish people that they may see our good works and give glory to the Father who is in heaven (Matt 5:16). Admittedly, this is not very congenial to the evangelical approach to mission. We do too much talking!

This brings up the issue of civility. We recall the oft-quoted observation of Martin E. Marty when recently asked to define the key problem American religion is currently facing. He said: "The problem is that the civil people are not committed, and the committed people aren't civil."[12] We've all observed this paradox. The more liberal people are, the more tolerant they are toward the free expression of diversity. In contrast, the more passionately people adhere to a particular religious commitment, the greater their tendency toward intolerance. What this means is that those who bear witness to what they regard as the truth are often castigated as implicit totalitarians. Karl Popper in his book *The Open Society* contends: "It is a short step from the confidence which says, 'I am sure' . . . to the tyranny which says, '. . . therefore I must be obeyed.'"[13]

This "short step" has been all too frequently taken by leaders—religious as well as political—down through history. Religious liberty is not a phenomenon that has seen progressive development over the centuries. Again and again, generations of people have suddenly found themselves tormented by intolerant enthusiasms and proletarian movements whose ideologies demand their adherence—or else! The struggle to maintain even elementary societal freedoms must be seen as a constant. There can never be the certainty of permanent success. The lure of new revelations promising societal renewal can mesmerize even those who have long been aware that societies that are seduced by such appeals seem totally unable to tolerate anything approximating full religious liberty, even varieties in religious belief.

Each successive generation must have leaders who have reflected deeply on the great debates in the seventeenth and eighteenth centuries, when men such as William Penn and his contemporaries contended for the ideal that error will be exposed and truth vindicated in any society that grants religious freedom to its members. This issue was foundational to the thinking of the British Parliament when it adopted the Toleration Act of 1686. Admittedly, this Act was flawed and political considerations largely dominated its members when this action was taken. Even so, by their decision to grant religious liberty to non-Anglican Protestants, the act was understood to acknowledge publicly that biblical revelation contained absolute truths that were essential to the well-being of individuals and the just ordering of society. The arena of public debate must ever be kept open. Because it was now accepted that truth will out, the right of free association must be protected by law.[14]

Today the mood is that our open society must reject all absolute truth claims and all the *a priori* assumptions that go with them. This mood largely characterizes nonpracticing Jewry. Attempts to assuage spiritual hunger are confined to such inadequacies as scientific rationalism, pantheistic monism, and secular humanism. And all the while, the Gentiles around them contend that what really counts is "religious experience"—the sort unrelated to anything approximating absolute truth. What people choose to believe is an utterly personal matter. If a particular subjective experience brings one to terms with a sense of one's own individual existence, then it is true for that person, although it might not be the "truth" for anyone else. And what this leads to is a form of tolerance that is "nothing more than a polite acknowledgment of our inability to convert the erroneous, a sign of the lack of religious depth of contemporary religionists."[15]

This rapidly growing form of tolerance is becoming increasingly widespread in mainline Protestantism. It is no longer a matter of the mere toleration of religious pluralism, but the adoption of a thorough-going secular apologetic that we can no longer judge which religion is true and which is false. In other words, absolute truth is not verifiable; the religions merely represent clusters of traditional opinions.

MISSION AND CIVIL LAW

It is inevitable in such a *Zeitgeist* that evangelicals inescapably encounter the issue of mission and civil law. At first glance, all is straightforward. As with our NYC case study above (p. 246), the issue of one's right as a citizen to give free expression to personal religious convictions and the obligations arising from them inevitably clashes with the interests of any segment of society that person seeks to evangelize.

During the period 1947–1951 I was a missionary in Southwest China and witnessed the disintegration of the government of Chiang

Kai-Shek through corruption, uncontrolled inflation, and Communist agitation. It was losing, as the Chinese put it, "The Mandate of Heaven." I also witnessed the period of anarchy that followed when no government existed. Then followed the euphoria that came to the people when the People's Republic began to extend its no-nonsense power over the nation. During this whole period I was occasionally asked the question: "Is there religious liberty in the Soviet Union?" My answer invariably began with a question: "What do you mean by 'religious liberty'?" I wanted our conversation to focus on the freedom we all have deep in our hearts to believe whatever we choose to believe. This inevitably brought the Gospel into the discussion. But when called back to the issue of religious liberty in the USSR I would speak of the long history of Christianity there and the probability that many of its citizens in their hearts knew about Jesus Christ and believed on him. On the other hand, I would state that the resources of the nation were behind official efforts to promote anti-religious propaganda. In contrast I would conclude by stating that I did not believe Christians in the USSR had the legal right to publish literature, distribute it publicly from house to house, conduct open-air or private meetings, or engage in various forms of worship and evangelistic outreach. Although the Communist party granted the people what was termed "religious liberty," the absence of civil laws protecting this liberty was quite apparent. Significantly, the state security police in Kunming got wind of my answers and cross-examined me on them when the issue was whether I should be granted an exit visa.

The U. S. Declaration of Independence (1776) establishes the issue of religious liberty on the postulate that all people are created equal by God. This assumption of equality was regarded as "self-evident." Hence, it was concluded that He had endowed one and all with the same inalienable rights to life, liberty, and the pursuit of happiness. In terms of mission, this included the right to the free expression of one's religious convictions—the right to publish, promote, and proclaim what one believes.

However, since the late 1970s, there has been considerable constitutional debate and struggle between the First Amendment protection of the religious person's right to the free expression of faith and the public's desire that the government exercise its right to intervene and protect the general welfare and general utility of its citizenry. By "utility" is meant "conducive to the happiness and well-being of the greatest number."[16] Fortunately, the outcome to date has been the recognition that the Bill of Rights protects individual citizens against majoritarianism. Americans still have "the constitutional right to be intolerant and dogmatic, and to believe in and peddle mental and spiritual poison, as long as they do so within the law."[17]

The function of a nation's civil laws is to provide security to this natural right by establishing forms and procedures for its protection. What this means is that civil laws can only secure the laws of nature, but not replace them. Even so, at all levels in our society we recognize that many attempts have been made and are being made to restrict the activities of disfavored groups and socially scorned religious movements, but to no avail. That is, to date!

Admittedly, no citizen may claim the right to be utterly free from all constraints. Only the complete absence of civil law would imply that the inalienable right to freedom is without restraint. Conversely, "if rights make sense at all, then the invasion of a relatively important right must be a very serious matter."[18] Indeed, any assault on this basic liberty is demeaning and injurious, for it strikes at the basic core of a person's values. All utilitarian rationalizations must be challenged when they in any way restrain the free exercise of the religious obligations a person feels committed, under God, to fulfill. In this connection Ronald M. Dworkin has summarized:

> The Constitution, and particularly the Bill of Rights, is designed to protect individual citizens and groups against certain decisions that a majority of citizens might want to make, even when that majority acts in what it takes to be the general or common interest.[19]

Whereas the Jewish community might rightly think that preventing the evangelization of their people is to their benefit, nevertheless, on utilitarian grounds alone, the Bill of Rights sees no warrant for negating this type of free speech. Along this line, and by analogy, Dworkin argues:

> The existence of rights against the Government would be in jeopardy if the Government were able to defeat such a right by appealing to the right of a democratic majority to work its will. A right against the Government must be a right to do something even when the majority thinks it would be wrong to do it, and even when the majority would be worse off for having it done.[20]

In a real sense this is a moral argument, not something to be classified under the rubric of legal right. By *principles*, moral arguments are identified and utilized to secure the fundamental right to freedom of expression—that is, to witness to Christ freely before the Jewish community. In contrast, *policies* designed to advance the collective goal of the Jewish people to immunize itself against any witness in favor of Jesus Christ cannot be allowed to bring about the transgression of *principles*, even when the Jewish community is certain that its people would be protected and even improved by silencing the Christian witness.

Unfortunately, civil law protection is being increasingly challenged in our day. The *Los Angeles Times Magazine* recently published an article by Nina J. Easton,[21] in which she describes the current widespread erosion of social forms and inhibitions that earlier kept aggressive compulsions contained in our society. "Couples hurl insults on TV dating shows, kids sing songs about killing their teachers, and soldiers march to chants about mutilating women." Although some call it humor, her contention is "America's funny bone is becoming a violent sledgehammer—with disturbingly serious results." When Easton referred to TV talk shows that were laced with obscenities and biting cruelty, and other syndicated TV series that contained anti-Semitisms and tirades against abortion activists that reduced their concerns to "deadly, sickly behavior," she pointed out the inevitable: "The ire of the Federal Communications Commission is being drawn, and the public is calling for legal restraints against this widespread abuse of the right of free speech."

Manifestly, we confront a complex matter. And since a concern for the evangelization of the Jewish people is far removed from the understanding of mission as advanced by WCC member churches and by the WCC itself, this complexity is aggravated by the media's penchant for utilizing prejudicial lingo in reporting on evangelicals engaged in Jewish evangelism. One wonders whether there will be an eventual erosion of civil law protection of this liberty.

CONCLUSION

How can this discussion be brought to a profitable conclusion? It seems quite evident that the time has come for evangelicals worldwide, through their churchly relations in the World Evangelical Fellowship and through their mission concerns defined in the Lausanne Covenant (1974)[22] and supplemented by the Manila Manifesto (1989),[23] to grapple with the issue of religious liberty. A comprehensive public statement is needed that reflects careful exploration of all the components under this rubric.

1. Arising out of conscience, religious liberty in its simplest expression means the freedom of the individual to think, believe, and worship in private.

2. It embraces the liberty of corporate worship, which includes interpersonal fellowship and association, and makes possible a social structure to maintain its existence—a community of those committed to its values.
3. It protects the freedom of the committed to share with others on a personal basis their religious values and spiritual experience.
4. It guarantees the right to teach the community's understanding of its distinctives to its members and their children.
5. It contends for the liberty of public teaching and evangelism within the local and national community.
6. This contending should be global, for the freedom to preach, evangelize, and teach should be sought throughout the world. Admittedly it should be sensitive to the distinct problems posed by ethnic and world religions.
7. Societally, religious liberty includes the free expression of one's conscience in matters pertaining to social service and to the prophetic search for ways to challenge customs and institutions that fail to bring to one and all genuine fulfillment in life.
8. Finally, religious liberty includes the freedom of believers to participate in all those government-directed activities that further good ends in local communities and in the state.[24]

One final question. What about civil law throughout the world and its relation to mission? Fortunately, the legacy of British common law remains in many countries as a result of the Western imperialism of the nineteenth and early twentieth centuries. But this legacy is rapidly crumbling before the resurgence of ethnic and religious nationalisms in many parts of the world. The freedom once granted Western missionaries is being increasingly curtailed. Fortunately, the emergence of a worldwide Christian movement from the churches they planted means that Western missionaries are no longer crucial to the completion of the task defined by the Great Commission. Vigorous missionary movements are spontaneously emerging in many parts of Asia, Africa, and Latin America. They represent the wave of the future but will probably increasingly confront a world more hostile to their witness than the hostility encountered by Western missionaries in the nineteenth century.

At present, after seventy years of Marxist domination, the peoples of the former Soviet Union are experiencing religious freedom. This freedom has also returned to the countries in Eastern Europe that the USSR formerly controlled. Whereas one is hopeful that a new day for the Christian mission is dawning, we fear present events in former Yugoslavia are preventing our being too sanguine as to the future. Will the resort to ethnic cleansing, endorsed by the Serbian Orthodox against Bosnian Muslims, stimulate other revengeful nationalisms to rise up and do likewise? This is always a grave possibility. Nationalism is always the last sin that Christians confess. Sadly, the long-standing unresolved ethnic and religious hostility between the Irish and British stands as an abiding demonstration of the tenacity with which such antagonisms are nourished and even sacralized.

EPILOGUE

The reader may be curious to know the outcome of that encounter in New York with the Jewish leader who challenged the rightness of my distributing Christian literature to the Jewish people, despite my awareness of the social disruption this brought to their families? Some time later that day I rejoined my companion and asked him what happened after the two had withdrawn from the rest of us. His reply was what I least expected. Apparently, when a friendly relationship had been established, their conversation focused on the possibility of personal relationship with God. It was then that this Jewish gentleman began to open his heart. He needed help. He was a true seeker. A New Testament was given him, and together my friend and he explored this subject. One may be sure this bit of exciting news truly made my day!

APPENDIX A
Luther A. Weigle and Religious Liberty

The twentieth century with its shameful record of destructive warfare and totalitarian tyranny brought great heaviness of heart to many Christian leaders. As a result, they increasingly realized that if "the Good News of the Kingdom of God" was their essential message (see Matt. 24:14), then proclaiming this Gospel at home and to the uttermost parts of the earth could not but involve them in seeking peace with justice and freedom among all peoples and nations.

It was in the midst of World War II that the leaders of the *International Missionary Council* began to recognize that more vigorous approaches to this task would have to be taken once hostilities ceased. They drew particular inspiration from an address delivered by Dean Luther A. Weigle of Yale University at Cleveland, Ohio, December 10, 1942. This address contained one of the most complete definitions of religious liberty and the rights of religious and nonreligious groups. While recognizing that his list was probably incomplete, Dean Weigle expressed the hope that it might serve as a basis for discussion and action. He grouped these rights in three classes.

I. The religious freedom of individuals includes the following rights:
   1. To believe as reason and conscience dictate. The terms "reason" and "conscience" are used, here and throughout this list, not as opposed to "revelation," but as denoting the human response to divine revelation.
   2. To worship God in the ways which reason and conscience dictate.
   3. To live and act in accordance with such belief and worship.
   4. To express religious belief in speech. This includes all forms of expression—art, journalism, books, the radio, etc., as well as oral speech.
   5. To express religious belief for the purpose of persuasion, to convince and convert others. This includes all forms of religious propaganda. It is the human side of Christian evangelism.
   6. To educate their children in their religious faith (including both belief and action).
   7. To join with others in the organized life and work of a church, congregation, or other religious fellowship.
   8. To withdraw from such affiliation with a religious organization or community; and, at the constraint of reason and conscience, to change belief, with corresponding changes in worship, action, speech, education, and affiliation.
   9. To disbelieve in God, to deny religion, and to act, speak, persuade, educate, and affiliate with others in ways appropriate to this disbelief or atheism.
II. By the term "church" we designate not only a local congregation but also national, supranational, and ecumenical bodies. With this understanding, the religious freedom of the church or congregation includes the following rights:
   1. To assemble for unhindered public worship.
   2. To organize for the more effective conduct and perpetuation of religious belief, worship, and action.
   3. To determine its own constitution, polity, and conditions of membership.
   4. To determine its own faith and creed—free from imposition by the state or any other group.
   5. To determine its own forms of worship—free from imposition by the state or any other group.
   6. To encourage and facilitate action by its members in accordance with its belief and worship.
   7. To bear witness, preach, teach, persuade, and seek commitment or conversion.

8. To determine the qualifications of its ministers and to educate, ordain, and maintain an adequate ministry.
9. To educate both children and adults. This affirmation of the right of the church or congregation to educate does not deny or exclude the right of the state to educate.
10. To hold property and secure support for the work of the church.
11. To cooperate or to unite with other churches or congregations.
12. Finally, the principle of religious freedom requires that these rights of the church or congregation be similarly the rights of organized groups of unbelievers or atheists.

III. The religious freedom of citizens includes:
1. The right of the citizen to hold the state itself responsible to the moral law and to God, and the right to labor to this end through appropriate judgments, witness, and constructive participation in the activities of citizenship.
2. The right of the citizen to dissent in the name of religious belief (reason and conscience) from an act or requirement of the state, and to express this dissent in action or refusal to act as well as in speech. This is the right of so-called conscientious objection. It is recognized that the state may rightfully require a penalty for such dissent, but the penalty for such behavior on grounds of conscience should take these grounds into account.[25]

In his closing remarks Dean Weigle stressed that "these freedoms are the right, not only of individuals, but also of churches and congregations, so far as these are made up of citizens. They are the right, not only of believers, but also of nonbelievers and atheists" (p. 36). He added:

It is a commonplace of history that every religious group stands for freedom when it finds its own liberty impaired. The question today is whether all who believe in God will stand together for the freedom of all mankind [p. 37].

This address closed with specific reference to mission and civil law.

In the list of rights claimed in the name of religious freedom, I have not made a separate classification of rights involved in the conduct of missions. That is not for lack of belief in missions; it is rather because the right to conduct missions is implied in all of the basic rights which we have named. It is not the special privilege of a favored group or race. It is involved in that free exchange of ideas and personalities which is essential to the progress of the world in freedom, in understanding, and in friendship.[26]

Note: Dean Weigle did not hope in vain! Over the years his perspectives have found expression and amplification in the occasional publications of the *Commission of the Churches on International Affairs of the World Council of Churches*. The most recent issue of CCIA/WCC *Background Information* dealing with this concern was 1987 No. 1 *Religious Liberty: Some Major Considerations in the Current Debate*.

NOTES

1. George Arthur Buttrick, *The Interpreters Bible*, vol. 7, New Testament Articles: Matthew, Mark (New York: Abingdon Press, 1951), 621.

2. By liberal Christianity we mean the freedom to formulate one's religion without being bound to the authority of Scripture. Doctrinal formularies, whether evangelical or traditional, are not regarded as criteria of truth, but simply vehicles of "religious" value. Hence, biblical affirmations are reconceptualized, such as the deity of Christ. The meaning is simply that "Christ" expresses the religious values attached to deity. Biblical concepts are reduced to mere symbols, reflecting a religious philosophy penetrated with agnosticism. Their cognitive value is reduced to meaninglessness.

3. James E. Andrews, Stated Clerk, Presbyterian Church (U.S.A.), Office of the General Assembly: "A Theological Understanding of the Relationship between Christians and Jews" (1988), p. 11.

4. Frederick Dale Bruner, *Matthew*, 2 vols. (Dallas: Word Publishing, 1990), 742.

5. *The Theology of the Churches and the Jewish People: Statements by the World Council of Churches and its Member Churches* (Geneva: WCC Publications, 1988), 742.

6. Ibid., 5.

7. Ibid., 186.

8. John R. W. Stott, *Christ the Controversialist* (Downers Grove, Ill.: Inter-Varsity Press, 1970), 18.

9. See Hyam Maccoby, *The Mythmaker: Paul and the Invention of Christianity* (New York: Harper and Row, 1986), 100–38, 139–205, 206–11.

10. Jeremiah S. Gutman, *Deprogramming: Documenting the Issue*, ed. Herbert Richardson. Typescript distributed by the American Civil Liberties Union and the Toronto School of Theology, 1977, p. 210. Also quoted by William C. Shepherd, "Legal Protection for Freedom of Religion," in *Cults, Culture and the Law*, eds. William C. Shepherd,

Thomas Robbins, and James McBride (Chico, Calif.: Scholars Press, 1985), 56. In this latter volume Gutman develops his thesis in "The Legislative Assault on New Religions," 101–10.

11. Francis of Assisi, "Preachers," chap. 17 in *Francis and Clare, The Complete Works* (New York: Paulist Press, 1982), 122.

12. Martin E. Marty—This appropriate reply was initially given to the key question directed to Marty by the religion editor of *The Chicago Tribune,* 5 January 1981, about the key problem American religion is now facing, and quoted by Robert Jewett, *Christian Tolerance* (Philadelphia: The Westminster Press, 1987), 9.

13. Karl Popper, *The Open Society and its Enemies* (Princeton, N.J.: Princeton University Press, 1977), quoted by Roy D. Clements, "Can Tolerance Become the Enemy of Christian Freedom?" *Cambridge Papers* 1, no. 1 (March 1992), (U.K., 41 London Rd., Stapleford, Cambridge CB2 5DE), 2.

14. Roy D. Clements, "Can Tolerance Become The Enemy of Christian Freedom?" 1.

15. John Murray Cuddihy, *The Ordeal of Civility: Freud, Marx, Lévi-Strauss, and the Jewish Struggle With Modernity* (New York: Basic Books, 1974), 10.

16. Clarence Lewis Barnhart, Editor in Chief, *American College Dictionary* (New York: Random House, 1957), 1339.

17. William C. Shepherd, "Legal Protection for Freedom of Religion," 99.

18. Ronald M. Dworkin, *Taking Rights Seriously* (Cambridge: Harvard University, 1977), p. 199.

19. Ibid., 133.

20. Ibid., 194.

21. Nina J. Easton, "The Meaning of America," *Los Angeles Times Magazine* (February 7, 1993): 16–18, 20, 43–44.

22. 1974: Lausanne Covenant, *Making Christ Known: Historic Mission Documents from the Lausanne Movement 1974–1989* (London: Paternoster Press, 1996), 1–55.

23. 1989: Manila Manifesto, *Making Christ Known: Historic Mission Documents from the Lausanne Movement 1974–1989,* 225–48.

24. See Appendix A: "Religious Liberty"

25. "Religious Freedom," *Biennial Report 1942,* Federal Council of Churches, 32–34.

26. Luther A. Weigle, "Religious Liberty in the Postwar World," in *Religion and the World Order,* ed. F. Ernest Johnson (New York: Harper & Brothers, 1944), 37.

ELEVEN

The Kingdom, the Church, and the Gospel in an Age of Pluralism

Edmund P. Clowney

WHAT IS THE CALLING OF Christ's church as contemporary American society disintegrates?[1] To be sure, the resolute plunge into pluralistic nihilism is more characteristic of what Peter Berger calls "the knowledge industry"[2] than of American society as a whole; and we do not know what mercies the Lord may yet show to our land. Yet as Christians feel the changing winds of political climate, the blasts against their values in the media, and the exclusion of the Christian faith from educational institutions, they begin to sense the dangers of complacency and of pietistical world flight. To what social testimony is the church and its members called? Is political action appropriate? How may threatened freedoms be protected so that the task of evangelism and Christian nurture can be carried forward?

Facing such questions, we reflect on the theological and practical options that may be available to meet the crisis we now perceive. From the left, the theology of liberation still finds in the Marxist dialectic the formula for social redemption. To deliver the oppressed, the Christian church is called to operate from within revolutionary movements—in the Third World for starters. From the political right comes the identification of the American experience with the manifest destiny of the kingdom of God, a vision that can also be made a call to arms, with weapons cached against the day of conflict.[3]

These options offered from the left and right are without appeal to most evangelical Christians. The World Council of Churches seems to have gone the way of the Communist Party with whose policies it so often identified. Both may have been written off too soon, but neither appears to offer the wave of the future. Notwithstanding, the fallacy and dangers of identifying the Christian faith with Americanism has been exposed in a recent tide of books analyzing American evangelicalism.

In thought and action, we must respond to the new understanding of democracy in the United States. Once it was assumed that moral law transcended political theories and grounded inalienable rights in the will of nature's God. While this assumption is still the conviction of most Americans, it is scornfully rejected by the so-called knowledge industry and is replaced by the claim that there are no moral absolutes, that all moral values are the product of a human community. Democratic government must therefore recognize a pluralism of values, not merely those of ethnic communities but also those individually held. The only values to be rejected are those that claim absolute validity; the assumptions on which our republic was founded are now the only assumptions held to be inadmissible in a pluralistic age.

To be sure, this attitude toward Christian morality did not begin with the so-called post-modern mind. It was already evident at the end of the nineteenth century when Oliver Wendell Holmes applied Darwinian assumptions to the structure of law.[4] As Christians become more aware of that radical shift in American legal philosophy, they must again consider the foundations of the state in law. They cannot be indifferent to the continuing reconstruction of the legal system by the assumptions of humanism.

Is the Christian response to seek a refounding of American government on Christian principles? Should the civil law of the Old Testament be made the basis of our legal system? Is the answer a national covenant and a Christian amendment to the constitution? Or can Christians support pluralism in some form, seeking an end to explicit discrimination against the Christian position and curbing the nihilist or statist drift of political philosophy?

Our answer must be theologically grounded. The biblical category that is crucial for the Christian view of the modern state is the category of the kingdom of God. The announcement of the kingdom is the distinctive message of the Gospels; the theology of the kingdom lies at the heart of the New Testament revelation. In the theology of the kingdom, the relation of the Gospel to the world in which it is preached is established.

The kingdom that Jesus proclaimed is not the kingdom of Israel; it is the kingdom of God. It comes not by human work but by God's will. Indeed, the very phrase *kingdom of God* defines the kingdom by the King. To be sure, the power of the kingdom of God forms a community of men; but that community is distinguished from all others by the simple fact that it is ruled by the King of heaven. The heavenly *polis* does not lack a political form; but the form of the kingdom is *theopolitical*, the saving rule of God.

To understand the politics of the kingdom, we must consider both the Lord of the kingdom and the community of the kingdom as they are joined in the salvation revealed in the New Testament.

THE LORD OF THE KINGDOM

The term *basileia* in the New Testament describes the *rule* of God rather than the *realm* of God, His dominion rather than His domain. In this sense it describes the immediate rule that is exercised by the Lord who comes in royal power: "The Son of Man coming in His kingdom" (Matt. 16:28 NASB).[5] People may be called into it or cast out of it; they may seek it or inherit it; but they do not compose it (cf. Matt. 7:21; 21:31; 23:13; Mark 9:47; 10:14–15; Luke 16:16).

The coming of the kingdom is one with the coming of the King. John the Baptist announced that the kingdom was at hand in the words of Isaiah: "Prepare ye in the desert a highway for our God!" (Isa. 40:3; Matt. 3:3). As in His Exodus deliverance, God will come to redeem His people.

Old Testament eschatology focuses on the coming of the Lord. On the one hand, the condition of God's people is so desperate that only God can deliver them. On the other hand, the salvation that God promises is so rich that it cannot be realized apart from God's own presence. Both of these reasons are developed and heightened in Old Testament history. From Israel's helpless slavery in Egypt to their dead bones in the valley of Ezekiel's vision, their need for divine help is constantly and increasingly emphasized. God's deliverance, in contrast, comes by His sovereign word. God does not need spears, swords, or battle chargers. He may save through Moses' staff, Gideon's trumpet, or even Samson's weapon, the jaw-bone of an ass. The theme of God's sovereignty in salvation is developed in the framework of covenantal history as outlined in Deuteronomy (30:1–6). After the covenant blessings have been granted to the people in the land and after the disobedience of Israel brings the curses of the covenant, issuing in captivity, then God will renew His covenant, circumcise the hearts of His people, and bring all His promises to realization.

As this history unfolds, the prophets dramatically declare that because all other help and hope is gone, God Himself will put on His helmet of salvation and come to deliver His own (Isa. 59:17; Ezek. 34:10–11). The nations are astonished, and even God's people marvel at the hidden treasures of God's bright designs (Isa. 52:14–15; Jer. 33:3). If the humanist category for the future is *possibility*, the divine category is *impossibility*. "Is any word too wonderful for God?" That question was put to the aged Sarah about the promised birth of Isaac; it became the reply of Gabriel to the Virgin Mary (Luke 1:37; Gen. 18:14).

There is another reason why God must come: not only because of the impossibility of the situation but also because of the glory of the salvation God has promised. God comes down in the Exodus deliverance not just to demand that Pharaoh let His people go but to bear them on eagle's wings to Himself (Ex. 7:26; 19:4). Not the liberation from Pharaoh's service but the imposition of the Lord's covenant is the meaning of the Exodus. "Salvation is of the Lord" (Jonah 2:9) does not only mean that salvation is from God but that salvation is found in Him: "I will walk among you and be your God, and you will be my people" (Lev. 26:12).

The mind of modernity makes the present time the hinge of history. All of the past is consigned to the dark ages; the utopian eschaton will come when science uses the tools of technology in the service of world government. Biblical eschatology cannot be reduced to another New Age mythology for the utopia that the Gentiles seek. The final blessing of salvation must be God's gift of Himself. That gift was given in the birth of Jesus Christ. The incarnate Lord cannot be made the symbol of either a new economic system or a new humanity more inclined to make it work. Biblical salvation is defined by the Savior in the reality of His person and His work.

Because the Lord Himself comes, all human complacency is shattered. Even the most oppressed must fear this Deliverer. But the Lord does not come in judgment; His hosts do not come as avenging angels to usher in His kingdom. Rather, they declare the sign of His humiliation: The shepherds will find Christ the Lord in the feed bin of a stable (Luke 2:12). The Lord has come to save His people—from their *sins* (Matt. 1:21).

The Lord of Glory has come as He promised; He cannot be barred by Caesar's decrees, Herod's soldiers, Satan's rage, or Aristotle's metaphysics. The foolishness of God is wiser than men. In the Incarnation, God comes both as Lord and as Servant, for He must fulfill both sides of His covenant with His people. When God meets humans, the smiting of His judgment must fall; and the worship of an obedient heart must be offered. God's salvation comes through the victory of His Anointed, who offers Himself as the final sacrifice and who is raised in triumph to the right hand of His Father.

Just as Christ's presence brings the kingdom, so His triumph established it. He is Lord over the wind and sea, life and death, men and demons. His authority to heal is one with His authority to teach and to forgive sins (Mark 2:10–11). His miracles are signs of cleansing, restoring God's creation from the pollution of evil. He casts out demons because He has bound the "strong man," Satan, in His wilderness ordeal (Matt. 4:10). Accused of being in league with the

Devil, He refutes the charge and adds, "But if I drive out demons by the finger of God, then the kingdom of God has come to you" (Luke 11:20).

None of the battles of history can compare with the encounter of the Son of God with the "prince of this world" in the desert. As God's chosen, called and endued with the Spirit, He must crush the head of the serpent in the conflict of His life and in the triumph of His death. Under the shadow of the cross Jesus says, "Now is the time for judgment on this world; now the prince of this world will be driven out" (John 12:31).

Paradoxically, Jesus' victory over Satan is accomplished by His own death on the cross. His "lifting up" in crucifixion is a lifting up to glory. At the cross, He finished His work of salvation and glorified His Father; from the cross He will draw men to Himself (John 12:32). The kingdom power of the cross does not rest in the cross as a symbol but as a sacrifice. "The Son of Man [is come] . . . to give His life a ransom for many" (Matt. 20:28). God's salvation cannot simply deliver some men from other men or even all men from global disaster. God's salvation must deliver men from themselves and from the power of the Devil. But above all, God's salvation must deliver men from His own wrath and curse. The Cross is God's gift of His only begotten Son; it is not another incident in the centuries of repression and rebellion but is the final deliverance for humanity made in the image of God.

To the politics of human power, the Cross is foolishness. Even John the Baptist was confused by the failure of Jesus to bring liberation through judgment. John had proclaimed Jesus as the coming One, the Judge who would wield the ax against every tree of injustice. But John found himself in prison, awaiting what proved to be a death sentence while Jesus went on performing miracles of kingdom power. John's faith was shaken. He sent messengers to Jesus asking, "Are you the one who was to come, or should we expect someone else?" (Luke 7:19).

Jesus' answer was to take John's messengers to witness His mighty works. Then, using words that recalled Isaiah's description of the great day of salvation (Isa. 26:19; 29:18; 35:5–6; 61:1), Jesus reminded them of what they had seen and heard and sent them back to John with a blessing to challenge his faith: "Blessed is the man who does not fall away on account of me" (Luke 7:23). Jesus did not come first to inflict the judgment but to bear it. Only in the temple did He lift the scourge of judgment, and then only to expel those who defiled God's house of prayer. No, He came rather to *bear* the scourge, to open the gates of life by receiving the thrust of death.

Christ's resurrection seals the reality of the salvation that is completed in His life and death. Christ does not provide a symbol for the liberation humans must find for themselves in later generations, nor is He an early example of the man of the future. Rather, His death is the great personal transaction in which the Son of God atones for sin by the sacrifice of Himself. So, too, His life provides the comprehensive and final fulfillment of kingdom righteousness. Apart from Christ there is no fulfillment of God's calling. Human culture celebrates the technology of war in the hymn of Lamech (Gen. 4:23–24) and raises the tower of Babel in the cult of the city, but all humanity's works are under the judgment of God. Only one Man is righteous, the Heir of all the promises of God and the observer of all the commandments of God.

Christ, the Second Adam, fulfills the calling of the first. Adam was charged to fill the earth and subdue it. Humanity's dominion, lyrically described in Psalm 8, is realized in the lordship of Jesus Christ as the author of Hebrews declares (Heb. 2:5–8). Further, in His resurrection glory at the Father's right hand, Christ fills all things. Paul describes Christ's filling both in reference to the church (His fullness as His body) and in reference to the world, which He fills with the sovereignty of His rule (Eph. 4:10; Jer. 23:23). In Jesus Christ, humanity's vocation of sonship as God's image-bearer is completely realized. The final depth of the covenant relation is not, "I will be your God, and you will be my people," but "You are my Son; today I have become your Father" (Ps. 2:7; Heb. 1:5). The beloved Son of the Father is the true Israel, the "minister of the circumcision" (Rom. 15:8) to fulfill the calling of the servant nation because He is the Servant Son. In Jesus Christ, God calls His Son out of Egypt (Matt. 2:15; Hos. 11:1), proves Him in the desert (Deut. 8:2; Matt. 4:1), offers Him on Mount Moriah (Gen. 22:1), and gives Him the nations as His inheritance (Ps. 2:8; Matt. 28:18).

In Christ, the old and new covenant people of God are united. Christ does not fulfill the old to clear the way for the new. He fulfills the new as well as the old in His own person and work. Neither does He provide a "cultic" service to initiate a new era of cultural flowering. The whole calling of humanity is fulfilled in the Son of Man.

Christ who brings the kingdom in His person and fulfills it in His work calls men into the kingdom according to His purposes. The kingdom comes in God's program, not ours; we are blessed if we are not offended by the Lord's way.

Christ calls us to take up a cross to follow Him. His way is the way of suffering that leads to glory. The delay of God's judgment means that those who preach Christ crucified must be prepared to suffer for His name. God's justice delayed is not justice denied. Rather, God holds open the door of mercy; He will not pour out the wrath to come until He has gathered in all that great host for whom He poured out His wrath on His only Son. With heavenly power, Jesus Christ now gathers in those other sheep from the ends of the earth. To that end, He restrains the wicked and disciplines His people. But He does not yet call the nations to stand before Him; not until the Second Coming will they know the day of the wrath of the Lamb (Rev. 6:16).

Christ's limitation of His judgment does not spring from any limitation of His power. Mysterious as His ways may seem to His persecuted saints, He pursues with divine wisdom His purposes of grace. The risen Christ is exalted as Prince and Savior to give repentance to Israel and remission of sins (Acts 5:31). In His dominion, He sends His disciples to the ends of the earth to proclaim life to the Gentiles (Matt. 28:18–20). His Spirit, the gift of His enthronement, gives not only His power for the task but His life, the new life of the coming age. The new creation has begun; the Creator Spirit is the breath of the Lord in the bosoms of new creatures in Christ Jesus (John 20:22; Rom. 8:10–11).

In and through the risen Christ, Christian hope is both realistic and realized. The future hope is not a mythic model, it is as real as the bread and fish eaten by the risen Lord. That future hope is also present through the Holy Spirit breathed by the Lord on His disciples. In the gospel of John, future and present hope is expressed in the formula, "A time is coming and has now come" (John 4:23; 5:25; 16:32). From the time that the Word became flesh, the hour of fulfillment began; the Resurrection was present in the Christ (John 11:25; cf. 5:21). The lifting up of the Lord assured the coming of the day when the dead shall hear the voice of the Son of God and live (John 5:25).

Paul says, "Now is our salvation nearer than when we believed" (Rom. 13:11 KJV), looking toward the day of the Lord's appearing. Faith in Christ looks forward to His coming again; it also brings the Christian into present possession of salvation and sonship (1 Cor. 15:2; Rom. 10:10; 8:15–17). The Spirit of Christ is the seal of present grace and the guarantee of future glory (Rom. 8:15–16; Eph. 1:13–14).

Christian hope, then, is not allegiance to the possible in a random universe. It is longing for the completion of God's work of restoration and renewal, longing for the new creation that is as real as Christ's resurrection body, which is its center and beginning. *Homo absconditus*, the dream man of secular utopianism, is but a mask of antichrist. In Jesus Christ, the *Deus Homo*, God is revealed in His grace and truth.

"He is the true God and eternal life. Dear children, keep yourselves from idols" (1 John 5:20–21).

THE COMMUNITY OF THE KINGDOM

The actualization of God's saving rule in Jesus Christ requires a real and heavenly form for the people of His kingdom. Christ the Lord came to gather a people, the remnant flock preserved for Him and given to Him, a flock that must include other sheep from the Gentiles as well as the chosen of Israel (Luke 12:32; John 10:16). The people, gathered by the Lord, form the new humanity, the full community of the kingdom.

God had called His covenant people to be His own possession, a people near to Him to praise Him before the nations (1 Pet. 2:9–10; Ex. 19:4–6; Isa. 43:21). Israel failed in this doxological task; but in spite of that failure (and even through it), God caused the nations to see His glory. The prophets promise the great day when God will gather the remnant of the nations with the remnant of Israel and pour out His blessing on both (Isa. 19:25; Jer. 48:47; Zech. 14:16). The preserved remnant of the people of God will be small indeed— like a piece of a sheep's ear taken from the jaws of a lion (Amos 3:12). But the saved remnant will be made a saving remnant. From the stump of the cedar will grow the shoot that will become an ensign to the nations (Isa. 11:1, 10). God's Servant is the shoot from the root of Jesse; and God says to Him: "It is too small a thing for you to be my servant to restore the tribes of Jacob, and to bring back those of Israel I have kept. I will also make you a light for the Gentiles, that you may bring my salvation to the ends of the earth" (Isa. 49:6).

The promised renewal of the people of God will be in depth as well as breadth. God will circumcise the hearts of His people (Deut. 30:6; Jer. 32:39; Ezek. 11:9). Continually, the history of God's covenant points to a greater realization in the future. The patriarchs confessed that they were pilgrims and aliens journeying toward the true city of God (Gen. 47:9; Heb. 11:10). Israel, at Sinai, was pointed to the land of promise and to the place where God would set His name. David established Jerusalem as his capital but confessed that he was an alien as his fathers had been (Ps. 39:13). At the dedication of the temple, Solomon acknowledged that the construction of men could not contain the living God (1 Kings 8:27).

God's final blessings therefore include unimaginably more than the restoration of a golden past. David and his throne, the Levites and the ark, the city and the temple—all these must be renewed, yet not by a restoration that would carry the people of God back in history to David's time. No, God's final restoration is a new creation;

and that new creation is begun in the resurrection of Jesus Christ (Isa. 65:17; 1 Cor. 15:42–57). Jesus is the Son of David, but His throne is as much above David's as God's right hand is above the earthly hill of Zion (Ps. 110:1; Zech. 12:8; Acts 2:33–36). It is in His risen glory that Jesus Christ will build His assembly as He raises up the tabernacle of David that is fallen down (Amos 9:11–12; Matt. 16:18; Acts 15:16–17).

"I will build my church"—Jesus Christ is the architect of the people of God. He speaks His word constituting the new Israel after He has elicited from Simon Peter a distinctive confession of faith in Him. With flattering unbelief, the multitudes call Him a prophet, yet they will not hail Him as Messiah, for He will not march on Jerusalem to set up a political kingdom. But in spite of Jesus' refusal of this popular messianic role, Peter confesses Him not only as the Christ, but as the Son of the living God.

"You are Peter, and on this rock I will build my church" (Matt. 16:18). Jesus is not contrasting Peter with the eleven, for he has just served as their spokesman in answering the question Jesus addressed to them all.[6] Jesus is contrasting Peter the apostle, the recipient of revelation from the Father, with the false teachers of the people of God who sit in Moses' seat and use the keys of the kingdom to lock out those who might enter (Matt. 23:2, 13). The true people of God confess the Son of God. To those who reject Him, Jesus says, "The kingdom of God will be taken away from you, and given to a people who will produce its fruit" (Matt. 21:43).

The word *church* asserts the unity of the new people of God. The Greek word *ecclesia* translates the Hebrew term *qahal*. Both mean "assembly." The definitive assembly of the Old Testament was the great covenant assembly at Sinai (Deut. 9:10). It was reflected in later assemblies gathered to renew the covenant and in assemblies at the three annual feasts. In assembly, the people stood before their covenant Lord; and that covenantal relation defined their existence. Israel was not defined genealogically as a tribe but covenantally as a holy nation, united in the presence of God.

The wind and flame of the Spirit made the feast of Pentecost the Sinai assembly of the new covenant. The author of Hebrews declares that Christians have not come again to Sinai but to the heavenly Zion where the festival assembly of saints and angels is gathered before Jesus, the Mediator of the new covenant (Heb. 12:18–24).

The New Testament assumes the continuity of the people of God even as it describes their renewal. It is no historical accident that the discipline, officers, and worship of the church are so closely related to the synagogue.

Paul declares, "For it is we who are the circumcision, we who worship by the Spirit of God, who glory in Christ Jesus, and who put no confidence in the flesh" (Phil. 3:3). Debating with a lawyer hired by the Jerusalem hierarchy, Paul insisted that Christianity is not a sect, but the way of the God of the fathers (Acts 24:5, 14). The controversy over circumcision highlights the claim of the church to be the true Israel. Had the church been understood as an assembly of "God-fearers" distinct from Judaism, the demand for circumcision would never have been made. The Judaizers were scandalized because Gentiles were being admitted into the number of the people of God without circumcision.

The final "people of God's own possession" must be one. As there is one Father over all (Eph. 4:6), so there is one family,[7] one "fatherdom" (*patria*, Eph. 3:15). Members of God's family form a "brotherhood" (*adelphotēs*, 1 Pet. 2:17; 5:9). Gentiles who were outside of Christ and aliens from the commonwealth of Israel are now fellow-citizens with the people of God and heirs of the covenant promises (Eph. 2:12, 19).

The Theopolitical Form of the Church

Because there is one true people of God on earth, there remains a theopolitical structure and calling for the church. It is not the structure of the kingdoms of the world. To apply to the world the form of the church is a sacralizing process that is just as illegitimate as the secularizing process that would apply to the church the forms of the world. Yet, the fact that the church does not possess a worldly political structure does not mean that it possesses no political structure whatever. The politics of the kingdom are the pattern, purpose, and dynamic by which God orders the life of the heavenly *polis* in the world. Only as it conforms to this heavenly pattern is the church a city set on a hill, given as salt to preserve the world from corruption and as a light to show the way to salvation.

Christ builds His church on the confessing Peter, the apostle whose faith is given by revelation of the Father. Since only the Son can reveal the Father and only the Father can reveal the Son (Matt. 11:27), human wisdom cannot bring in the kingdom. Long ago, the Qumran covenanters recognized from the Old Testament that the community of God must be founded on the truth, the revealed mysteries of God.[8] But only in Jesus Christ is that foundation of truth laid. We have seen how efforts to build society in a post-Christian era have generated new mythologies that soon pass, such as the cults of Hitler, Lenin, and Mao.[9]

The heavenly discipline of the church corresponds to the

heavenly origin of its apostolic faith. Jesus commits to Peter and to the other disciples (Matt. 18:18) the authority of the keys of the kingdom, giving earthly form to the heavenly community. The keys of the kingdom close the fellowship against the one who refuses apostolic doctrine or who will not receive correction for an offense against a brother (Matt. 18:17–18).[10] The sanction in heaven of judgments made on earth assumes, of course, what Peter confessed, Christ's divine authority. Christ gives the keys even as He brings the kingdom. The authority of the keys is *only* spiritual in the sense that temporal judgment awaits God's judgment on the last day.[11] It is *fully* spiritual in the sense that a final and heavenly authority is effective; the person who refuses to hear the word of Christ is at last outside God's eternal kingdom.

Paul reflects on the eschatological character of judgment in the church when he rejects with dismay the practice of permitting secular courts to adjudicate disputes between Christians. Since Christians will one day judge the world and even the angels, the least of the saints is well qualified to settle disputes about affairs of this life (1 Cor. 6:1–4). The Spirit of the age to come already gives His wisdom to the church.

The exercise of heavenly judgment must in fact begin in the house of God (1 Pet. 4:17). The church is not now called to judge the nations; those outside the church of God will judge (1 Cor. 5:12–13). But those within must judge themselves (1 Cor. 11:13) and be judged by their brethren (1 Cor. 5:12).

As a heavenly community, the church must deal with the temporal concerns of its members; yet its discipline remains spiritual, not temporal. For example, the church could require a Christian storekeeper to refund purchases that had been gained by misleading advertising. But if the member refused, the church's final sanction would be excommunication, not economic boycott.

The heavenly community of Christ is called to an earthly pilgrimage. The people of God may not abandon the program of His kingdom—"if indeed we share in His sufferings in order that we may also share in His glory" (Rom. 8:17). Paul rebukes the triumphalists at Corinth: "You have become kings—and that without us! How I wish that you really had become kings so that we might be kings with you!" (1 Cor. 4:8). We may not wish to condemn the Camisard Christians in the Cevennes mountains of France who, under the savage persecution of Louis XIV, turned on their persecutors, but Christ does not call His church to rebellion. Rather, He gives the grace that enabled the Huguenot galley slave to call his chains the chains of Christ's love.

"For here we do not have an enduring city, but we are looking for the city that is to come" (Heb. 13:14). There is no earthly city that abides—not Babylon, not Rome, not Jerusalem. Every kingdom of man will be shaken, every wall shall fall (Heb. 12:27; Ezek. 38:20). Yet the author of Hebrews is reflecting not only on the fact that there is no abiding city here but on the truth that Christians are not given one. The military and police power needed to maintain a political community in this world cannot be sought in Christ's name. Christians are called to go with Christ outside the walls of the city, bearing His reproach (Heb. 13:12–13).

Christ commanded Peter to put away his sword (John 18:11). He declared to Pilate, "My kingdom is not of this world. If it were, my servants would fight" (John 18:36). Yet Christ is not helpless against Pilate; His kingdom that is not of this world rules over all the kingdoms that are of this world. Pilate's power is given from above (John 19:11). By the will of the Father, Pilate rules; by the will of the Father, the Beloved Son is given up.

Christ's servants *need* not fight because God's kingdom does not need their weapons; they *may* not fight because God's kingdom of redemption cannot be established by the sword: "For though we live in the world, we do not wage war as the world does. The weapons we fight with are not the weapons of the world. On the contrary, they have divine power to demolish strongholds. We demolish arguments and every pretension that sets itself up against the knowledge of God, and we take captive every thought to make it obedient to Christ" (2 Cor. 10:3–5).

God takes the helmet of salvation and the breastplate of righteousness to deliver His people (Isa. 59:17); these are the weapons of the Spirit that Christ gives for the struggle, not against flesh and blood, but against principalities and powers (Eph. 6:12–18). The sword of the Spirit prevails where physical weapons are useless.

Three principles apply, then, in God's restraint on the sword for the community of His kingdom. First, God has taken the sword of judgment into His own hand because the time of the judgment of the world has come. To be sure, God in rich mercy delays the day of His wrath. Yet the Judge of the nations is already seated on the throne of His power; the message of the kingdom does not call for soldiers to put the King on His throne, but for penitents to confess their ruling Sovereign and sue for His mercy.

Second, the Lord's restraint of the sword reflects His moving of the conflict to deeper levels. His triumph over the powers of darkness is a triumph not only of spiritual judgment but of redeeming grace. Paul, the chief of sinners, is made a captive of Christ's love, chained by grace to the chariot of Christ's triumph (2 Cor. 2:14). To effect His victory, Christ refused the temptation to use the authority of the kingdom to provide earthly bread, to gain visible assurance of God's protection, or to receive the political reality of rule from the prince of this world. Christ calls His church to the same conflict and the same obedience.

Third, God restrains the sword because the bringing in of His kingdom is related to God's sanction of the sword in the hands of the rulers of this world. God did not first give the sword to Israel as a priestly nation but to "all flesh" after the flood to restrain violence (Gen. 9:6). The holy wars of Israel were divinely commissioned not for this purpose but to foreshadow the final wrath of God's judgment. Apart from these judgments, Israel was to bring blessing to the nations and their rulers. The value of God's wisdom for governors is a major theme of the wisdom literature. In Israel's exile, Daniel was counselor to kings; the role of Cyrus as God's servant in restoring the nation from captivity anticipates the messianic Deliverer. "My servant Nebuchadnezzar, king of Babylon" (Jer. 27:6) is granted dominion by God not only over Judah but the surrounding nations of Edom, Moab, Ammon, Tyre, and Sidon.

The captives in Babylon are told to build houses and dwell in them, give their children in marriage, and be multiplied. "Also seek the peace and prosperity of the city to which I have carried you into exile. Pray to the LORD for it, because if it prospers, you too will prosper" (Jer. 29:7).

The members of the new Israel in dispersion are to pray for the rulers in the lands where they are scattered (1 Tim. 2:1, 2). That duty does not conflict with the Christian's service of the Lord. Jesus' answer to the question about paying taxes to Caesar had a double edge.[12] The rule of Caesar is acknowledged even while His claims to deity are set aside. Since the image on the coin is Caesar's, those who are under His rule have an obligation to give Him what is His. And since humanity itself bears God's image, it must render all to God.

The Kingdom and the State

Paul elaborates on this teaching of Christ when he charges Christians to obey human government for conscience's sake, since "the authorities that exist have been established by God" (Rom. 13:1). Paul assumes that rulers are ministers of God for good. It is a fair implication of His teaching that if a ruler so subverts the business of governing that the state becomes a terror to good works rather than evil, the Christian conscience would be no longer bound. In judging the good or evil performance of the state, the Christian may not, however, judge the state as a form of the people of God but only as an ordinance given to all men to preserve life.

The distinction between the state as the form of the city of this world and the church as the form of the heavenly city remains essential. Christ's heavenly authority controls the nations, but they are not thereby made His disciples. His headship over all things is distinguished from His headship over the church which is His body, the fullness of Him that fills all in all (Eph. 1:21–23).

To be sure, the life of the worldly kingdoms is influenced by the life of the church in their midst; the people of God are like salt to preserve the world from its corruption; the kingdom works as a leaven, penetrating the world with the influence of Christian faith, hope, and love. Yet, even the worldwide spread of the Gospel cannot remove Christ's prohibition of the sword as a means of bringing in or maintaining His kingdom.

The church and only the church is established by Jesus Christ as the earthly form of the new and heavenly people of God. It cannot be set beside other structures of human life, for it is the structure of the new humanity in Christ. The family remains as God's institution for the propagation of life; the state remains as God's institution for the preservation of life. The church is neither competitive nor correlative to family or state. It does not give institutional form to one aspect of human experience, the "spiritual" aspect, or the life of faith. The church visible is not an association set up only to conduct public worship. To suppose that the transcendent body of Christ finds institutional expression in both the church and the state as religious and political spheres is to substitute a sociological concept of the church for the teaching of the New Testament. Christ does not give the keys of the kingdom to Caesar nor the sword to Peter before the *parousia*. The church is the new nation (1 Pet. 2:9), the new family of God (Eph. 3:15). The covenantal family of the patriarchal period and the covenantal nation after Moses demonstrate that God forms His people in a way that respects the structures of life in the world, but those forms also demonstrate that the electing grace of God's kingdom points beyond those structures.

Christ Himself provides the new form with the new life. The church has the spiritual and eschatological form that the kingdom demands. It is contrasted not with the family or with the state but with the *world* as the corporate structure of unbelief.

The relation of the church to the social structures of this world varies with the nature of the structure. The family, as a form of God's creation, is restored in relation to the church in a way that the state, an institution made necessary by the Fall, is not. In God's kingdom there is restoration of creation, fulfillment of the ordinances of God for a fallen world, and anticipation of the new creation. Each of these principles applies to families within the church of God. Monogamous marriage is restored; the husband's headship of the home is maintained but also transformed. In the church, the family structure is honored by the place of men in rule, yet the calling of men and women in the church also anticipates the new order in Christ in which there is neither male nor female. Even the family is not identified with the new order of the kingdom. Those who are not willing to renounce family ties for Christ's sake cannot be His disciples (Matt. 10:34–39). Christians are further instructed in the holiness of the kingdom that permits them to remain in marital alliance with unbelievers—in sharp contrast with the requirements of the ceremonial law of the old covenant (1 Cor. 7:14).

The church as the family of God provides the earthly bonds of fathers, mothers, brothers, sisters, sons, and daughters that constitute the eternal reality foreshadowed in the creation ordinance of the family (Matt. 3:34–35; 10:29–30). The marriage bond itself is more than an allegory of the mystery of Christ's union with the church. It is a prefigurement, a unique union of jealous love that prepares us to understand something of the intensity of devotion that joins the Lord with His people.

Since the church anticipates the form of the world to come, it transcends the social and political forms of this world. Yet the church cannot for that reason be set over these institutions. The claim of Boniface VIII to the two swords has been rightly discredited in biblical ecclesiology. The discipline of the church may declare a man outside the kingdom of heaven, but it cannot prejudice his earthly citizenship or dissolve his marriage. We have seen the folly of papal interdictions that place kingdoms under the ban to accomplish political ends. Liberation theology follows the same course in support of world revolution.

Christianity cannot be revived by linking it to man's political hopes, nor can Marxism be given a new dynamic by the infusion of Christian hope. Moltmann has sought to politicize Christian theology by orienting it to the future. His "pro-ligion" joins "faith in God with hope in the liberation of man on a new earth and under a new heaven."[13] A Christian universalism of hope "makes meaningful and relevant the political humanism of Christianity."[14]

But Christian eschatology cannot be cut loose from the past of redemption. The choice is not between past and future but between the Gospel and humanism. Christian eschatology cannot link with political utopianism any better than Christian soteriology can link with political messianism. Christian hope awaits the return of Jesus Christ, the same Lord who rose from the dead on the third day and who will come to judge the living and the dead (2 Thess. 1:7). The world of the future is not the better world of the humanist dream but a new world when creation itself will be delivered from the bondage of corruption into the liberty of the sons of God (Rom. 8:20–21). "For our citizenship is in heaven; from whence also we wait for a Savior, the Lord Jesus Christ: who shall fashion anew the body of our humiliation, that it may be conformed to the body of His glory, according to the working whereby He is able even to subject all things unto Himself" (Phil. 3:20–21).

Does the firm hope of the Christian in the coming of the consummation kingdom remove all concern for the bettering of the political kingdom? Since the state is not authorized to use the sword to advance the saving kingdom of God, does doing so fall outside the sphere of Christian activity?

There is, of course, an important difference between the opportunities and responsibilities of a Christian citizen in a modern democracy and those of a church member in the Roman Empire. Not only does our citizenship give us a vote, locally and nationally; our freedom to associate enables us to apply to our governing representatives the political pressure of voting blocks. The use of such pressure in lobbying now plays a major role in the functioning of our government.

Even so, it would be a mistake to suppose that the contemporary political scene has created a situation for which the New Testament offers no guidance. The apostle Paul was, after all, a Roman citizen; he exercised his right for a trial before Caesar to defeat the plots of his countrymen. But he made no effort to organize political action in Rome to secure a government more just than that of Nero. Even more to the point is the example of Jesus Himself. Not only did He refuse to seize power in Jerusalem as the crowds demanded, He devoted all of His efforts to the establishment of His spiritual kingdom when there were opportunities on every hand for Him to influence political life. His popular following, not to speak of His own powers, made Him a force to be reckoned with in the political setting of His ministry.

By example and precept, the New Testament makes the priorities of the kingdom clear. The presence of the kingdom of grace does influence the kingdoms of this world. It does so by the indirect influence of light, salt, and leaven, not by the use of temporal power.

It is in the indirect influence of the kingdom of grace that the Christian calling for political life must be found. The Christian must do all to the glory of God; he or she must be a citizen to the glory of

God and vote to the glory of God. But to vote to the glory of God is not to vote to set up a theocracy. The Christian citizen must support God's plan for the state in this time between the first and second coming of Christ. God has not commissioned the state to conform the behavior of its citizens to the law of love to God and neighbor. Its purpose is rather to restrain lawless violence that would threaten life.

It may be supposed that such a goal is too ambiguous to be viable. If the governor is to be a terror to evil works but a praise to those who do well, how are good and evil to be discerned apart from God's revelation? And has not God told us quite specifically in the civil legislation of the Old Testament what actions are evil and, indeed, what sanctions are to be applied—death, for example, in the case of homosexual or bestial practices?

But as we have seen, the Old Testament theocracy does not provide the model for the kingdoms of the world. The successor to Israel is not the national state, but the church of Jesus Christ where the sanctions are spiritual. Old Testament law anticipated the last judgment by outwardly enforcing the ethics of God's kingdom. Kingdom ethics are now applied inwardly in the government of the church through the Word and the Holy Spirit.

The worldly kingdom cannot and must not seek to legislate and enforce the holiness that God requires. The apparent anomaly that continues to trouble us is how a pagan kingdom like Nero's Rome, aptly likened to a beast out of the sea (Daniel 7), can be called God's servant to praise the good and avenge evil, so that our obedience is not simply prudent but conscience bound (Rom. 13:1–5). What creates the anomaly is the delay, for a time, of God's judgment, so that the people of God may be gathered in from the ends of the earth and at end of God's appointed time. If God's own judgment is to be withheld until His spiritual kingdom is completely established, there must be temporary restraint on violent evil so that life in the world may go on. It is for this task that the authority of civil government is given.

Christian citizens have the responsibility to use such authority as they possess to direct the state in its proper role. The touchstone of their activity in this sphere is their insistence on using such political power as they possess in concert with others willing to seek the same objectives. Failure to do this must inevitably convert their actions into an effort to seize power in Christ's name. Christians have every right to meet as members of Christ's church to analyze civic issues and to consider the application of biblical principles to social and political questions; they are free to expose evil and identify good in the society at large or in the government in particular. They cannot, however, seek power to enforce Christian morality. Further, the focus of the church on the Gospel and its acknowledgment of the authority of Scripture must hold its teaching office close to the proclamation of the Word: fearless in loyalty to the truth of God, clearly applying the truth to contemporary situations. The church must not claim an authority it does not possess in the interpretation of social and political questions.

Even in the advocacy of righteousness in government, Christians must be willing to take the pragmatic position that working with non-Christians involves. Our confidence is in God's common grace by which He restrains men from the evil and folly that their own rebellious wickedness would produce. While God in judgment does give men up to their own sins, He has appointed a day of judgment and now calls sinners to repentance. The appointment of a day when Jesus Christ will sit in judgment means that God limits the time of reckoning; but it also means that until that day comes, God's wrath, though revealed, is restrained. Life continues and the gospel of grace is proclaimed.

In this time, we must not reduce God's demand for total obedience, the righteousness of His kingdom. We must beware of leading others to suppose that there is a lower standard of civic decency that God will accept. The Lord God, by the pressure of His general revelation as well as in the summons of Scriptural revelation, continually requires that men hear, repent, and turn to Christ in whom alone they may find atonement for sin and the gift of perfect righteousness. Although men rebel against the call of God, they cannot escape its pressure; and they are often willing to do things that are in themselves right.

The knowledge of God and of right and wrong that divine revelation constantly provides makes men accountable for their sin, but also at times it restrains their sin. In this situation we must be willing to work in civic affairs with any and all who advocate policies of relative justice, even those who deny the very existence of God. Our confidence is not in them, but in God's restraint of the outworking of their own rebellion. Only in such a context can we find an advantage in the position of one who theorizes about natural law while rejecting the true and living God.

There is a calamitous difference between a people who have been immersed in paganism for centuries and a post-Christian society. While the culture of the latter may carry a deep tradition influenced by Christian values, its posture of rebellion will give it a direction that is more explicitly and consciously anti-Christian. Apart from a great revival of true religion, we may expect hostility and persecution from the powers that be in the West. Nevertheless, Christians must not only keep their testimony clear but be ready to acknowledge even against a darkening horizon the relatively just and decent policies that may continue to appear, however inconsistently, in a postmodern world. The politics of the kingdom of heaven is the politics of faith, hope, and love—faith that confesses the risen Savior, hope that looks for His appearing, love that is inflamed by His sacrifice on the cross. Only the realism of resurrection hope can sustain the Christian as a pilgrim traveling home.

Christians will often be accused of otherworldliness, aloofness, and noninvolvement. They cannot forget their heavenly citizenship to be conformed to this world. They refuse to make patriotism or revolution their religion, or a socialist utopia their hope. They see the naiveté and the apostasy of secular hope.

Yet the church is not a retreat where the pious await the *parousia*. The church has an agenda set not by the world but by the Lord. Christ commissioned the church to live for the purpose for which He lived and died. The urgency of the priorities of His Father's will governed His earthly obedience. In His heavenly glory, He sends His disciples to the nations with the same purpose. Christ's great commission expresses the political objectives of His kingdom—the evangelization and edification of the nations in adoring fellowship with the triune God.

The church is organized for these ends: the worship of God, the nurture and growth of God's people, and the bearing of witness to the world. For each of these ministries, the church is endued with gifts of the Spirit by the exalted Christ. First, the Word of God must be ministered to these ends; Christ enables every Christian to confess His name before men and exhort His brethren in the truth. Christ grants gifts of order to discipline the church in love. The pilgrim church must also minister mercy, caring for the poor and the distressed among the brethren, and, as God grants opportunity, to all men.

Christ has not promised to make us wise in world politics, skillful in technology, or talented in the arts. Love of the Lord brings fruitful living in all His creation. But Christians live as stewards, respecting the priorities of the kingdom. The Christian labors not to amass wealth but in order to give to the needy; the man who has everything lives only to give it to the Lord in faithful stewardship. He lives as possessing nothing. The man who has nothing is a child of the King, possessing everything. Christ's redemption does not improve our efficiency in worldly living. It is the purchase of the King who claims us for Himself and His program. To do all to the glory of God does not mean that any conceivable activity can glorify God.

The world cannot be sacralized by the fiat of a worldly theology to form the community of love Christ came to establish. The world lacks the new life of the Spirit who sheds abroad the love of Christ in human hearts. It cannot be governed by the spiritual structure of Christ's kingdom. It is the church that possesses the Spirit and is possessed by the Spirit to manifest on earth now the realities of heaven and the age to come. The politics of the kingdom demand that Christians take seriously the structure of the church as the form of the people of God on earth. Today in many major denominations, preachers of another gospel are not only tolerated, they control the church. In Bible-believing churches, there is often another form of Babylonian captivity to secular goals and values. While radical theologians still serve the political left, there is no lack of conservative preachers to proclaim nationalism in the name of Christ. Only feebly does the church's ministry of mercy bear witness to the compassion of Christ's gospel. Instead, Christians spend on extravagant luxuries the funds Christ has entrusted to them for the relief of the poor and needy.

The deep fellowship of love that joins the Lord's people finds little expression in churches that continue to meet for one brief hour of formal boredom every Sunday morning. Evangelism has been shifted by default to para-ecclesiastical organizations, many presenting a truncated gospel, and most by their very specialization detaching the Gospel from the life of a serving and loving community.

It is time for judgment to begin in the house of God. Let the church break with the deadening customs that have stifled its living service of the Lord. Let it put into practice the politics of the kingdom. Then a renewed and reformed church will show the world the meaning of true life in community. There is no better way to bear witness to a postmodern society than to manifest in the midst of it the radical fellowship of love and obedience to Christ that marks the society of heaven on earth. Let the church be the church, and it will find an open door that no man can shut in proclaiming Jesus Christ, the Alpha and Omega, the Lord of history and salvation.

NOTES

1. Included in this chapter is material published in "The Politics of the Kingdom," *Westminster Theological Journal* 41, no. 2 (1979): 291–310.
2. Berger includes in this "new class" educators, communicators, therapists, lifestyle engineering bureaucrats, and lawyers. See "Different Gospels: the Social Sources of Apostasy," in *American Apostasy: The Triumph of "Other" Gospels*, ed. Richard John Neuhaus (Grand Rapids: Eerdmans, 1989), 4, quoted in Donald A. Carson, "Christian Witness in an Age of Pluralism," in *God & Culture*, eds.

D. A. Carson and John D. Woodbridge (Eerdmans, 1993), 37.

3. Religious survivalist sects may be expected to multiply as the year 2000 nears.

4. See Herbert W. Titus, "God's Revelation and the Common Law" in this volume.

5. All Scripture in this chapter, unless marked otherwise, is from the New International Version of the Bible.

6. This is further supported by Jesus' giving the power of the keys to all the apostles in Matthew 18:18.

7. The phrases *pasa patria* (Eph. 3:15) and *pasa oikodome* (2:21) are best translated "the whole family" and "the whole building."

8. The "council" *sodh* of the community is founded on the "counsel" *yisodh* of God. See G. Vermes, *The Dead Sea Scrolls in English* (Penguin Books, 1966) 1QH 6:25, 26; 1QS 5:5; 9:3f. Such passages as 1QH 7:6–10; 10:4; 11:4, 9, 16; and 12:12 show the linking of the secret truth with the foundation of the congregation and the individual.

9. Cf. Jacques Ellul, *Les Nouveaux Possedes* (Payard, 1973).

10. "Binding" and "loosing" was applied both to practices and to persons in Jewish usage. The teaching and governing aspects of apostolic authority are both in view.

11. Although God may visit judgment sooner: Acts 5:1–11.

12. See Oscar Cullman, *The State in the New Testament* (New York: Scribner's Sons, 1956), 34–37.

13. Jürgen Moltmann, *Religion, Revolution and the Future* (New York: Scribner's Sons, 1969), 41.

14. Ibid.

A Summary Statement of the Consultation on Theology and Civil Law

Carl F. H. Henry

AS EVANGELICAL CHRISTIANS we met in consultation on the subject of theology and civil law.[1] We gathered in Washington D.C., from March 17 through 20, 1993, to consider what Christ and the Church expect of us as believers and citizens in a free society, and what we may contribute to and expect from society as evangelicals.

The purpose was to explore biblical principles and to set forth theological underpinnings of civil law. Within the Christian community this statement addresses in particular those who make, enforce, or interpret laws or who are engaged in the practice of law.

The following affirmations and denials have been drawn to address our fellow citizens of like faith for their exhortation and also those of different convictions. The intent is to make known our concerns and to submit such principles as we believe may properly be considered by the whole society in its quest for liberty, justice, and social harmony. In three days of dialogue and discussion, illuminated by a series of eleven papers, we shaped the following twenty affirmations and denials. These represent a consensus shared by the sixteen participants, thus not every participant may agree with every individual item.

Participants in the consultation were:

Gary Amos, Ph.D., Author and Lecturer, Virginia Beach, VA
Gleason Archer, Ph.D., Professor Emeritus of Trinity Evangelical Divinity School, Deerfield, IL
Dr. Harold O. J. Brown, Professor of Biblical and Systematic Theology, Trinity Evangelical Divinity School, Deerfield, IL
Daryl Charles, Ph.D., Colson Scholar in Residence, The Wilberforce Forum of Prison Fellowship, Washington, D.C.

Edmund Clowney, Th.D., Adjunct Professor of Practical Theology, Westminster Theological Seminary, Escondido, CA

John Eidsmoe, D.Min., J.D., Professor of Law, Faulkner University, Montgomery, AL

Arthur Glasser, Th.D., Dean Emeritus, Fuller Seminary School of World Mission, Pasadena, CA

Carl F. H. Henry, Ph.D., Evangelical Theologian and Author, Visiting Professor of Theology, Trinity Evangelical Divinity School, Deerfield, IL

H. Wayne House, Th.D., J.D., Professor of Theology, Michigan Theological Seminary, Plymouth, MI; Professor of Law, Simon Greenleaf School of Law, Trinity International University, Anaheim, CA and Deerfield, IL

Douglas Kelly, Ph.D., Professor of Systematic Theology, Reformed Theological Seminary, Jackson, MS

Forest Montgomery, J.D., Counsel, Office of Public Affairs, National Association of Evangelicals, Washington, D.C.

R. C. Sproul, Ph.D., Professor of Systematic Theology and Apologetics, Reformed Theological Seminary, and President of Legioner Ministries, Orlando, FL

William Stuntz, J.D., Professor of Law, University of Virginia School of Law, Charlottesville, VA

Herbert W. Titus, J.D., Editor of *Forecast,* and former Dean, Regent University School of Law, Virginia Beach, VA

Larry Walker, Ph.D., Professor of Old Testament and Semitic Languages, Mid-America Baptist Theological Seminary, Memphis, TN

Tuvya Zaretsky, Director, Southern California Jews for Jesus, Los Angelas, CA

GOVERNMENT AND THE STATE

The Sovereign Creator

We affirm that all human beings are created by God and are subject to His sovereign rule.

We deny that people are autonomous or a law unto themselves.

Divine Institution of Government

We affirm that all human government is ordained and instituted by God.

We deny that any human government has absolute and sovereign power.

Role of Government

We affirm that the purpose of government is to preserve and protect the life, liberty, and property of all persons subject to its jurisdiction.

We deny all claims that government is the source or owner of those rights.

Imposition of Taxes

We affirm the authority of the government to impose taxes upon all those within its jurisdiction to pay for services lawfully rendered by it to all.

We deny that the government has the power to expropriate or redistribute wealth by means of confiscatory tax rates on income or inheritance.

Church and State

We affirm that the church and civil government have separate and distinct roles and spheres of authority.

We deny that the separation of church and state means the separation of the state from God.

CIVIL LAW

Transcendent Moral Absolutes

We affirm that just law is based on transcendent moral principles that are absolute and universal.

We deny that the subjective preferences of any culture, generation, community, or individual can form the foundation of a just legal system.

Supernatural Origin of Rights

We affirm (as does the American Declaration of Independence) that inalienable rights to life, liberty, and the pursuit of happiness are a divine endowment, and that civil rulers are bound to secure those rights.

We deny that government has authority to create or abrogate fundamental human rights and responsibilities.

God's Law and the Nations

We affirm that God the Creator reveals His moral law in created by God, are human conscience and preeminently in the Scriptures of the Old and New Testaments, and that God's moral law has applicability to all people and nations.

We deny that God's law in the Scriptures is irrelevent to the modern world.

Limitations of Government

We affirm that it is proper for government to punish immoral behavior that is detrimental to the family and public order, but that exercise of such power must be limited to prevent abuse by imperfect civil rulers.

We deny that each person in society has the right to define morality solely by individual choice apart from ethical absolutes.

Pluralism, Diversity, and Tolerance

We affirm that social diversity and community tolerance are among the defining strengths of a nation.

We deny that this rich tradition of diversity and tolerance should be imposed by laws or regulations enforcing political correctness or multiculturalism.

The Source of Rights

We affirm that the source of inalienable rights is God (as attested in the American Declaration of Independence) and that those fundamental human rights are secured—not granted—by government (as in the United States Constitution).

We deny that the source of rights is to be found only in the First Amendment to the United States Constitution.

CITIZEN

Citizenship and Obedience

We affirm that God has called all citizens, Christian and non-Christian alike, to seek the good of the community and country where He has placed them.

We deny that the imperfections and abuses of duly consituted governments release citizens from the divine mandate to conscientious obedience under God.

Promote Justice

We affirm that Christian citizens should properly use such political power as they possess in concert with others willing to seek the same civic objectives.

We deny that Christians may legitimately seek political power for the church or exercise political power to the prejudice of the just interests of other citizens.

The Pursuit of Rights

We affirm that the concern over the infringement of human rights is one way in which Christians exhibit their devotion to justice and commitment to an adequate public philosophy.

We deny that taking a stand for one's human rights is an improper endeavor for Christians.

Law and Morality

We affirm that civic virtue and moral discipline are vital for the continuance of a free society.

We deny that legislation can be separated from moral concerns or that public officials should attempt to separate public policy from moral standards.

Respect for Authority

We affirm that the Bible imposes solemn obligations to honor, respect, and obey civil authority.

We deny that Christians are bound to obey civil authority when it forbids what God commands and commands what God forbids.

Education of Children

We affirm that a democratic society is best served by the education of its citizens according to the choice of their parents.

We deny that the civil authority has primary determination regarding the education of children.

America's Founding Fathers

We affirm that the nation's founders were predominantly Christian in belief and practice, and we encourage present day American Christians to contine this heritage through local and national political involvement.

We deny the distortion of history that alleges that America's founding had little or no Christian base.

CHURCH

Unity of the Church

We affirm that Jesus Christ, who is the Lord and Head of the chruch calls Christians to demonstrate in a fragmented world the unity of the Spirit in the bond of love and peace.

We deny that the barriers of human prejudice should restrain the church from manifesting this unity.

Light, Salt, and Leaven

We affirm that the church is called to serve as light, salt, and leaven in the world, influencing life and culture by its example and prophetic witness.

We deny that the church is called to coerce or control those outside its bounds.

Global Mandate

We affirm that the Christian church is divinely mandated to go to every community and nation to proclaim the Gospel.

We deny that the Christian witness is to be confined to areas where it is welcomed or approved.

State and Church Jurisdiction

We affirm that what God commands or forbids takes precedence over what civil government prohibits or requires.

We deny that the civil government has jurisdiction over religious institutions in matters that God has relegated to those institutions.

Free Exercise

We affirm that the free exercise of religion includes the right to propagate, proselytize, or evangelize.

We deny that this right extends only to Christians.

NOTES

1. Sponsored by the National Association of Evangelicals.

Index

340.11
H 8422

97648

LINCOLN CHRISTIAN COLLEGE AND SEMINARY

3 4711 00150 6726